The New Mandarins

By the same author

The Uncommon Commoner
Inside the Foreign Office
'Special' No More
The Boys on the Bongo Bus

JOHN DICKIE

The New Mandarins: How British Foreign Policy Works

I.B. TAURIS

LONDON · NEW YORK

Published in 2004 by I.B.Tauris & Co. Ltd
6 Salem Road, London W2 4BU
175 Fifth Avenue, New York NY 10010
www.ibtauris.com

In the United States of America and in Canada distributed by Palgrave
Macmillan, a division of St Martin's Press, 175 Fifth Avenue, New York
NY 10010

ISBN   1 86064 978 5 hb
EAN   978 1 86064 978 3

A full CIP record for this book is available from the British Library

A full CIP record for this book is available from the Library of Congress
Library of Congress catalog card: available

Set in FF Arnhem and Futura Bold by Ewan Smith, London
Printed and bound in Great Britain by MPG Books, Bodmin

Contents

Preface

In the old days the conduct of foreign affairs was entrusted to a small international elite who shared the same sort of background and who desired to preserve the same sort of world. Sir Harold Nicolson

We have to adapt our diplomacy to the new environment, a world of rapid change, dominated by the superpowers, racked by violence and torn by the dissensions of ideology and race. Lord Trevelyan

WHEN I first travelled to an international conference in Geneva a member of the Foreign Secretary's delegation, Sir John Russell, gave me this advice: 'Don't forget your tennis racket.' In the course of the next thirty years of travelling with prime ministers and foreign secretaries around the world, the pace and complexity of diplomacy changed momentously. No longer have diplomats – or diplomatic correspondents – any time for a leisurely morning on the tennis court. The laptop computer, the mobile phone and the tape recorder keep the hands too busy for tennis.

How the Foreign Office is meeting the challenge of change is a matter of increasing public concern, particularly since the terrorist attack on New York's twin towers on 11 September 2001 resulted in international politics being catapulted into a state of almost constant turmoil. In this new frenetic atmosphere the question is often posed as to how British foreign policy works. Having observed it at close quarters inside the Foreign Office and at embassies on all continents, I realized that the answer lay in assessing how a quiet revolution begun by Young Turks in the Foreign Office has changed the system and made it more open to ideas from the new mandarins as well as to influences from outside.

A definitive study of all aspects of the quiet revolution – how diplomats are selected in a series of exacting tests, how they are trained and promoted for high office in the Diplomatic Service, how the formulation of Britain's foreign policy is being transformed with greater transparency, and how the conduct of that policy is affected by pressures from Parliament and the media – is a project that could only be undertaken if a great number of doors were opened inside the Foreign Office and elsewhere in Whitehall, as well as in missions abroad. In this instance unusual access to inner sanctums in the corridors of power was made possible with endless patience – and significantly without any conditions – by Sir John Kerr as Permanent Under-Secretary of State and subsequently by his successor, Sir Michael Jay. Many members of the Diplomatic Service at all levels provided rare insights into the system under challenging questioning about its merits – and weaknesses still to be eradicated – in long interviews conducted off the record to enable observations to be made with complete frankness.

Their contributions were matched by interesting comparisons provided by former members of the Foreign Office and diplomats from many other foreign services. There were also illuminating observations offered by MPs, officials of non-governmental organizations, directors of think tanks, activists in lobby groups, and journalists. To all of them who took part in over 125 interviews I am extremely grateful for their openness and trust. I am also deeply indebted to the very helpful staff of the library at the Royal Institute of International Affairs under the innovative librarian, Catherine Hume, for invaluable assistance in checking details; to Steve Priestley, Chief Clerk of the House of Commons Foreign Affairs Committee, for his generous help with statistics and parliamentary documents; to Christopher Lee for his commitment to the launch of the project; and to Lisa T. Gamandi, editor of the Diplomatic Service List. My greatest thanks are due to my wife, Inez, who endured long periods of isolation throughout my research and writing with immense tolerance and kept me going with her sumptuous cordon bleu cooking.

Finally, an apology: at the risk of offending the purists I have used the term 'Foreign Office' instead of the formally correct 'Foreign and Commonwealth Office' since throughout the diplomatic world it is affectionately known as the 'FO'.

John Dickie
'Brooklands', Oxshott

To Inez, Lorna and Nigel for so many
happy memories

Introduction

*Diplomacy is not necessarily a mysterious process. It is thought to be
so because matters of great importance have, for reasons of discretion,
practicality and mutual confidence, to be discussed in private by unknown
people, and while this is happening Foreign Offices and Embassies present a
surface which may look anything from vacuous to defensive. In fact, behind
this surface, a lot of ordinary but varied human beings are trying to make
international relations work.* Lord Gore-Booth, *With Great Truth and
Respect*, 1974

FOR three entire days all Her Majesty's Ambassadors Extraordinary and Plenipotentiary were absent from their posts in every capital in the world. This
unprecedented Meeting of the Mandarins addressed by the Foreign Secretary
at the Queen Elizabeth II Conference Centre in Westminster in January 2003
was summoned to assess how Britain should face an unprecedented series of
challenges across the globe. The buzz word around the conference hall was
'strategy'. The collective wisdom of the mandarins was focused on how to work
out policies in terms of the 'strategy and innovation' required for Britain's
increasingly complex role in the international diplomatic arena.

All the optimism at the end of the Cold War that a new world order could
be established had been swept away in a series of upheavals threatening an
era of extremely perilous disorder. Havoc wrought by international terrorists,
the war in Afghanistan and the crises leading to military intervention in Iraq
intensified the clash of cultures between Islamic fundamentalism and the
Western democracies. The Middle East melting pot spilled its tensions into
areas well beyond the Euphrates and the Nile. Globalization swept across every
area of the globe, leaving everyone, not just the HIPCs – the Heavily Indebted
Poor Countries – struggling to cope with its consequences. State-of-the-art
information technology and medical research, while advancing knowledge at
a previously unimagined pace, still failed to stem the horrendous death toll
of victims of HIV/Aids and drugs. Since solutions to such problems depended
on stability in the international arena, the first requirement was meeting the
challenges of terrorism and the spread of weapons of mass destruction.

Members of the Diplomatic Service entrusted with ensuring 'the best
for Britain overseas' always have before them the mantra formulated by

Palmerston in his speech to the House of Commons on 1 March 1848: 'We have no eternal allies and no perpetual enemies. Our interests are eternal and perpetual, and those interests it is our duty to follow.' But therein lies the rub. Where those interests lie and with whom Britain should work most closely to achieve them has remained a problem of bewildering complexity for the policy-makers when policies have to be defined and redefined almost daily at times. Although the so-called Anglo-American 'Special Relationship' which Churchill forged with Roosevelt in their Atlantic Charter of August 1941 faded away when the USA emerged as a virtually unchallenged superpower after the dissolution of the Soviet Union, the strong legacy of transatlantic cooperation continued to be almost as central to the Labour government of Tony Blair as it was to the Conservative government of Margaret Thatcher.

What complicated the task of Tony Blair was that, unlike Margaret Thatcher, he was concerned to be 'at the heart of Europe' with his partners in the European Union, and yet there were many occasions when he saw Britain's interests as being closer to those of the Americans than what the French and Germans perceived the best interests of Europe to be. Once President George W. Bush set his sights in his State of the Union address in January 2002 on taking on the 'axis of evil' in Iraq, Iran and North Korea, the prospect of a widening gulf between him and some of the leaders of Europe became inevitable as each phase of the crisis over Saddam Hussein's regime unfolded. It often left Prime Minister Blair trying to ride two political horses pulling ever more vigorously in different directions, threatening the authority of the United Nations Security Council, the integrity of the NATO alliance, the unity of the European Union and the cohesion of the Commonwealth.

Ironically – and fortuitously – the impact of these challenges coincided with a vibrant period of innovative change in the Whitehall department where they had to be handled. Virtually unnoticed, a quiet revolution had been taking place directly across the road from No. 10 Downing Street. Amid the barrage of political, constitutional and economic changes launched by the government of New Labour under Prime Minister Tony Blair following its election in 1997, few people realized that an equally fundamental transformation was under way at the Foreign Office. Nothing like it had ever been witnessed before in the corridors of power in Whitehall. The elitist culture with which the first Foreign Secretary, Charles James Fox, surrounded himself on taking office in 1782 had survived for over two centuries, with senior officials being perceived like Sir Humphrey Appleby in the television comedy *Yes Minister* as supercilious Whitehall warriors armed with tightly rolled umbrellas. The persistence of that perception was highlighted in the confidential valedictory of the distinguished

Arabist, Ambassador Sir David Gore-Booth, when he wrote to Foreign Secretary Robin Cook at the end of his career, stating: 'One of the great failures of the Diplomatic Service has been its inability to cast off its image of bowler-hatted, pin-striped and chinless characters with a fondness for champagne.'

Yet even as that complaint was being filed, and the advocate of the 'Cool Britannia' project to rebrand the United Kingdom's image abroad, Mark Leonard, was inveighing against what he called 'archaic and ageing diplomatic missions filled with Chippendale furniture, pompous heraldry on official publications, titled diplomatic envoys', the reason for the ridicule was gone, the ivory tower swept aside by the tide of events. Rumblings of revolution surging throughout the lower ranks of the Foreign Office had been gathering strength from the middle of the 1990s. Frustration among the young ambitious diplomats at having to mark time for years because of the snail's pace of promotion, irritation at the hierarchical system of making policy assessments, and exasperation at the outmoded means of communication and at being behind every other Whitehall ministry in introducing new technology, all combined to produce the tinder awaiting a spark to launch the movement for radical reform.

That came from Robin Cook within days of his becoming Foreign Secretary, when he summoned the Foreign Office staff to the gilded splendour of the Locarno Room, where his predecessor Austen Chamberlain signed the treaty with Aristide Briand and Gustav Stresemann on 1 December 1925 settling the disputed frontier between France and Germany. The lower ranks were sitting, hushed, at the back, some in awe of the grand salon they had never seen before with its ornate ceiling and majolica plaques depicting the emblems of twenty countries. But if the case for reform needed any justification it was the sight that greeted the new Foreign Secretary as he scanned the front row: a phalanx of sombre-looking, dark-suited men, the senior mandarins. One observer watching at the side of the salon described the scene: 'It was like a parade of undertakers who had met beforehand to choose the first hymn and were ready to sing it in perfect harmony. They expected to hear a few familiar homilies, nod patronisingly in approval, and carry on as before.' Instead, Robin Cook delivered an announcement to shock the system: it was time for change, a big change. The new Foreign Secretary's proclamation of an agenda for reform was the equivalent of firing the gun for the revolution to start.

It did not happen overnight, however. The newly appointed Permanent Under-Secretary of State heading the Diplomatic Service, Sir John Kerr, had not taken over at that stage, and having just returned from being ambassador in Washington was still sizing up the problems. Robin Cook had to immerse himself in the role of being the first Labour Foreign Secretary for eighteen years and prepare to take on the added duties of Britain's presidency of the European Union for the first six months of 1998. It was not until the following year that the various strands of the modernization movement were brought together to thrust the revolution into top gear. Ironically it was in the middle of the 'arms for Africa crisis' over Sierra Leone, when Robin Cook seemed to be totally besieged by his critics, that he paused to peep above the parapet and give the go-ahead for a group of young officials to 'think the unthinkable' and draft proposals on how the Foreign Office should operate as 'the best of British'. This released all the pent-up energies of the Young Turks, who immediately embarked upon a massive consultation exercise called 'Foresight', the details of which are disclosed for the first time in the following chapter, that resulted in liberating the Foreign Office from the stranglehold of a tradition dating back over two centuries.

As the largest staff inquiry ever undertaken in the Civil Service, the Foresight team set up more than a hundred contact groups at home and abroad in posts all over the world to obtain ideas from over a thousand members of the Diplomatic Service. The ninety-seven-point findings set the Foreign Office's Board of Management back on its heels. They were prepared for change by now, but the range of the Young Turks' manifesto was far more extensive than most of the senior mandarins expected. For their part, the Young Turks recognized two basic facts of the challenge they had posed: radical change could not take place if the Foreign Secretary was not willing to give it his blessing and let it happen and, even more important, the revolution could not achieve its ends without a positive response from Sir John Kerr to authorize the ways and means – and, significantly, the finance – for it to go ahead.

As a shrewd judge of a situation and its possible consequences, which earned him high praise from Foreign Secretaries Robin Cook and Jack Straw, as well as from Prime Minister Margaret Thatcher (who once saluted him as her 'golden pen' for his drafting skills), Sir John Kerr saw the way the wind was blowing, persuaded the Foreign Office Board of Management to change tack and wisely steered the changes through at a faster pace. He recognized the need for 'quick wins' to convince the Young Turks that it was results not rhetoric which mattered, and saw the need for top priority to be given to a complete revamp of the plans to introduce state-of-the-art communications technology despite the high cost of catch-up. In setting up working groups to implement the recommendations of the Foresight Report in a smoothly managed transition, he encouraged a new sense of partnership and commitment to change throughout all ranks and ensured that the quiet revolution was rolling forward with vigour when he passed the baton to his successor in January 2002.

For the momentum of the revolution to be maintained the choice of successor was crucial, and in Sir Michael Jay the Young Turks were heartened to find a modernist after their own heart who had practised what he preached about modern public diplomacy in frequent tours de force on French radio and television as ambassador in Paris. He surprised even those whose best expectations were that the process of reform could be continued unabated. He stepped up the pace. In a matter of a few months the new Permanent Under-Secretary astounded the old guard by abolishing some of the historic pillars of the Foreign Office establishment in a whirlwind of structural changes from the top downwards.

Once initial steps in modernization began to produce results throughout the system, the aloofness of the Foreign Office – in the way it conducted itself and its policies – which caused James Callaghan as Foreign Secretary to complain that 'foreign policy is not an idol to be hidden in the temple, untouched by profane hands', was steadily eroded. The traditions of exclusiveness were superseded in most – but perhaps not all – parts of the Foreign Office by an awareness of the need to be inclusive in terms of the new mandarins being attracted to the Diplomatic Service and the cooperation sought from outside it in the formulation of policies, as will be revealed in the chapters that follow. One interesting example of the inclusiveness is that Muslims and Hindus now work together in the Foreign Office at levels formerly beyond the aspirations of ethnic minorities in an environment that used to be characterized as 'white, male, and Oxbridge'.

Another key aspect is the acceleration in the promotion of women. They were not allowed to become mandarins until after the Second World War. They were only able to apply for the Administrative grade of the Diplomatic Service when the Eden reforms of 1943 were implemented. Even then women were required to resign on marriage until the regulations were changed in 1972. When Sir John Kerr took over as Permanent Under-Secretary in 1997 none of the twenty-one under-secretaries was a woman. At the end of the Kerr regime three of the thirteen under-secretaries were women – and the process continued to accelerate. For both male and female mandarins the new system allows them to choose where their careers take them. Under the old dirigiste system a diplomat could be consigned to Ulan Baatar without having any say on whether being Second Secretary at 30 Enkh Taivny Gudamzh in the Mongolian capital for three years was an acceptable reward for joining the Foreign Office to travel and see the world. Now the bidding system for posts inside the Foreign Office and abroad enables diplomats to map out their moves on the way to the top as mandarins, rather than wait for promotion on the old basis of Buggins's turn.

Policy-making used to be a highly confidential operation carried out with a level of secrecy rarely seen outside a Trappist monastery. Submissions on action to be taken had to be authorized and signed by the Permanent Under-Secretary before being sent to the Foreign Secretary as the recommended policy. They were the product of in-house analysis based on top-secret telegrams from embassies. No outside expertise or opinions were sought. Nowadays, as will be demonstrated in Chapters 6 to 10, the formulation of foreign policy is usually the product of many sources outside as well as inside the Foreign Office, with input from Members of Parliament, on-the-spot staff of non-governmental organizations (NGOs), academic experts, businessmen with experience in the problems being faced in an unstable region, and foreign correspondents whose contacts with opposition factions in a country are not easily matched by diplomats. It is a much more inclusive process now that the speed of communications in the IT era requires much quicker responses than in the days when it took hours to decode telegrams. Partly because of this, and partly because the changes have greatly reduced the hierarchical procedures that used to keep the lowly in their place, junior diplomats are now able to get their ideas and recommendations through to the policy-making level more swiftly without sending them step by step up the spiral.

It may be more than a coincidence, therefore, that the popularity of a career in the Diplomatic Service soared as the impact of the quiet revolution percolated to the common rooms of academia. Surveys of 6,000 final-year undergraduates at forty-two British universities have put the Foreign Office among the top two choices for where they would like most to work. In 2001 it was number one, well ahead of the Virgin Group at number two, and Accenture at number three. In 2002 it yielded first place to the BBC but came second in front of British Airways at number three. Universum Communications, a company specializing in graduate recruitment which carried out the surveys, gave as its reason for the FO being so popular: 'The work environment is challenging and exciting. Graduates are given responsibility and a structured career path at an early stage. They are able to make a real difference.' But the competition for a place in the Diplomatic Service is more severe than in any other profession. Only one in a hundred of the country's highest-qualified graduates applying to the Foreign Office is successful, a situation that makes the new generation of mandarins and the challenging opportunities opening up for them as key players in the policy-making for tomorrow's world a fascinating subject for examination.

ONE

The 'Foresight' Saga: The Manifesto of a Revolution

The fundamental premise of a revolution is that the existing structure has become incapable of solving the urgent problems of development of the nation.
Leon Trotsky, 1935

Change is not made without inconvenience, even from worse to better.
Samuel Johnson, 1755

FROM the moment Robin Cook became Foreign Secretary in May 1997 hardly a day passed without what he said or what he did hitting the headlines. It was one controversy after another in the newspapers. First came the furore over the contradictions in New Labour's 'ethical foreign policy' – a phrase he never actually used, although he laid himself open to accusations of cynicism by seizing the moral high ground with a commitment to an 'ethical dimension' in the conduct of foreign policy. Then there was his grilling in Parliament over the Foreign Office involvement in the arms-to-Sierra Leone row, with further trouble over military supplies to Zimbabwe and Indonesia. A visit to Israel ended in a snub from Prime Minister Binyamin Netanyahu, who cancelled a dinner after Robin Cook omitted the ritual homage at Yad Vashem, the Holocaust memorial, and laid a wreath instead at the memorial for Deir Yassin, the massacre of Palestinians by the Stern Gang in 1948. Another visit, accompanying the Queen to India, was overshadowed by a bitter row over remarks about Kashmir attributed to him in Pakistan. On top of that there was the melodrama at Heathrow Airport, as his turbulent private life was about to be exposed in a Sunday newspaper, when he chose to abandon his wife and go off with his mistress. Even in his last days at the Foreign Office in April 2001 in the heat of the general election campaign, Robin Cook swept the 'battle of the £' off the front pages over his argument for 'legitimate immigration' that chicken tikka masala, not roast beef and Yorkshire pudding or fish and chips, was 'Britain's truly national dish'.

His four years at the Foreign Office made him the most controversial Foreign Secretary since the Second World War. Not for him the sort of affection in which Ernest Bevin and Sir Alec Douglas-Home were held at all levels of the Diplomatic Service. Inside the Foreign Office Robin Cook quickly acquired the reputation of a testy loner with the temper of George Brown and the arrogance of Anthony Crosland without the compensating ability to command admiration as a dominant figure in the international arena. Those who dealt with him frequently always entered his room treading very carefully, not knowing which of his moods would predominate. 'He was a cat, not a dog' was one knowing assessment of how cautious people had to be with him in his moods. As one of his staff put it: 'He has a waspish wit. People do not cross him – they take great care not to do so.' Another diplomat who spent much time in his company admitted: 'It was not easy to warm to him. He was not a man of the heart.'

Yet he will be remembered in the corridors of power not just for the endless controversies and arguments swirling round him but for starting the revolution inside the Foreign Office which transformed the way this great department of state was run and the careers of those working in it – without any recognition outside the Foreign Office of the significance of what he had set in train. Even so it was not an achievement that he particularly regarded as a badge of honour. For him it was part of his political philosophy to be a tradition-breaker and a reformer. Nonetheless it was a historic moment when, within days of establishing himself in the elegant first-floor room overlooking St James's Park where his predecessor Sir Edward Grey lamented the lights going out all over Europe in 1914, Robin Cook sent the first salvo of the revolution reverberating throughout the palatial building created by Sir Gilbert Scott and down to the diplomats' club in Pall Mall, the Travellers'.

After acknowledging in his mission statement about what he saw as the role of Britain in the world that he counted on 'the professionalism, the expertise and the dedication' of the Diplomatic Service, Cook sent a shudder through the Locarno Room, where the senior mandarins were sitting in front of the assembled staff, by announcing that the time had come for change – and substantial change – to modernize the Foreign Office. It was a conclusion he had been pondering for a long time in opposition which was thrust to the top of his agenda for reform when he looked at the staff list and saw that most ambassadors were in their fifties, that there was little evidence of equal opportunity from the numbers of women among the upper echelons of the mandarins, and that the overwhelming majority of faces around him were white. The speech went down well with the people at the back of the room behind the senior mandarins, and they waited enthusiastically for the follow-through in practical terms.

Cook was not the first to recognize the urgent need for modernizing the Foreign Office. Tentative starts had been made through the introduction of objective-setting in the years before New Labour came to office. There were proposals for the creation of focus groups from Rob Young as Chief Clerk (a Dickensian title changed in 2002 to Director General Corporate Affairs), but they failed to find favour with the board. One of the major avenues for proposing change, however, was through the comprehensive spending review that the Treasury imposes on all Whitehall departments and which requires them to examine how efficiently they are being run. After the 1995 spending review, when the Treasury observed that other departments had streamlined their top-heavy structure while the Foreign Office had left it undiminished, a more determined effort was made by a steering group for the comprehensive spending review, chaired by Rob Young, which was given an external perspective by the inclusion of Lord Marshall, chairman of British Airways.

At this stage there was an infusion of innovative ideas from Fiona Moore, who became deputy head of what was then the Resource Planning Department after achieving an MBA at Imperial College sponsored by the Foreign Office, the first person to do so. During her MBA she produced a dissertation on 'Cultural Change at the Foreign Office' which led her to recommend a broader and more rigorous system for recruitment and promotion. At that time secondments were rare – none from NGOs and just a few both ways from the Department of Trade and Industry – so she suggested that more people should move from department to department throughout Whitehall. The dissertation was circulated in the Foreign Office and reached Robin Cook through his Minister of State, Derek Fatchett, and his special adviser, Andrew Hood. However, the Foreign Secretary was so absorbed in international affairs that he could not devote the necessary time to considering structural ideas and organizational matters.

This lack of availability was aggravated by the problem that many experts with ideas experienced throughout Cook's term as Foreign Secretary: no adviser had the ear of Cook in the way that Charlie Whelan had access to the Chancellor, Gordon Brown. None knew how to play the system in the Foreign Office as it was operated at the Treasury. Cook was not a team player – a trait that won him few friends. He would often lock himself away to brood over the draft of a major speech or a sudden problem. Unlike most leading politicians, he was emotionally incapable of reading out a speech composed entirely by someone else. While he would ask his speech writer to prepare a text he would usually set it aside and start again. That meant issuing a 'Do Not Disturb' edict to his staff. One of them admitted: 'No one would dare interrupt him – not even if there was a fire in the building – and he could seal himself off for hours.'

Cook thought nothing of cancelling all engagements at short notice – sometimes without any apology to those he had been due to see – and devoting himself to the one issue at hand, leaving those with other matters requiring an answer to bide their time for another opportunity. It was the communication problem which created tensions at times with senior mandarins, including the Permanent Under-Secretary, whose relations with Cook in the first eighteen months were often categorized by officials around him as 'quite difficult'. As he arrived with a certain amount of suspicion of a Foreign Office that had had eighteen years of Conservative ministers, his relations with diplomats often became what they described as 'very awkward'. Those who undertook special missions for him often received neither appreciation nor thanks.

When Sir Ivor Roberts was on a sabbatical at St Antony's College, Oxford, in 1998 after being ambassador in Belgrade, he was summoned to the Foreign Office and asked to make a clandestine visit back to Yugoslavia. As there had been difficulty in assessing the intentions of President Slobodan Milošević over Serbia and Kosovo, it was decided that since Sir Ivor had established easy access to Milošević during his term in Belgrade he was best placed to sound him out. The mission was successfully carried out without it leaking to the media, and a lengthy report was duly submitted through the Permanent Under-Secretary to Robin Cook. It was exactly what the Foreign Secretary required, but he neither called in Sir Ivor nor sent a note of appreciation. There was little enthusiasm in the Office for a Foreign Secretary who kept himself so aloof and, although there was some easing of the tensions as time went by, the best that one diplomat who was working closely with him could say at the end was 'we were rubbing along'.

Nevertheless, ideas kept bubbling up through the Resource Planning Department, which was then headed by Michael Aron, an inventive counsellor who had been seconded to the European Commission and had served on the British mission in New York. One of the suggestions which was subsequently adopted was to have non-executive members on the Board of Management. Another proposed a services organization to deal with all the supply requirements of the Foreign Office from furniture to air tickets, which was the genesis of an internal market. Other proposals on reforming the Senior Management Structure were not so well received, particularly one that questioned the necessity for an array of deputy under-secretaries at the top of the hierarchy. That did not go down well with the senior mandarins.

It was ironic, therefore, that a momentous leap forward in modernizing the Foreign Office occurred when the Foreign Secretary and the Permanent Under-Secretary were under fire from all sides in Parliament and the press for seemingly being totally at sixes and sevens over its conduct of affairs. At the height of the row over the involvement of the British company Sandline in supplying arms to Sierra Leone, Robin Cook broke away in a move that seemed to go against his normal instinct of concentrating intensely on the issue of the day and took a decisive step on reform. He called in his speech writer, Matthew Gould, a young high-flyer who had joined the Foreign Office after taking a degree in Philosophy and Divinity at Cambridge, and told him to take time off and create a reform group of young officials. Their task was to think the unthinkable, ignore the taboos about changing the hierarchical system, and devise means of modernizing the Foreign Office to enable it to meet the challenges of the decade ahead with 'the best of British'. It was Cook's second salvo after the celebrated 'Declaration of Intent' in the Locarno Room a year earlier, and it gave the Young Turks the licence to pave the way for the quiet revolution.

Significantly, Cook was astute enough not to issue a detailed mandate for reform to the Young Turks. He made his views clear about the need for a lot more openness, more diversity, an increased intake of secondments from the private sector, and a sharper focus on serving the public better. But he realized that if the impression spread through the Foreign Office that the reforms and modernization plan were being imposed like a political programme it would arouse the same sort of antagonism as that which greeted the 'Cool Britannia' rebranding project and would fail to evoke the wholehearted enthusiasm of staff at all levels of the Foreign Office. Equally important, the Permanent Under-Secretary deliberately did not try to take over the organization of the grass-roots movement or intervene in its directives. Subtly, however, he arranged for Michael Aron – a modernist but not one to count himself a Young Turk – to be available to chair the modernization group initially, while Matthew Gould was the group secretary and chief organizer. Other senior mandarins in his position as Permanent Under-Secretary would have been alarmed by revolting peasants in the ranks of the Foreign Office and would have manoeuvred to stifle the movement. But as one of the Young Turks acknowledged afterwards: 'We were lucky John Kerr was there at the time because he saw himself at times as a revolting peasant too!'

As Permanent Under-Secretary, Sir John Kerr had very sharp antennae, able to gauge very quickly how strongly any proposition was supported. Having satisfied himself that the Young Turks had widespread backing, he concluded it was better to have such people working inside the tent than outside. The tactic employed to great effect by Kerr was to say to them, 'Tell us what you think' – without ever having to admit to them that the management had got it wrong. By what was regarded afterwards as a typical Scottish trait – although he would no doubt deny it was learned at Glasgow Academy – Sir John convinced the uprising that he was just waiting to join them once he knew what they wanted. The message conveyed to all those calling for change was that the senior management was ready to cooperate.

The first phase was for the Young Turks to put some of their ideas down on paper. This resulted in a small group of people – self-selected from various parts of the Foreign Office – working as a ginger-group, meeting at lunchtime and weekends in their own time for months to thrash out ideas. At times there were twenty-four people engaged in heated debates, mainly from front-line and administrative departments from all grades up to first secretary, and not all graduates from the fast stream. Their search for ideas was helped by a series of lunchtime talks to the Young Turks from outsiders. They were particularly impressed with Sir David John, chairman of the British Oxygen Company, who explained how the problems of modernization had been tackled in his company through a task force chosen from all over the world to present recommendations to the board. Among the most forceful members of the ginger group was Sir John Kerr's former private secretary in Washington, Karen Pierce, who was then deeply involved in the Bosnian situation. She produced some radical new ideas for a paper on 'Personnel Assessment and Personnel Management', which went into the pool of some ten provocative proposals set down on four pages of A4 paper.

One of the Young Turks' first decisions was to determine the time span of their vision for the future. Military planning is usually projected twenty or thirty years ahead. For the Foreign Office that was considered too much like an academic ivory tower projection. Bringing the vision down to what was required for 2005 was not thought stretching enough, especially since budget forecasting was already focused on that. In the end the target was set at what the Foreign Office should be and what it should be doing in 2010. This vision was described in a draft paper ten pages long by Matthew Gould entitled 'Creativity', which examined why the Foreign Office appeared to have run out of new ideas and why it needed to change. It portrayed the big picture of how the Foreign Office should be pursuing its objectives overseas and how it should be operating at home, spreading its talent more effectively, improving working practices, and ensuring that it was an efficient global player for the rest of the Whitehall departments. Among five other draft papers was one with provocative new proposals on knowledge management by Karen Pierce.

When the Board of Management read the drafts they swallowed hard and realized that the best course was to go with the flow. There was one defining moment in discussions on a section of 'Creativity' which stated that one reason for a shortage of ideas was that people were nervous about putting up radical proposals for fear of a harsh put-down from a senior member of the board. The experience of having 'RUBBISH' written in capitals across a submission, it was emphasized, was enough to ensure that a bold young rising star would not want to risk another such stern put-down. When Sir John Kerr bristled at this suggestion and asserted that nobody did that nowadays, a voice piped up, insisting, 'You do, PUS!' This brave interjection struck the first blow against the hierarchical system that Foresight was aiming to destroy once and for all. With the Permanent Under-Secretary obliged to recognize the validity of the case made in the 'Creativity' paper, the decision-making process on reform shifted up a gear.

Formal authorization for the Young Turks to produce a manifesto for the revolution under the title 'Foresight' was given in the grandiose country house setting of Chevening, some four miles from Churchill's house at Chartwell in Kent. The home of seven Earls Stanhope since 1717, Chevening was bequeathed to the nation in 1967 and became a residence for Prince Charles from 1974 to 1980 before being assigned as a weekend retreat for foreign secretaries to entertain and hold brainstorming sessions. The history-making pre-revolutionary session was convened – without Robin Cook but with his sanction – by the Board of Management as an away day for brainstorming, with modernization as one of the items on the agenda in July 1999. Members of the board went down to Chevening on the eve of the meeting. At the bottom of the hierarchical pile, the Young Turks had to make a 6 a.m. start from London on 16 July to be there in time for the opening session, even though their item was halfway down the agenda. Climbing the magnificent wooden carved stairway to the drawing room with its Gainsborough portraits, the Young Turks delegation, led by Matthew Gould and newly appointed professional consultant Sheena Matthews, awaited their turn to tell the board what was required from a revolution.

After the other items on the agenda about modernization, with papers by senior mandarins Anthony Brenton on whether the Foreign Office should become a spending department like the International Development Department and David Reddaway on immigration, the Young Turks were invited to address the meeting. Karen Pierce delivered her thesis on knowledge management over the lunch period, followed by Matthew Gould on the theme of a new beginning with 'Creativity'. They had been apprehensive of the reaction of Establishment figures whom many in the Office regarded as old fogeys. Instead the board took its cue from Sir John Kerr and greeted the papers with enthusiasm. The only mutterings of resistance came from the administration side and certain heads of department. Guiding the two sides into alignment, Sheena Matthews secured agreement for a massive worldwide consultancy exercise as the basis for the Foresight Report to chart the future for the Foreign Office to 2010.

The group of Young Turks was expanded to take in representatives from all grades in the Foreign Office and authorized to issue a series of question-naires to 1,400 members of the Diplomatic Service at home and abroad in over a hundred contact groups. The fact-finding was concentrated on six themes: Vision 2010, led by Matthew Gould; Personnel; Information Technology and Working Practices; Communications; Resource Management; and Customer Service. What would normally take professional pollsters six months was com-pleted in eight frantic weeks. Each team working on the six themes had a senior mandarin as coordinator, encouraging them, not curtailing their scope. The teams sent out a series of questionnaires with up to twelve questions to their contact groups for responses from members in embassies. For Vision 2010 Matthew Gould wrote to all senior ambassadors, some of whom, such as Sir Roderic Lyne in Moscow, responded enthusiastically with several pages of suggestions for radical change.

At the same time Sir John Kerr took action to resolve the IT problem, which had left the Foreign Office lagging behind the rest of Whitehall. He called back one of the bright stars in the Diplomatic Service seconded to the European Sec-retariat in the Cabinet Office, Matthew Kirk, and asked him whether he could work out how to set up a state-of-the art system that would put the Foreign Office on top of the IT league. He was given ten days to assess the challenge and returned to the Permanent Under-Secretary with the assessment that it could be worked out in three months. Sir John Kerr was impressed, gave him the title Project Director for Global Communications – and a budget of £250 million, scraped together without selling too much of the 'family silver' in terms of property. To find out the specific requirements from posts abroad and departments at home, Matthew Kirk appended queries to the Foresight questionnaire. He also went to the private sector to learn from the experience of Reuters, the BBC, British Airways and BP.

The new IT strategy resulted in the systems on people's desks, which were ten years out of date, being modernized with the Firecrest system for confi-dential communications. The next step was the connection of the Firecrest system to FTN (Foreign Office Telecommunications Network), linking posts abroad and keying them into the Government Secure Intranet (GSI). The third

step was the introduction of Prism, providing a management system, a financial accounting system, a personnel management system and a knowledge
management system for the whole network. Matthew Kirk's solution ensured
a single point of responsibility on each issue, enabling decision-making processes to be transparent, fully accountable and properly recorded for storage
in the archives. Under the new system a submission from a desk officer put to
the Foreign Secretary cannot be altered by the Permanent Under-Secretary. He
can add that he does not agree with it, give his reasons and suggest something
different. The choice is left to the Foreign Secretary, and future historians will
see the differences of view. Posts have much more freedom, being able to communicate directly without going to the centre and not having to clear a draft
with somebody else. Security is ensured by having access at three levels: Secret,
which requires a diplomat to go into a separate room for a special terminal;
Confidential; and Private Unclassified. Only 2 to 3 per cent of the traffic is
Secret; 42 to 43 per cent is Confidential; 55 per cent is Private Unclassified.

Although the complexities of IT problems are never easy to resolve, they were
much less difficult than the problems relating to working practices, personnel management, deployment of resources and the role of the Foreign Office
at home and abroad, because their solutions depended more on changing
attitudes and reorganizing ways of working than on extra funding. The results
of the consultation exercise, which were published as the Foresight Report
in January 2000, surprised even the Young Turks. They certainly stunned the
Establishment. They expected a crisp twenty-page document. Instead they were
faced with a 104-page report far more radical and comprehensive than they had
ever imagined. It would have been longer, with 100 key findings, not ninety-
seven, because, although Robin Cook insisted that the report should not be
made public, some excisions were made in case parts were leaked to the press
which might have highlighted criticism of the Foreign Office and not balanced
it with an account of the good aspects that the report was recommending be
enhanced.

Cook's concern, although at odds with his repeated aspiration of transparency, was not unexpected, since any smugness about the Foreign Office
being a Rolls-Royce service was demolished in the first chapter of the report,
which examined the way in which it was prepared to face the challenges of
the world in 2010. Many old mandarins compared the Diplomatic Service with
what they saw in other countries and concluded that it should stay as it was,
whereas the real yardstick for the Young Turks was not just being better than
the French or the Germans but being the very best of British. There may have
been some cause for self-satisfaction in the report's seventeen-point list of

what the Foreign Office was considered to be good at: among other things, handling crises, understanding foreigners, hard language skills, multilateral negotiations, cultivating contacts, and attracting good people. But against that the board was presented with a list of twenty-two items where the Foreign Office, in the view of those working for it, needed to make a vast improvement in its performance.

Top of the negative list was long-term strategy planning, followed by planning for worst-case scenarios, recognizing failure and learning by mistakes, setting and following priorities, identifying and dropping unnecessary work, and reallocating resources to meet new priorities. Farther down the list of aspects requiring attention were the need to draw upon outside experience, to get rid of under-performers, create a culture of genuine equal opportunities, delegate responsibility, and have a better relationship with the rest of Whitehall. The findings stressed that expertise in hard languages was not enough. There had to be deeper expertise in technical issues such as climate change and capital markets, which required more time on training and secondment and more specialization in regions and issues. The assumption that the Foreign Office was the only department able to understand foreigners and to handle international issues had to be abandoned to ensure that such arrogance did not become a barrier to a good working relationship with other Whitehall ministries.

The report called for a greater pool of European Union experts by starting such specialization earlier in careers. It highlighted the fact that the number of first posting appointments to the delegation in Brussels was insufficient compared with their opposite numbers in other ministries, which resulted in a shortage of first secretaries with EU experience in London. Alongside the specialists, the report emphasized, all members of the Diplomatic Service should be 'EU-literate', and there had to be a greater number of them able to speak European languages. The need for more expertise in negotiating and managing complex contracts was also highlighted, and for this the Foreign Office would have to develop more open relationships with commercial partners. But with other Whitehall ministries forging their own international links, the report stressed that it had to be recognized that the Foreign Office could no longer be the unchallenged coordinator of Britain's international business and therefore had to ensure that its international networking skills were fully deployed to continue to be the leading player. At the same time, while the rest of Whitehall had its own narrow perspective on what was important to each department, the Foreign Office had a great opportunity to use its capacity to see the entire international picture and give a lead in directing attention to the big issues ahead.

One of the most radical analyses of the use of Foreign Office skills was focused on the most effective spread of talent at home and abroad. Since a diplomat abroad costs much more than one in London, the Foreign Office was urged to ensure that work was not undertaken overseas which could be done in London. By the same token, it urged that there should not be duplication in London of work that could be more efficiently done at an embassy. However, the report underlined the need to review staffing levels abroad to see whether, as many suspected, fewer could achieve as much if not more. It drew attention to the suspicion that an ambassador's staff was sometimes unnecessarily large simply because of his own rank in the Diplomatic Service. On the other hand, the report made the point that too many burdens were put on small posts and that if they had less to do they would produce a better quality of service.

Where the report echoed an anxiety felt throughout the system at home and abroad was in highlighting what it called 'the curse of long hours'. While crises were accepted as inevitably involving extra work, the main blame was directed at overloading, bad management and the work culture. Many responses from the staff emphasized the pervasiveness of 'presentism' – the belief that being on duty regardless of what was being done was important in itself. The report called on senior management to stop working long hours themselves, thereby encouraging others to follow their lead. By giving this example senior management would accord recognition to the fact that by reducing hours and concentrating on important matters staff would be able to improve their standards of performance. One key recommendation was that in assessing priorities in the workload at the Foreign Office there should be greater readiness to query questionable projects – including those from ministers and senior officials – and where necessary they should be rejected as not representing a justifiable use of time. As an added pressure to reduce excessively long hours a proper overtime payment scheme was recommended with a strict cash limit on directorates so that senior officials would be penalized if they went over the limit.

What turned out to be the most provocative part of the Foresight Report was a section headed 'Memo to Ministers'. It sent a shudder right to the top which resulted in it being returned from the Foreign Secretary's office with strict instructions that it should be kept secret. Any disclosure was considered likely to confirm that Robin Cook was not running a happy ship. In fact, not every member of the Young Turks group was at ease with all the thirteen points set out as recommendations to improve relations between ministers and staff in the Diplomatic Service. Some thought it should have been balanced with a parallel list of what the organization could do to serve ministers better. The memo, however, was drafted – mainly by Matthew Gould and Sheena Matthews

– with the best intention of ensuring better two-way communication between ministers and officials. It emphasized that a clear lead – clearer than had been provided by the Foreign Secretary and his ministers up till then – was required in order to produce more enthusiastic cooperation from staff in achieving greater efficiency.

For a start, it urged ministers to set out what their priorities were so that the staff could concentrate on them and assign less attention to other matters. The memo made the sharp point to junior ministers that they should focus on a limited number of subjects; otherwise, if they tried to cover everything with the same amount of commitment, they would just be going through the motions. It indicated that diplomats were often left in the dark about the direction to take on ministerial requests and stressed the need for honest feedback so that staff would be able to gauge whether their submissions were on the right lines or whether they were wasting their time. To underline the importance of getting it right, the memo insisted that ministers had to realize that officials could take constructive criticism.

Ministers were advised to lead from the front and to be seen to be doing so, rather than staying remote, working through senior staff and letting their ideas trickle down haphazardly. It was not a question of having ministers embark on royal-style walkabouts along the corridors of the Foreign Office every Friday when ministers were not at Westminster, but of encouraging them to walk into hard-pressed departments, see how they were coping with the flood of telegrams, and express appreciation for their work. This tradition of ministerial aloofness was affirmed when Lord Hurd recalled his days in the Diplomatic Service in a review of Richard Thorpe's biography of Eden in *The Times* on 16 April 2003: 'In the early Fifties we newcomers never saw the Foreign Secretary. Every now and then a submission of ours, stately in its paper jacket, would come back from his Private Office and we would gather round to gaze at the initials A.E. in red ink which showed that he had actually seen our handiwork.'

What was never properly realized by the Establishment was how over the years morale inside the Foreign Office had sunk to such a low ebb. How deeply young diplomats were irked by often being taken for granted by ministers – and how much that sense of disappointment undermined morale – was underlined in the last item in the thirteen-point memo, under the heading 'Appreciation': 'Small amounts of praise from ministers go a long way. So always say Thank you. Make a point of writing to staff who have done exceptionally well, and copy it into their personnel files. Turn up at departmental parties and drinks, if only just to put in an appearance.' That such a recommendation had to be made left no one in any doubt about how large the gap had become between ministers and their diplomatic staff. This disgruntlement with the ministerial 'Us and Them' attitude was met head on by the memo, which made the strong recommendation that ministers break down barriers by engaging all levels of Foreign Office staff in discussion. Its advice was emphatic: broaden the debate on issues by inviting junior staff as well as senior members to meetings so that the strength of a case, not the rank of the person making it, should decide the outcome.

The memo put most of the onus for promoting innovative ideas on ministers. It argued that ministers were better placed than anyone to make the Foreign Office more creative and urged: 'Force us to come up with radical ideas. Chair brain-storming sessions. Make us defend our assumptions. Encourage creative thinking. Praise innovative and fresh ideas, even when they are impractical or you do not agree.' While it advised ministers to call in groups and listen to their concerns, the memo steered them away from becoming a counselling service, but made the basic point: Do know what is going on in your own organization.

With the Foreign Office at last accepting the need to modernize, it struck the Young Turks as extraordinary that management had deliberately kept the new information technology out of ministers' offices, thus sending all the wrong signals inside and outside Downing Street. It was a point with which Peter Hain concurred when he arrived at his office after being appointed Minister of State and asked where his computer was, having used one at the Welsh Office. He was told there wasn't one. It took several months before one was installed – and for a long time he was the only minister in the Foreign Office who worked on his own computer. The memo advised all ministers from the Foreign Secretary down to start using a computer all the time and send the staff e-mails – advice not taken very readily.

This catalogue of complaints apparently touched a raw nerve. An advance copy of the Foresight Report was sent to Robin Cook in January 2000, at the same time as the Board of Management received their copies. No adverse comment was ever made officially. There was no meeting, however, between Sheena Matthews as head of Change Management and Robin Cook during the subsequent eighteen months of his term as Foreign Secretary. It left many of the Young Turks surprised, since he had presented himself as the great modernizer in politics and had come into the Foreign Office as the man ready to blow the wind of change throughout the organization. Although he had a habit of losing interest very quickly in issues that were not making big headlines, no one found any reason to doubt Cook's commitment to reform. But he left the impression that he was worried about the consequences, which called for more of his attention than he seemed to those around him prepared to give.

Not so Sir John Kerr. For him the peasants' revolt and its outcome in the manifesto for a revolution were confirmation that the time for change had been recognized throughout the Foreign Office at home and abroad, and that the modernization movement could not be stopped, only accelerated. What could be stopped was publication of the Foresight Report, and because of the risk of further bad publicity for the Foreign Secretary, Sir John Kerr bowed to the sensitivity of Robin Cook about the Memo to Ministers. It was agreed that not only should the report not go into the public domain but that there should be no disclosure that the Foresight saga had taken place – an edict which, surprisingly, survived until the disclosures in this chapter.

The immediate follow-through was Sir John Kerr's promotion of 'quick wins' to convince the staff that the Foresight exercise had not been a flash in the pan. In hindsight some of them appear trivial. Friday was proclaimed Dress Down Day, with many young officials choosing to come into the Foreign Office in their leisure gear, although not many of the senior mandarins were spotted in chinos or Levi's. More modern pictures appeared on the walls and colourful plants brightened the gloom of the corridors. The colour code for papers – one colour for one grade of official and a different one for a higher-grade official – was abandoned. A fitness centre was set up in the Old Admiralty Building with classes not just in aerobics, Pilates and yoga, but also in kick-boxing, which attracted almost as many women as men. The use of first names was another attempt to make it seem that the hierarchical system was being abandoned at a stroke. Instead of junior staff having to be formal in address-ing their boss as 'Ambassador' or 'Sir', they were encouraged to call him by his first name – unless he was the Permanent Under-Secretary, as he was still called 'PUS'. The really big changes were to come in the transformation of the antiquated communications system into state-of-the-art satellite communica-tions under Matthew Kirk.

The pace of change was quickened in the operations of the action groups mandated to take the new ideas forward into the various spheres of personnel, management, resources, working practices, the way IT was used not only to speed up but to improve performance, and the working environment. When Michael Arthur, then Economic Director General, took over as chairman of the Foresight Group on Resources in March 2001, it defined its core functions as supplying new ideas to put to the administration, acting as a sounding board for ideas from the administration, exercising a check on actions by the board, tracking the progress of resource decisions, and promulgating best practice.

Its London-based group was expanded to fifteen members and a worldwide group to pull in views from overseas was established, with members contributing through Firecrest from such places as Los Angeles, Nairobi, Paris, Geneva, the Seychelles, New York, Port Villa and New Delhi.

Keeping the momentum going was a task assigned to Andrew Key, another young high-flyer, with the responsibility for facilitating the work of ginger groups on new ideas and taking all the proposals for change to the board. Once they were approved he had authority to apply pressure on the various directorates and departments to ensure that specific action was taken to implement what was authorized by the board. New ideas are continually being sought on managing resources better to ensure more efficient delivery of services and policy, a search that seeks to set up new projects with action groups derived from an e-mail list of 300 activists on Foresight. Staff seconded to the private sector are expected to return with insights into different ways of making strategic decisions which could be applied to the Foreign Office. Discussions are held with people who run projects outside government so that lessons in achieving change can be gained from tapping into the experience of business companies and NGOs.

An assessment of where the Foreign Office stood was undertaken nine months after internal publication of the Foresight Report through a special survey of reactions among 300 of the staff at home and abroad, in large missions and small posts, through a Culture Inventory and Experience of Change questionnaire. It indicated what people wanted from the organization: that it should encourage staff to perform to their maximum capability, foster more open communication and closer cooperation across the boundaries of geographical and functional specialization, and offer incentives to challenge current practices and try out new ways of working. On the negative side, however, it indicated shortcomings still remaining in the system: a tendency to dodge responsibility in order to avoid blame; pressure to conform and avoid the risk of making mistakes; resistance to criticism resulting in the curbing of initiative; and the legacy of the hierarchical culture persisting in the idea of controlling subordinates and yielding to superiors.

A wider stocktaking took place in January 2002 at a modernization conference for the upper echelons of the mandarinate – some hundred heads of mission and heads of departments at home – organized by Sheena Matthews. Four themes were discussed in the first part: flexibility at the FO, managing talents effectively, ensuring high-quality services, and the way the organization operated. In the afternoon the entire session concentrated on how to provide the best leadership. Each session was recorded and a transcript sent out to every post so that everyone in the Diplomatic Service could be brought up to date on all the changes that had helped to modernize the Foreign Office and what remained outstanding from the agenda originally set when the Young Turks embarked upon thinking the unthinkable.

Even more important was the message Sir Michael Jay issued on 14 January 2002, the first day he took charge as Permanent Under-Secretary: modernization must keep going. Significantly, it was delivered in the same place as Robin Cook launched the first salvo of the quiet revolution in May 1997: the historic Locarno Room. Hundreds of eager young officials crammed into the gilded salon or craned to listen from the corridors as he promised that Foresight would not be allowed to run into the ground. The Young Turks were cheered to know that the newly installed head of the Diplomatic Service was convinced that one of his important tasks was to have a permanent ginger group thinking all the time about change. He gave them the pledge they wanted: that there would be constant evolution; people had to accept it, learn to adapt to it and see it as a challenge to be faced every day in the Foreign Office and in every post abroad. No one expected instant total modernization of the system set in stone two centuries earlier. But the commitment from the top to radical reform was quickly demonstrated in a stream of significant structural changes put in place by Sir Michael Jay. Such evidence that the wind of change generated from the grass roots had begun to transform the Foreign Office and the assurance of continual striving to ensure the best use of some of the brightest brains in the country – these are the legacy of the quiet revolution, which is a magnet for the new generation of mandarins.

TWO

The New Generation of Mandarins

Mandarin: not a Chinese word but one given by the Portuguese colonists at Macao to officials – from the verb 'mandar' to command. The whole body of Chinese mandarins consists of 27 members. They are appointed for (1) imperial birth; (2) long service; (3) illustrious deeds; (4) knowledge; (5) ability ; (6) zeal; (7) nobility; (8) aristocratic birth. Brewer's Dictionary of Phrase and Fable, 1894

The Foreign Office is staffed by dedicated and often brilliant people.
Lord Owen, *Time to Declare*, 1991

UNTIL 1907 all aspiring mandarins seeking admission to the Foreign Office were chosen personally by the Foreign Secretary. As they needed to be recommended by a highly placed relative, the Diplomatic Service in the nineteenth century acquired the reputation of being 'the outdoor relief department of the aristocracy'. The nominees were required to have an annual income of £400 – a considerable sum in those days – for the first two years of their probation. When Lord Clarendon introduced an entrance examination in 1856, successful candidates had to have what was described as 'a high qualifying standard in French and handwriting'. After the introduction of a proper competitive examination in 1870 candidates had to pass demanding tests in French, Spanish, German and Italian as well as geography. It was not until the Diplomatic Service was formally merged into the Foreign Office in 1918 that the requirement of a £400 annual income was dropped.

For many examiners thereafter the necessary qualities for a mandarin were those described by Sir Harold Nicolson in his classic volume *Diplomacy* in these terms: 'Truth, accuracy, calm, patience, modesty and loyalty.' Then he added: 'But the reader may object: "You have forgotten intelligence, knowledge, discernment, hospitality, charm, industry, courtesy and even tact." I have not forgotten them. I have taken them for granted.' Such virtues were not thought to be found in women in those days. Apart from housemaids, who used to be accommodated in bedrooms on the top floor in Downing Street, the first woman engaged in the work of the Foreign Office was Sophia

Fulcher, who was employed in 1889 as a typist with the official title of 'Lady Typewriter'. No woman was allowed into the Administrative grade until after the Second World War. The implementation of the Eden White Paper of 1943, stating 'Every member of our Foreign Service should be in the fullest sense representative of our whole nation, of every class and section of the community', opened the door for Monica Milne to become the first woman admitted to the Administrative grade and be appointed Second Secretary in the Washington embassy in September 1946. Over the next eight years seventeen other women gained places in the Administrative grade, but because women were obliged to resign on marriage in those days seven of them had left the Diplomatic Service by 1954.

Britain lagged behind many other countries in lifting the barriers for career women. Mrs Ruth Bryan Owen was appointed United States ambassador to Denmark in 1933, and at that time Chile, Turkey and Spain were among those who encouraged women with posts in their diplomatic and consular services. Barbara Salt was due to become Britain's first woman ambassador with an appointment to Israel in 1962, but she had to withdraw because of illness. It was not until 1976 that the first woman ambassador was appointed: Anne Warburton then became 'Our Woman' in Copenhagen.

Since the abolition of the marriage barrier in 1972 there has been a drive to ensure that women have the chance to achieve their potential more quickly, but the pace of progress has still been slow. The first married woman to become an ambassador was Veronica Sutherland, who went to Abidjan in 1987, accompanied by her husband, Alex, who worked there as UK Director of the African Development Bank. A year later Juliet Campbell, once the star briefer of the press in the News Department, went with her husband, a retired professor, to head the embassy in Luxembourg, where, for the first time, the majority of diplomatic spouses were male.

Only in the past few years, however, has the quiet revolution begun to show signs of a significant acceleration in the appointment of women. In 1994, with women forming 28 per cent of the Diplomatic Service staff and 36 per cent of the Foreign Office's London-based staff, only 3.4 per cent had positions in the senior grades. When Sir John Kerr was appointed Permanent Under-Secretary of State and Head of the Diplomatic Service in 1997, not one of the twenty-two directors and heads of strategy units in the Foreign Office was a woman. Three years later seven of the twenty were women. In 1995 there were only three diplomatic missions headed by women. In 2004 there were seventeen – thirteen by ambassadors or high commissioners and four by consuls general.

One of the great tradition-breakers achieved a 'double first': in 1999 Kathryn

Colvin became the first woman appointed Vice-Marshal of the Diplomatic Corps, and in July 2002 she became the first woman – a married woman, too – appointed ambassador to the Holy See in the Vatican. Nonetheless, there have been grounds for grievance in that none of the top-ranking diplomatic posts, such as Washington, Moscow, Beijing or Paris, has as yet had a woman appointed as ambassador. The nearest to such elevation so far has been Pauline Neville-Jones, a brilliant deputy under-secretary of state as Political Director, who left the Diplomatic Service in 1996 and took up an appointment with NatWest Bank after the plum of the Paris embassy went to Sir Michael Jay.

In an attempt to promote a quickening pace, at least at a less elevated level, the Foreign Office recruited Melanie Allison, who was national campaigns manager of Opportunity Now, with a title straight from a manual on political correctness: Gender Diversity Adviser. The Permanent Under-Secretary of State, who launched a Gender Action Plan to address issues causing problems for women in the Foreign Office, chairs a Gender Advisory Group, which is a forum for a cross-section of the staff to discuss, among other questions, ways of making the Diplomatic Service more family friendly. As part of the 'charm offensive' there have been two innovations: all members of staff are given five days' honeymoon leave (whether only on one occasion is not clear) and a crèche was opened in September 2001 with places for thirty-six children in the old telegram room, redecorated with tigers painted on the walls, alongside the King Charles Street entrance, to replace the limited facilities formerly available at Westminster. Although it is not a free service it is subsidized, with smaller fees for junior members of staff, and priority is given to those women who might otherwise find it hard to resume their work at the Foreign Office. The fitness centre has been modernized with new facilities and now offers a ten-week course on t'ai chi.

Arrangements are made for flexible working hours and job sharing. Special unpaid leave, formerly limited to five years, was extended to ten years to allow a career break for family reasons or for women to pursue their career elsewhere and then return. Sir John Kerr issued an appeal in November 1999 for women who had left the service to come back, saying: 'We are making rejoining easier – it makes sense for us to look for people who know us and our work and would fit in easily.'

To attract graduates to consider a career as mandarins, the Foreign Office brought the Nicolson test up to date by describing what it takes to be a successful diplomat in these terms: 'You must be able to think quickly and analytically, have good interpersonal skills and an interest in international affairs ... You will need good communication skills and be a good organiser ...

You will also need plenty of motivation and be driven by a fascination for your work.' For Denise Holt, the personnel director until her promotion as ambassador to Mexico in 2002, her job entailed conducting an exacting search for the high-flyer who had the ability to produce good-quality advice under pressure, the determination to achieve objectives, and the potential to be a good manager. Foreign Office teams travel the country for such paragons, inviting them to come forward as applicants at recruitment fairs, universities and community groups, as well as organizing seminars for university careers advisers. To tempt them to apply to deploy their talents in the Diplomatic Service rather than in the City or the multinational companies, they emphasize the varied opportunities available around the world in 232 posts, including ninety-nine embassies, forty-six high commissions and ten diplomatic missions to international organizations. Graduate applicants, who used to be called candidates for the Administrative grade, are now part of the Fast Stream Recruitment Programme for what are termed the Policy grades.

One of the projects designed to attract students, the Overseas Undergraduate Attachment Scheme, has been stepped up in recent years and is now a major operation. It offers work experience for between two weeks and two months at British embassies to undergraduates in their penultimate year, but they have to pay their air fares and living costs. In 2000 there were fifty-one undergraduates – 45 per cent women and 10 per cent from ethnic minorities – participating from twenty-four universities, including Glasgow, Edinburgh, Newcastle and Sheffield, as well as Oxford and Cambridge. In posts such as Bucharest, Rangoon and Canberra they had first-hand experience of consular problems which throughout the 232 posts operating in 190 countries involved 45,000 British citizens seeking assistance for illness, bereavement, arrest or lost passports.

The Foreign Office website projects a vivid sense of importance – and excitement – for potential new mandarins in 'playing a leading role' in Policy grades. It sets out the following scenarios:

- A high-ranking official from an African country is due to meet the Foreign Secretary to discuss human rights. As the desk officer for the region, it is your job to write a brief explaining the issues and suggesting points for discussion.
- A member of the Royal family is touring your host country. It is your job to oversee arrangements and see that the visit goes according to plan.
- Civil unrest has broken out in a remote part of the country where you are based. London needs detailed information about why this has happened and who is involved.

- A British company contacts you asking for advice on exporting its products to your host country. It is your job to help identify some suitable trading partners.
- As the UK representative at an EU working group you have to negotiate the inclusion of some wording to which the Government attaches great importance.

The website targets impressionable graduates:

As a policy entrant in the Diplomatic Service you could be dealing with any one of these situations or indeed all of them, or something similar, from your first few months in the office. You will change jobs every two or three years: the only thing they have in common will be the challenges and stimulation they offer. People in policy grades in the Diplomatic Service help to formulate policy on political, commercial and economic matters. That could mean anything from writing a progress report on complex arms negotiations in Geneva to briefing a minister on the latest plans to expand the European Union. Although you will concentrate on policy work, you may have the opportunity to try Press and public affairs, consular, immigration or management work as well.

Despite these enticingly portrayed opportunities, the success rate in recruiting members of ethnic minority groups has been, in the admission of the Civil Service Fast Stream Recruitment Report published by the Cabinet Office in July 2000, 'unacceptably low'. That was presumably why one of the two recommendations used on the Foreign Office website came from a recently recruited diplomat, Priya Guha, working as Second Secretary at the British embassy in Madrid. She is quoted as saying: 'It's a great opportunity to live and work in a different country. Every day I am dealing with people from the Spanish Ministry of Foreign Affairs and, of course, in touch with colleagues back in the UK. The work is really interesting and varied and I'm given a lot of day-to-day responsibility.'

Another 'happy entrant' the Foreign Office featured in its report for 2001 was Irfan Siddiq, who described his first two years with spells on the nuclear disarmament and NATO desks before preparing for a posting to Cairo. 'As it happened, the second Palestinian intifada broke out just a few days after I joined the Department, and so my time there was especially busy and interesting. I am now learning Arabic. The fact that I am going to work in an unfamiliar part of the world armed with the local language is a huge bonus, and I greatly appreciate the investment that the Office is making in me.'

In campaigns to attract more applicants from the ethnic minorities their special role has been highlighted in the initiative begun in 2000 of sending

Muslim members of the Foreign Office as consular officials to help the 20,000 British Muslims attending the Hajj in Mecca – the first non-Muslim country in the world to do so. Lord Patel of Blackburn led the supporting delegation of eight doctors (to take care of the elderly pilgrims unused to the strains of being in a crowd of two million Muslims), three counsellors from the British Muslim community and a small team from the Foreign Office – which had many more volunteers than were required – all wearing a Union Jack emblem on their white djellabas, working alongside diplomats from the British consulate-general in Jiddah. On-the-spot assistance eased the distress of British pilgrims who had lost their identity documents and the grief of the relatives of an aged pilgrim who died during the Hajj. This Foreign Office initiative has had a significant impact upon the Muslim community in the United Kingdom, making them much more willing to encourage their academically successful graduates to seek a place in the Diplomatic Service.

Although the number of serving officers from ethnic minorities is still very small – 289 out of a total staff of 5,436 at the end of 2001, amounting to a mere 5.3 per cent – the fact that in the upper echelons there has been a marked increase in recent years, with fourteen now serving as first secretaries and thirty-four at third or second secretary level, is being emphasized to those who used to regard the Foreign Office as out of their reach as an argument for reconsidering their prospects as applicants. At the same time there has been concern at the high rate of withdrawal by candidates from ethnic minorities. Research showed that candidates often lost interest because of the length of the selection process. As a result a monthly newsletter has been introduced to give candidates more information and keep them in touch with developments as they progress through the various stages of the tests. Significantly, it was tacitly recognized that there was not always a level playing field for ethnic minority candidates. The Fast Stream Recruitment Report published in July 2000 stated: 'Following a review of assessor training, we commissioned consultants to develop and deliver a refresher training programme, designed to increase assessors' awareness of *cultural diversity* in the context of evidence-based assessment. Guidance has been incorporated into both the Assessors' Handbook and the training programme for new assessors.'

Waverers among those targeted by recruitment teams are reminded of the way in which Dr Vijay Rangarajan, a brilliant Cambridge mathematician and son of a distinguished Indian civil servant, made his mark in the Foreign Office and was appointed in 1999 private secretary to the Permanent Under-Secretary and Head of the Diplomatic Service, a post traditionally regarded as a springboard to the upper echelons. Sir John Kerr had been private secretary twenty-five years earlier to Sir Michael Palliser, who became Permanent Under-Secretary and Head of the Diplomatic Service twenty years after he had served as private secretary to Sir Ivone Kirkpatrick. Dr Rangarajan had the basic qualification for an aspiring mandarin: a very good degree – his was a first; nothing below a 2.2 is acceptable – and the ability to impress in a severely competitive environment.

One of the biggest promotions from the ethnic minorities was the appointment in April 2004 of Anwar Choudhury as High Commissioner in Bangladesh at the age of forty-four. A late entrant into government service, he spent six years as a consultant engineer with Siemens Plessey before joining the Ministry of Defence. Choudhury was so impressive when he served in the Cabinet Office for three years that, despite never having worked at a post abroad or headed the administration of a mission, he was chosen as the outstanding candidate for the British High Commission in Dhaka.

The severity of the competition facing every candidate is demonstrated by the statistics for fast stream recruitment to the Diplomatic Service. In 1999/2000 there were 1,577 graduates who applied for a place in the Diplomatic Service; thirty were recommended for appointment, a success rate of only 1.9 per cent. Applications in 2000/2001 rose by an amazing 82 per cent to a total of 2,743 candidates, which amounted to 54 per cent of the number of graduates applying to the entire Civil Service. Even so, only twenty-six appointments were made to the Diplomatic Service from the fast stream candidates, a success rate of only 0.95 per cent. As long ago as 1968 the Foreign Secretary, Michael Stewart, a former schoolmaster, summoned vice-chancellors from provincial universities for a one-day seminar at the Foreign Office in an attempt to get the message across that their graduates could compete successfully against those from Oxford or Cambridge. It took over three decades for the message to be accepted and for the notion that an Oxbridge degree was essential for aspiring mandarins to be convincingly discounted.

Nonetheless, Oxbridge has continued to dominate the selection of the new mandarins. Of the twenty-six new entrants chosen from the 2000/2001 applications eleven were from Oxford and five from Cambridge. Edinburgh University supplied two successful candidates, with one each from Bristol, Hull, Kent, Leeds, London, Newcastle, Sheffield and Wales. Women won twelve places against fourteen won by men. In the previous year Cambridge candidates secured eight places, Oxford seven. The other fifteen successful candidates came from seven provincial universities and one Scottish university. Three from Southampton University won places, as did two from Bristol University, two from Durham University, two from Exeter University, two from

York University, one from Keele University, one from London University and two from Glasgow University. In the entire fast stream programme 42 per cent of the successful candidates were newly qualified graduates, 13 per cent were unemployed, and the remaining 45 per cent of successful applicants had jobs and were switching to become civil servants. The average age of candidates at the time of their application was twenty-four.

Among the 2001 intake of mandarins-to-be were three very impressive graduates from ethnic minorities. One was an applicant of Sri Lankan extraction who went to a comprehensive school in East London and fell under the spell of a brilliant teacher who inspired him to get a place at New College, Oxford. Alongside him were an outstanding Afro-Caribbean scholar from Croydon and a highly talented Muslim of Pakistani origin from Yorkshire. Their breakthrough represented one more successful application than the previous year and a much applauded improvement from zero the year before that. In the fast stream applications for the Civil Service as a whole, seventeen ethnic minority candidates were recommended for appointment – 6.2 per cent of the total compared with 2.2 per cent in 1999/2000.

They were with the front runners in a process begun in September each year with the deadline for applications and continuing over eight months until the results are announced. The first hurdle is the Qualifying Test, including what is termed a bio data questionnaire, at a day of written examinations held at various government test centres throughout the country. There is no essay writing, no test of ability in a foreign language. Although the United States State Department tests candidates on their knowledge of current affairs, the Foreign Office does not rate that as important. Nor is any great store set at this stage on language qualifications or even linguistic aptitude. It is basically an IQ test to evaluate a candidate's skills in verbal and numerical reasoning, plus a number of psychometric tests to assess suitability for the demands of government service. At the end of the testing there is a substantial fall-out every year, sometimes as many as one out of five applicants.

The next stage is the main hurdle: two days at CISB – the Civil Service Selection Board, which is a sophisticated, updated version of WOSB, the War Office Selection Board for choosing service personnel for officer training – held in London. It is a gruelling test, not only of the candidates' skills but also of their mental strength under pressure – and under the close scrutiny of psychologists. They are assessed under a number of competency headings, each being linked to what are termed 'behavioural indicators'. Measurements of performance are made against a 'behavioural checklist' drawn up by a firm of occupational psychologists to meet the requirements of the Foreign Office

– a process that appears to vindicate all the forebodings of Lord Strang, former Head of the Diplomatic Service, who wrote in his memoirs: 'The modern candidate can dispense with much of the book-learning and most of the old-fashioned social graces; but he must possess in place of these accomplishments a thick armour of brass, for he is exposed to all the wiles and probings of the professional psychiatrist.'

It begins with much tougher tests of verbal and general reasoning ability than were faced in the Qualifying Test. A candidate is confronted with a fictional problem such as an asylum issue or the ethical aspect of an aid programme which could be encountered by a desk officer. Three options are given for a recommendation on the policy to be adopted. The candidate is required to put forward a course of action and the reasons for choosing it in preference to the others. Next there are group exercises which are intended to test 'interpersonal, leadership and negotiating skills'. Each person is given a role to play in an imaginary crisis situation and the examiner controls each development in the situation in order to assess how well each person acts out the role allocated. It presents each candidate with the dilemma of deciding how strongly to project leadership qualities without appearing to go over the top and seem arrogant, attention-seeking and domineering.

Candidates admit that it is a very stressful experience, mainly because they are conscious all the time of what is at stake and realize that an ill-judged answer could jeopardize their prospects of a career in the Foreign Office. One criticism that even successful candidates acknowledge is that the pressure applied by the psychiatrists rewards those who have a facility for quick responses. It has prompted those who have come through the test with the best grades to ponder whether the preference for speed rather than profundity engendered by the tests may not undermine the quality of advice if that priority is maintained when they enter the Diplomatic Service.

The third part is a series of interviews which are designed to explore the 'background, intellect and motivation' of the candidate – a process much more probing than it used to be. Sir Pierson Dixon, who rose to be Ambassador at the United Nations, recalled that some of the questions he faced at his entrance exam were farcical, such as 'Who was the French poet who never wrote anything of note after the age of seventeen?' and 'Is there any resemblance in the mentalities of the ancient Greeks and the modern Athenians?' The first question that Lord Gore-Booth, who became Permanent Under-Secretary, faced at his entrance exam interview was: 'What is your view about sterilization?' Nowadays, when the interviewer explores the candidate's attitudes, there is a tendency for a smart-Aleck or smart-Alexandra to assume that points can be scored by the intensity of references made to humanitarian issues such as HIV/Aids, Heavily Indebted Poor Countries and the IMF, and environmental pollution. In fact, a demonstration of balanced concern and an awareness of the complexities of demands upon national resources are more likely to impress examiners.

From the original 2,743 hopefuls in 2001 only sixty survived to face the last hurdle – Final Selection Board – which decides who is recommended for the vacancies. They arrived at the board classified in four categories on the basis of the assessors' verdicts on their performance at CISB: (1) outstanding – a rarity, (2) very good, (3) good, and (4) borderline. The board is usually chaired by the personnel director. Alongside are four other members, two from inside the Foreign Office – one of whom would be an assistant director of personnel, the other the head of a front-line department – and two outsiders. The latter are usually experienced panellists either from the business world or academe.

The report from CISB usually indicates the areas in which candidates should be probed to reveal how strong their sense of dedication is likely to be. Attitudes to postings in challenging areas and the depth of motivation beyond a normal interest in travelling around the world are explored. In the course of a forty-five-minute interview the candidate is given the chance to make assessments of the current agenda of international affairs as an indication of how global their interests are. Judgement rather than expertise is the quality being sought by examiners, who seek to bring out how committed candidates are to accepting responsibility in a variety of situations likely to be faced in posts across the world.

Candidates usually rate the final interview as the most interesting part of the entire selection procedure, since it gives them the opportunity to take the initiative rather than being locked into the defensive situation of reacting to observations, as happens during the CISB tests where the assessors make the running. The good talkers relish the chance to direct the exchanges with the board into areas where they can show their ability to give an intelligent appraisal of situations for which they have prepared – sometimes by astute borrowings of arguments gleaned from the pages of *The Economist*. Even at this late stage there is no requirement to prove fluency in any language. At the end, however, candidates are given a language aptitude test. It is not the final determinant of success or failure but is used as an indicator of the sort of initial appointment that would be most suitable for a candidate prior to specific language training at a later date.

When the successful candidates are notified that they are to be admitted to the Diplomatic Service their appointment is subject to their passing two final checks: a medical examination and a security vetting. The medical test is usually routine, without the high fitness qualifications required when a multimillion-pound football transfer depends upon the outcome. However, there was one occasion, in 1993, when it did alter the list of appointments. Andrew Gilchrist was informed that he had come thirteenth when there were vacancies for twelve. Two weeks later he was admitted because a successful candidate had been medically examined and found to have only one kidney. As he explained : 'Thereupon, having been certified as possessing the correct number, I duly took his place. Later I learned that the regulation was based upon the severe strain imposed upon Foreign Service staff stationed abroad by the pressure of the social round of representational life to which their kidneys are regularly and inevitably exposed.' It was fortunate for the Diplomatic Service that he slipped into it unexpectedly since Sir Andrew Gilchrist proved a valiant ambassador in Reykjavik and Djakarta, in both capitals defying angry demonstrators attacking the British embassy by blasting back with a skirl of bagpipes.

Since the end of the Cold War the security check, termed PV (TS) – Positive Vetting (Top Secret) – has become less rigorous. Investigations of candidates were to be, in the words of the official notification, 'concerned not only with their political sympathies or associations but also with revealing any characteristics which may be a potential risk to security'. Nowadays there is much less probing into the political background of candidates unless there are strong suspicions about their reliability. Equally significant, the automatic ban on homosexuals being admitted to the Diplomatic Service was lifted. Changes were introduced by John Major as Prime Minister in July 1991 'in the light of changing social attitudes towards homosexuality in this country and abroad, and the correspondingly greater willingness on the part of homosexuals to be open about their sexuality, their life-style and their relationships'. However, being a homosexual is still regarded as a disadvantage in a bid for promotion to the higher echelons, as was evident from John Major's statement: 'The susceptibility of the subject to blackmail or pressure by a foreign intelligence service will continue to be a factor in the vetting of candidates for posts involving access to highly classified information.'

Apart from the main route to the status of mandarin through the fast stream recruitment of graduates, there are three other ways of getting on to the escalator to the upper echelons: direct recruitment of those with specialist skills; late entry examinations, usually for those between thirty-five and forty-five years of age; and a specialist entry system for economists. People with successful careers outside the Foreign Office are headhunted either on a

short-term contract for five years or for full-term engagement. Throughout the
Civil Service in recent years there has been a growing realization of the need
to attract more people with scientific backgrounds. Successful applicants with
degrees in non-arts subjects constituted only 26 per cent of total admissions
in 2000. The Fast Stream Recruitment Report stated in July 2000: 'Like many
other organisations we need generalists who are familiar with scientific issues
and the interpretation and presentation of numeric data.'

Those with specialist skills are recruited for specific jobs mainly inside the
Foreign Office but sometimes abroad. Dianna Melrose, who was renowned for
her innovative ideas as Policy Director at Oxfam, was recruited in February 1999
to be the deputy head of the Planning Department – the first woman and the
first outsider appointed to the think tank inside the Foreign Office, reporting
directly to the Permanent Under-Secretary on policy issues. Less than two years
later, after passing the tests for entry into the Senior Management Structure,
she was appointed head of the team of twelve planners. Sheena Matthews, an
independent consultant, took over the Change Management Unit until it was
disbanded in 2002, and John Williams, an experienced political journalist,
was brought into the Foreign Office by Foreign Secretary Robin Cook as his
spokesman and head of the News Department – the first person from outside
the Civil Service selected for that appointment.

People in their mid-thirties who have had successful careers outside the
Foreign Office have been recruited intermittently and have proved highly successful entrants to the Diplomatic Service. Two outstanding examples were
in the British High Commission in Harare together in 2000, during the crisis
over the invasion of white farms by so-called war veterans: Peter Longworth,
formerly a distinguished diplomatic correspondent, was High Commissioner
and Ian Hay-Campbell, the Deputy High Commissioner, had been a highly
esteemed BBC World Service producer for twelve years before joining the
Diplomatic Service. Their journalistic background combined with their diplomatic training proved invaluable in helping them to stay cool and resolute
in situations that were often made deliberately provocative by members of
President Mugabe's government.

For the second time in three years a special competition for late entrants
to join the Foreign Office was held in 2001. Candidates from NGOs, universities, the law, business and the armed forces answered the advertisement
announcing fifteen places at first secretary level for people between the ages
of thirty-five and fifty-two. Anyone accepted at the upper end of the age limit
is admitted on a five-year contract, those at the other end being offered up
to twenty-five years' service. None of the fifteen posts was a specialist ap-

pointment, in keeping with the demand for generalists with wide experience. But there are times when specific posts are advertised. One such was for the Director of Trade Promotion in Toronto when Peter Agar was recruited from the Confederation of British Industry after a very competitive examination. As there is a need for diplomats with an ability to manage large budgets and big projects, the Foreign Office has adopted a policy of seeking such talents from the business world. Once inside the Foreign Office, these recruits can move on when their particular specialist project is functioning smoothly to a generalist job at a higher level where management skills would be an advantage.

The third alternative route into the upper ranks of the Foreign Office is through the Diplomatic Service Economists Scheme. The Foreign Office realized – somewhat belatedly – that keeping pace with globalization, the European Union's increasing involvement in eastern Europe and the technological challenges of the Pacific Rim required priority to be given to acquiring a much more extensive range of economic expertise among its new mandarin class. It launched a recruitment campaign for 'talented economists who are original thinkers and can apply their core economic skills and specialist knowledge to policy issues in international macroeconomics, trade, financial markets and development, supplying the economic policy element of foreign policy issues'.

The people they are targeting are described as 'ambitious self-starters who have strong economic skills and want to put them to good use in a front-line policy environment'. Candidates are given the sort of incentive designed to seduce them from the ivory towers of academe: 'We want to make maximum use of your theoretical and applied economics training but to use it on real life cases – there are no backroom jobs at the Foreign Office.' Apart from theoretical knowledge, other qualities are necessary in the modern world of diplomacy: 'You will need excellent interpersonal and communication skills. You will need to sell technical ideas to a non-technical audience, working in multi-disciplinary teams. And you will need to demonstrate that you can, with appropriate training and experience, learn how to build networks of key contacts overseas which form the core of diplomatic work.'

Mobility and flexibility are highlighted as added attractions for applicants with the basic requirement of at least a second-class honours degree in economics, preferably with some macroeconomics training and experience; if they have a mixed degree, then economics should have accounted for at least 50 per cent of the course. During the first two years of the appointment, spent in London working on global economic policy or European Union matters, there is the possibility of becoming what is termed a country economist, 'working on a region of hot political interest like the Middle East or South East Europe'.

The appointment involves cooperation with economists in other government departments, particularly the Treasury, the Department of Trade and Industry, and the Department for International Development. Thereafter there is a move abroad covering economic developments in a country such as the United States or Brazil, or an appointment to the British delegation at the United Nations in New York or the Organization for Economic Cooperation and Development in Paris. An extra incentive was introduced in September 2001 when the Foreign Office agreed to sponsor one of the top entrants from the entrance competition for a post-graduate MSc in economics. Once established in the service, economists are free to switch to other core areas of foreign policy work with a view to becoming ambassadors, or they can seek secondments to do international economic work elsewhere in Whitehall, at international organizations or in the private sector for a time as part of a career in the Foreign Office.

For all three routes into the Foreign Office, not even the most ardent recruiting officer would claim that the financial rewards for new entrants are a powerful magnet. The new pay and grading scales introduced in September 1999 replaced the cumbersome system of ninety-three grades and seventy different pay scales with a flexible system intended to reward staff eager to make the most of their potential. But although the starting salary of £20,240 per annum in April 2003 for fast stream entrants to the Policy grade was substantially above the average annual earnings of £17,880 at that time, it remained well below what graduates could expect elsewhere. In the City a graduate entrant to an investment bank could be offered £36,000 with the prospect of doubling it within five years. Even when older Foreign Office fast stream entrants have impressive experience after graduation, the most they are offered is £34,544 per annum, which is also the maximum starting salary for economist entrants. A week after one high-flyer, Neil Wigan, accepted an appointment to the Policy grade following two years working for an investment bank, he received an offer from the private sector with a salary package worth three times more than the Foreign Office entrance salary – but the challenges of diplomacy were enough to nullify the financial seductions of the City.

Casting their eyes farther ahead, however, those hoping to become senior mandarins could take heart from the financial rewards at the top. The pay of the Head of the Diplomatic Service, like that of all thirty-three permanent secretaries in Whitehall, is based on recommendations to ministers from the Remuneration Committee on permanent secretaries' pay, and was given a substantial boost by the Senior Salaries Review which the government accepted in February 2003. Stating that it was necessary to encourage recruitment from the private sector and to 'reward people properly' for their contribution to public service, the review recommended raising the upper limit from £179,000 a year with new pay scales ranging from £118,750 to £251,500 – much more than cabinet ministers at £127,791 (including a £56,358 salary as an MP). The Prime Minister, whose salary of £175,414 is the highest of EU leaders, accepted the recommendation with the proviso that the limit should be capped at £200,000 until 2004. The salaries of the twelve Grade 1 officers – nine of whom serve abroad – range from £115,000 to £189,999. Only two earn over £140,000. Below them are nineteen other senior mandarins with salaries between £90,000 and £114,999. The rest of the 430 diplomats in the Senior Management Structure earn between £40,000 and £89,999, with the majority earning between £50,000 and £69,999.

However alluring these ultimate rewards may seem from the first rungs of the ladder at the Foreign Office, they look much less attractive to the aspirants in the private sector, where the latest statistics on executive pay show that diplomats are well down the salary league tables. In a Chief Executives Pay Survey published in the *Guardian* on 25 September 2002 the list included three who earned over £1 million, headed by Clive Thompson of Rentokil with a salary of £1,543,000, followed by Michael Bailey of Compass Group with £1,337,000 and John Hawkins of Anite Group with £1,047,130 (which incorporated a bonus of £529,000). Behind them were twelve chief executives earning more than £500,000, such as Brian Staples of Amey with £612,339, John Roberts of United Utilities with £598,600, Steve Maine of Kingston Communications with £580,000 and Oliver Whitehead of Alfred McAlpine with £529,000. The average chief executive salary in the leading organizations surveyed was £391,547, which was more than that of the only woman in the list: Bridget Blow of IT Net with £367,000 (incorporating a bonus of £121,000).

In terms of take-home earnings, where the private sector basic salary is augmented with bonus payments and cash from the exercise of long-term incentive plans, the gap is much wider. A *Guardian*-Inbuchon survey published on 5 October 2002 on the packages earned by the top 136 FTSE directors on the millionaire executives list revealed that Tony Ball who ran British Sky Broadcasting transformed his basic salary of £725,000 into take-home pay worth £7,779,310. Similarly Bart Becht of Reckitt Benckisser earned £9,062,000, Jean-Pierre Garnier of GlaxoSmithKline pocketed £7,044,843, Lord Browne of BP took home £5,521,348 and Martin Bandier of EMI earned £4,950,550. The only woman chief executive in the FTSE 100 did not make the millionaires' club. Marjorie Scardino, of the Pearson publishing group, turned down a bonus of £117,000 after a poor year for the company and limited herself to a basic £525,000.

Cynics are apt to scoff when young diplomats put the satisfaction of serving their country before the lure of financial rewards, but the dedication of
aspiring mandarins was amply demonstrated when a notice was sent round
the Foreign Office in November 2001 asking for volunteers to spend six or eight
weeks in Afghanistan immediately the Taliban were ousted from Kabul. They
were warned that they would experience rough living while helping the special
envoy, Stephen Evans, to reopen the embassy in Kabul and re-establish contacts in Herat and Kandahar. No special hardship allowance was mentioned
in the notice circulated on a Friday afternoon, yet there was a queue of 220
applicants for the six vacancies on the Monday morning, eager to go.

One of the advantages which the Foreign Office has over other organizations seeking high-quality graduate recruits is that its structure has been
modernized to deal with the many new facets of international relations and
thereby offer a much wider variety of outlets for trained minds seeking new
challenges. Instead of being channelled into progressively more specialized
financial operations, as can happen in the City, the graduate entrant into the
Foreign Office is attracted by the opportunity to pursue his interests in various
directions in London and abroad. The chance to make changes was set out
in the mission statement issued by Robin Cook within a week of becoming
Foreign Secretary in May 1997. As well as the traditional objectives of promoting the national interests, ensuring the security of the United Kingdom
and boosting trade abroad, it set out two objectives on the quality of life and
mutual respect which reflected the ambitions of aspiring mandarins.

On quality of life the mission statement made this pledge: 'We shall work
with others to protect the world's environment and to counter the menace of
drugs terrorism and crime.' On mutual respect it promised: 'We shall work
through all international forums and bilateral relationships to spread the
values of human rights, civil liberties and democracy which we demand for
ourselves.' Allied to these objectives, alongside the usual pledge to use Britain's
position as a permanent member of the United Nations Security Council
to achieve more effective action to keep the peace, there was a commitment to
combat poverty in the world. Strong emphasis was put on fostering 'a people's
diplomacy through services to British citizens abroad and by increasing respect
and goodwill for Britain among the peoples of the world'.

The strategy for such wider objectives reinforced the drive to modernize the
organization and structure of the Foreign Office in London. In 1965 there were
only thirty-nine departments, mainly organized geographically except for a few
functional ones such as the quaintly named Scientific Relations Department
and that concomitant of the Cold War, the Atomic Energy and Disarma-

ment Department, subsequently called the Arms Control and Disarmament Department. The organization then was top heavy with seven deputy under-secretaries and ten assistant under-secretaries. Radical changes introduced six directors general, changed the structure of departments, swept away the entire tier of assistant under-secretaries and replaced them with fourteen directors in charge of geographical or functional areas (these used to be called commands – a militaristic term that Sir Michael Jay abandoned on becoming Permanent Under-Secretary in favour of directorates). The largest is the Personnel Directorate, which supervises nine administrative services concerned with recruitment, training, promotion and deployment (see Appendices 1 and 2).

As other Whitehall ministries have become increasingly involved in European regulations, the Foreign Office has expanded its organization dealing with the European Union. The Director General Europe, Kim Darroch, supervises the work of three directorates: European Union (External), covering relations with other EU countries and enlargement of the Union, European Union (Internal), handling internal economic and institutional policies, and European Union (Bilateral), concerned with political and economic relations with those on the Mediterranean, including the Holy See and Monaco, as well as what are termed 'post-Holocaust issues'. Under him there is a team leader responsible for handling issues concerned with the professed aim of a Common Foreign and Security Policy in Europe, which, for some experienced diplomats, is a matter of expecting hope to triumph over experience. The range of opportunities in the ten teams assigned to European affairs attracts many ambitious young diplomats, as they are seen to be a fast-moving escalator to promotion.

Turbulence in the Balkans led to the creation of the Eastern Adriatic Department, with increased opportunities for appointments in Croatia, Bosnia, Macedonia and Albania. A Counter Terrorism Policy Department was hived off from the Drugs and International Crime Department, which had become overloaded with the expansion of the international drugs trade. Environment policy, which was assigned to a department dealing with matters such as international energy policy, wildlife protection and international space, broadcasting, postal and telecommunications issues, was given the status of a separate department after mounting international concern over climate change, the ozone layer, nuclear clean-up and the movement of nuclear materials.

Human rights questions have been given a much higher priority than they used to receive. Looking back on the early days of his service as second secretary, Sir John Coles, who retired as Permanent Under-Secretary in 1997, observed: 'In 1964 I was the Human Rights Officer in the Foreign Office and I cannot say that much attention was paid to my work (it was at that time that a Labour Foreign Secretary initially decided that the United Kingdom would not ratify the United Nations Convention on the Elimination of Racial Discrimination).' Now there is a special Human Rights Department with a staff of twelve responsible for ensuring compliance with obligations at the United Nations, the Commonwealth, the Council of Europe and the Organization for Security and Cooperation in Europe, not only in terms of the United Kingdom's overseas bilateral relations but also (with other Whitehall departments) domestic applications. At the instigation of Foreign Secretary Robin Cook an annual report on human rights is drawn up so that a record is available on what has been achieved by its campaigns and where more progress needs to be made.

One of the impressive innovations was the creation in April 1998 of the Human Rights Projects Fund, which enables diplomatic missions to secure funding to achieve their human rights objectives in the country in which they are stationed. In its first three years it dispensed more than £15 million to fund 400 projects in ninety countries. The projects were directed at helping vulnerable groups such as the disabled and children facing sexual exploitation, promoting prison reform and combating torture. The establishment of a Global Citizenship Unit by the Foreign Office in March 1999 won praise in the annual audit of Amnesty International. It welcomed the acknowledgement that British business had a major role to play in the context of the Foreign Office's objectives in terms of 'mutual respect' and claimed it recognized that 'British firms operating overseas generally have much more impact on the people in the countries in which they operate than does the British Government'.

Through careful husbandry, Sir John Kerr was the first Permanent Under-Secretary to avoid cuts in the Foreign Office budget in the Treasury's expenditure round and prove to the auditors that there is value for money in the services of the 5,436 on the staff – fifty-three fewer than the Crown Prosecution Services' 5,489 and almost 44,000 fewer than the Inland Revenue's 49,383. The cost of running the Foreign Office and the Diplomatic Service – excluding grants-in-aid to the British Council, the BBC World Service, and certain peace-keeping commitments – amounted to £817 million in the year 2002/2003. While the cost has escalated enormously since 1954, when it was under £20 million, rising to £467 million in 1991, the latest rise accruing from a dramatic expansion of commitments following the end of the Cold War did not arouse dismay when compared with Liverpool City Council's budget of £1,017 million.

Since the new Labour government laid down that where there was a country or a problem of concern to British interests there should be a British diplomatic mission, the Foreign Office has secured more funds for expanding the activities of the Diplomatic Service. Following a visit by Sir John Kerr to North Korea, diplomatic relations were resumed and a new post opened in Pyong-yang. It was one of twenty-seven new diplomatic missions created between 1997 and 2001. Embassies were opened at Bishkek, the capital of Kyrgyzstan; Chişinâu, the capital of Moldova; Tarawa, capital of Kiribati; and Dili in East Timor, as well as five new posts in China and six in India. They are mainly commercial, in keeping with the renewed emphasis on promoting trade which accounts for 38 per cent of the activities of the Diplomatic Service.

Although expansion of missions is a continuous process, Sir Michael Jay was also cost-conscious and regularly reviewed posts in terms of value for money. As a result of reassessing diplomatic representation in Central America in the light of changing strategic priorities, radical reductions were made in the latter half of 2003. The embassy in San Salvador, which once had a staff of six diplomats, was closed and British interests were left in the care of an honorary consul. Ambassadors were withdrawn from Honduras and Nicaragua and replaced with a chargé d'affaires. The ambassador to Guatemala was accredited to all three governments. The reason given to the Foreign Affairs Committee was the need 'to strengthen the UK's diplomatic network in other parts of the world now more critical for UK interests' – a view not likely to win friends and influence people in Central America.

To enhance the competitiveness of British firms there has been an expansion of Trade Partners UK, the key unit working overseas for British Trade International which coordinates activities across government departments and whose Group Chief Executive, Sir Stephen Brown, an ex-army officer who rose to be High Commissioner in Singapore, reports directly to the Foreign Secretary and the Trade and Industry Secretary. It is responsible for commercial work at 200 diplomatic posts where the priority is to provide up-to-date, reliable market information to enable British firms to compete effectively. It has also built up its services enabling inexperienced small exporters to acquire the know-how to develop their export potential. One of its major target markets, Brazil, has been given special attention after 100 British firms attended the Rio oil and gas exhibition. Trade Partners UK raised its sights by aiming to achieve a 50 per cent increase in British exports to Brazil by 2005.

In this new era of modernization, with a determination to make the most of expanding opportunities, the Foreign Office is evolving through its quiet revolution with a new breed of dedicated mandarins who have established a high reputation throughout Whitehall as the crème de la crème. There is still a long way to go before it will become evident whether the old Whitehall warriors have really been succeeded by a 'Generation of All the Talents'. Much depends upon the extent to which the new mandarins benefit from the training designed to make the fullest use of their talents, and how well they utilize their experience to prepare themselves for the challenges of the testing times for diplomacy in the decades ahead.

THREE

Preparations for the Mandarinate

When I entered the British Foreign Service in 1949 I received absolutely no formal training whatsoever. One entered the pool at the deep end. Sir Peter Marshall, *Positive Diplomacy*, 1997

I joined the FO on 3 September 1964 and was despatched two weeks later to learn Arabic at the Middle East Centre for Arabic Studies (MECAS) in Lebanon. The choice of Arabic (made for, not by, me) turned out to be pivotal. Sir David Gore-Booth, *Valedictory*, 1998

JOINING the Diplomatic Service used to be just like joining a club in Pall Mall. In the days before the strict security precautions sealed off all the approaches to Downing Street, a new entrant could pass through the tall wrought-iron gates opposite No. 10 and be welcomed into the Foreign Office by a commissionaire as if he were entering a club. The new member would be shown round the high-ceilinged rooms of the palazzo created by Sir Gilbert Scott and then be introduced to other members. It was a leisurely initiation into the rites of the mandarinate. Before the storm clouds of the Second World War began to gather, it was the custom of the Head of the Diplomatic Service, Sir Robert Vansittart, to invite a new member to have lunch with him at his club.

In those carefree times of the early 1930s, as Sir Bernard Burrows, a legendary figure in the Foreign Office, wrote in his memoirs at the age of ninety-one in 2001: 'Work did not start until eleven o'clock in the morning. This gave time for riding in Richmond before a late breakfast. We had a longish lunch break, then later all assembled for tea in the Department and left as soon as we decently could after six. The most tiresome part of the programme was that we had to work on Saturday mornings, so that weekends were somewhat curtailed.' When he started there were no training courses: 'You were assigned to a slightly older mentor who told you the mechanics of the business and then you gradually worked yourself in.' Not so today.

Preparations for a professional career vary considerably from country to country, none more so than in the profession of diplomacy. There is much debate in governments about the best way of making the most of the talents of the successful candidates in their diplomatic services. In the Foreign

Office there have been many changes in recent years, with regular reviews of the length and content of induction programmes. The constantly increasing range of expertise required of diplomats, and the way training systems to meet these requirements are being developed in other countries, has resulted in frequent reappraisals in Whitehall. Some foreign ministries maintain that a novitiate learns more by working in a mission than by spending time in a lecture theatre. Others prefer to give an extensive grounding in all the aspects of a diplomat's functions so that the new entrant is fully equipped for most eventualities before being appointed to a post.

The flexible system in the United States of America has attracted much interest in other countries. Because the US State Department is committed to 'equal opportunity and fair and equitable treatment without regard to race, colour, national origin, sex, religion, age, sexual orientation, disabling condition, political affiliation, marital status, or prior statutory, constitutionally protected activity', a wide variety of entrants emerge from the Foreign Service examination, which is a one-day series of written tests and a second day of interviewing, role-playing and discussions. Few entered straight from graduation in the unusually small intake of twenty candidates in April 2001: with ages ranging from twenty-eight to fifty-eight the average age was forty-three; among the eight women and twelve men, eleven were married, four had PhDs, five had law degrees and thirteen already had overseas experience.

The next Foreign Service intake following an examination held on 29 September 2001 – and an increased budget from the administration of President George W. Bush to cover the cost of replacing the large number of retired officers recruited just after the Second World War – was assigned to fill 466 openings in five career tracks: eighty-nine Administrative Officers, seventy Consular Officers, ninety-seven Economic Officers, 103 Political Officers and 107 Public Diplomacy (information services and public affairs) Officers. They were selected at a Final Review Panel by two examiners who did not take part in the oral assessment or the personal interview. The candidates choose which of the five tracks they wish to enter – and stay with it for their entire career, although switching tracks is sometimes possible – and their results determine their position on the career track register.

All new entrants, regardless of the track they choose, begin initial training at what is termed the A-100 course at the National Affairs Training College in Washington. During the six-week induction period they learn about the structure of the State Department and the objectives of the policies implemented by the Foreign Service. As well as being instructed on the procedures of departments and embassies there are courses on what is described as 'behaviour and etiquette'. There is no requirement to have any knowledge of a foreign language, although those who wish to specialize can take courses in Arabic, Japanese, Russian or any other hard language.

Training is continued abroad when appointees are posted to embassies, where they are virtually on probation for a period of up to five years. During the induction course they submit a list of ten overseas jobs in order of preference and state the reasons for their choices. After two years abroad they are allowed to select where their next probation period will be served as certain posts at embassies are set aside for second-posting candidates. After thirty-six months they are tested by the Commissioning and Tenuring Board to ensure that they have acquired the right qualities for a career in the Foreign Service. If they are not 'tenured' they have one final chance to satisfy the board of their suitability twelve months later.

Canada also operates a five-year training programme which dealt with the 100 candidates who entered the Foreign Service as a result of the 2001/2 recruitment campaign; this allowed the Graduate Recruitment Test to be taken online under supervision at various Canadian missions abroad. The Foreign Service Development Programme has a stricter testing regime than that of the US State Department. Entrants without the necessary proficiency in French and English (Canada's two official languages) are required to undergo training for up to twelve months, during which period they receive only 80 per cent of the official salary. If candidates fail to reach the standard of fluency in twelve months they have to leave. After formal classroom instruction and on-the-job training in Ottawa or at overseas missions there are four performance tests spaced out over eighteen, thirty-six, forty-eight and sixty months.

France's Foreign Service has obtained its recruits from the prestigious Ecole Nationale d'Administration for generations, and until recently did not consider it necessary for them to have any formal training programme in order to deploy their talents in the diplomatic world. After a short tour of the Quai d'Orsay the practice was to assign them – without any choice being offered – to a department where they stayed for two years and acquired the techniques for dealing with problems by watching what their more senior colleagues were doing. At the end of twelve months a formal interview took place as a matter of routine, after which the new entrant would be confirmed in the diplomatic service. This seemingly irreproachable elitist system was severely criticized by Prime Minister Lionel Jospin following a damning report in July 2000 on the French diplomatic service by a national commission of inquiry headed by François Heisbourg. As a result Jospin called for radical reforms and the establishment of a new training institute by 2004, which was greeted with undisguised glee in a comment in *The Times*: '"Arrogant" French diplomats have been told to go back to school and to model themselves on their British and American counterparts to win back influence on the world stage.'

This general reform movement did not divert the Japanese from their traditional training system, unchanged for the past twenty-five years, which gives the twenty graduate entrants each year a living allowance – not a salary – during their two years' probation. The initial three months are spent at the Foreign Ministry Training Institute, which runs courses in Japanese culture alongside lectures on the state system, economics and international law. There are no special courses on the environment, human rights or international crime and drug trafficking. The next twenty-one months are spent as a trainee at a department in the Foreign Ministry. While most candidates have a good standard of English after ten years of learning the language at school, those who are being assigned to a country where a knowledge of English is essential are sent to an English-speaking country for two years to become fluent. They remain full time at a university and go to the Japanese embassy only to take their examinations.

Spain's Foreign Ministry gives fifteen graduate entrants a one-year course at its Diplomatic School with classes in politics, economics, law and current affairs. During this period they are not paid a salary or an allowance. Only after they have passed the exam at the end of their course are they admitted to the diplomatic service and given a diplomat's salary. It is similar in Sweden, although there is no Diplomatic School, just a training department at the Foreign Ministry. There is a three-week induction course for new entrants, who then spend a year as a trainee learning in a department and attending lectures – but not being paid as a diplomat until the end of their probation.

The Germans have the most intensive training of all countries for their aspiring diplomats, with a two-year course intended to teach them all they need to know for the rest of their career. From the moment the forty new entrants (twenty-three men and seventeen women) in 2001 arrived at the Foreign Office Training Centre in Bonn they knew they had to concentrate entirely on the lectures, with much emphasis on the legal aspects of diplomatic work, and they were not able to go into an embassy except to watch what diplomats were doing. It is an up-front cramming programme covering every aspect considered necessary for a career in which they may end up as an ambassador in a major capital. At the end of two years in the Diplomatic School a newly qualified diplomat may spend a further five years in Berlin before being posted abroad. No special courses are considered necessary in mid-career, not even when a diplomat is about to become head of a mission for the first time.

Although aspiring British mandarins are sent to the German embassy in London during their introduction to the Diplomatic Service, to see how its system works in its political, economic and consular divisions, there is no inclination to copy the cramming programme of the Germans. The Foreign Office is renowned for having the most comprehensive ongoing training systems – envied by governments around the world – for keeping diplomats up to date and up to the highest standards of their profession so that they can be influential throughout their career. Where it has been less sure of its handling of talent – and in consequence has been experimenting with various formulas – is in getting the new entrants thoroughly primed for the years ahead during the induction period.

Before the actual training starts the new entrants attend a pre-induction day when they are briefed on what to expect at the preliminary training course and have their nerves calmed by meeting the previous year's intake over lunch. They are required to attend what used to be called the Diplomatic Service Language Centre and is now the 'FCO Language Group', where their aptitude for languages is assessed and they are tested in French. After the board decided in 2000 that the level of French throughout the Diplomatic Service was not high enough, it was decreed that all new entrants should have as a minimum what is termed passive functional standard French – that is a moderate level of understanding in reading or listening. Once they reach that standard they are encouraged to carry on and improve their fluency, since it is a Diplomatic Service regulation that all Policy grade officers should acquire a good command of French at an early stage in their career and maintain it throughout their service, regardless of where they are posted. Their language programmes are designed to be taken without disrupting their initial training. They can do two hours before their normal working day starts or two hours in the evening.

The induction course for the Policy grade has been extended twice in recent years from three weeks to five weeks plus two days. These extra days were introduced to give an outline of the policy work on top of the basic programme, which some of the new entrants regarded as too basic for graduates with a first-class degree in PPE. In lectures and briefings by a minister, the Foreign Secretary's speech writer, one of the Foreign Secretary's private office staff and the Director for Strategy and Innovation, they are told about the objectives of British foreign policy, how diplomats are expected to work with ministers, and what sort of briefing papers are required for meetings with foreign ministers at home or abroad.

Much of the initial training is practical work, setting out the basic skills of drafting submissions and minutes, précis writing and speech writing. Every-one is expected to be competent on a computer, but there is a short refresher course as an introduction to the IT system used at the Foreign Office. The importance of trade promotion is instilled into the high-flyers during a day at British Trade International, and the high profile given to human rights is underlined in a whole-day session conducted by an outsider, usually from the organization Justice or Amnesty International. Lectures are given on key issues such as the environment and on the way international crime and drug running are being tackled. Extra sessions have been added on finance systems in the Foreign Office and the resource accounting system as a result of the increasing emphasis on managerial skills.

Until recently there was no instruction on how policies can be presented to gain maximum coverage in the press and on television. The Press Department, which deals with enquiries from the media, has now been given a place in the entrants' programme. But newcomers to the Diplomatic Service admit that this brief introduction is not adequate preparation for encounters with journalists. One of the difficulties has been the downgrading of the department in terms of its status inside the Foreign Office and outside in Fleet Street. The department itself has lost much of its direct contact with the media since it abandoned daily briefings for correspondents, who used to come to the Foreign Office for forty-five minutes every afternoon to raise points of policy and ask questions about what they thought were newsworthy issues – often a good indication to briefing officers of what might be top of the agenda in the next day's national newspapers. First-hand knowledge of how the media operate is difficult to acquire when even staff in the department rarely get the experience of face-to-face encounters with enquiring journalists or have the chance to see how correspondents work in a newsroom under the pressures of deadlines. Apart from attending a media interview with a minister, these diplomats are usually functioning merely as a telephone answering service.

There are two visits outside the training course at the Old Admiralty Build-ing – one to Parliament, the other to Brussels. Before going to Westminster the fledgling diplomats are given lectures on guidelines for the Foreign Office's relationship with Parliament and the ethical standards required of civil servants in their dealings with ministers as Members of Parliament. They are made aware of the nature of briefings expected for ministers and the Permanent Under-Secretary before they face questioning by the Foreign Affairs Select Committee. Their visit to Brussels lasts three days and is preceded by two days of lectures on the European Union and how the departments in the Foreign Office and the Cabinet Office deal with various issues. They meet officials at UKREP (the delegation to the European Union), the EU Commission and the British embassy, where they have talks and question-and-answer sessions.

To get away from the lecture theatre atmosphere, there are two sessions of virtual reality in a Foreign Office department: one a situation faced in a geographical department, another about a problem encountered in a functional department. A typical simulation exercise is that of a trafficking case handled by the Drugs and International Crime Department. Each group of new entrants is supplied with all the information available from a variety of sources. They are required to analyse how best to deal with the problem and whom to consult before taking action – without seeing any of the actual submissions or conclusions reached in dealing with the case. When the group reaches a decision and sets out the reasons for choosing the way in which they think the problem should be solved, they are then given the details of how the issue was actually resolved. This sort of exercise often makes people wonder why more practical experience of working in various departments is not included in the course, even if this resulted in the induction period being extended to three months. There have been suggestions that the best introduction to the Foreign Office would be achieved by putting the new entrant directly into a department to learn the ropes from others doing the work and then having a general induction course.

Unlike other foreign ministries the Foreign Office does not conduct any tests at the end of the training programme for new entrants. Although some ways of measuring performance have been considered, the idea of tests has been rejected on the ground that it would change the atmosphere for new arrivals and introduce pressure to conform to standards. The current philosophy is that freedom from further exams encourages newcomers in the era of the quiet revolution to be more creative in their responses and more ready to challenge what has been regarded as the orthodox approach to the situations with which they are confronted.

At the same time the recruitment campaigns for graduates make it clear that their career progression – and their salary – will depend on their closely monitored performance. As soon as the new entrants are informed of their first appointment to a department – which happens when envelopes are passed to them during the induction period – they are made aware that they are being monitored through a continuous process of appraisal. This is done by a line manager who acts as a sort of mentor, discussing performance regularly with the new diplomat. There is a written appraisal six months after entry, another after twelve months and then further appraisals each year after that. It is blandly pointed out that the purpose is simply 'to ensure that you know how you are performing'. In fact it is for the Personnel Directorate to know how you are performing and to have it in writing. The line manager's appraisal will be counter-signed by a more senior officer, who will add further comments. Then the line manager will show the appraisal to the aspiring mandarin and reveal what the Office think of his or her performance and allow written responses to be added. The sting comes at the end with the statement: 'You will also agree objectives – performance targets for specific areas of your work – for the coming months.'

Apart from these performance targets further training targets are set. In the first twelve months the new entrant is expected to take advantage of the extensive training system by signing up for three initial courses – one on the appraisal system, so that its full implications are realized from the start, another on management skills, and a third on management inclusion, which is the politically correct term for equal opportunities. As staff appraisal is re-garded as a core competence through all ranks in the Diplomatic Service, the high-flyers are urged to take the one-day course soon after their induction so that they can learn how to identify in themselves – and later in staff they will manage – the objectives to be achieved and how to meet them.

Management skills are being given increasing emphasis in the development of a senior mandarin. To take the first steps in acquiring them the new entrants are expected to apply for a three-day course held at a London hotel, where they will be instructed in the techniques of organizing work, making decisions and ensuring that they are properly carried out, and dealing with problems and con-flicts over action plans which may arise. The third initial course is intended to develop management inclusion techniques to deal with what are described as 'increasing challenges regarding the extent and breadth of differences that have to be accommodated in the workplace' and instilling 'a more complete under-standing of how the treatment of people can affect performance' – descriptions illustrating the care taken to be politically correct in the light of race relations initiatives following the Macpherson Report on the Stephen Lawrence case.

Training programmes are not organized on a 'beginners only' basis. They are intended to develop the talents of diplomats and staff at all grades of the Diplomatic Service at all stages from their first year to their final posting before retirement, which is compulsory on reaching the age of sixty – and even as that time approaches there are courses on planning their financial resources and a three-day workshop on preparing for post-retirement employment. Since 2000 more than twenty new courses have been introduced with extra financing from the government's Invest to Modernize Fund, bringing the total to over a hundred.

Apart from certain courses with a predominantly confidential content, such as those dealing with security, consular issues and the handling of visa applications, most of the courses are contracted to outside agents whose experts set up and conduct the programmes. Currently there are more than thirty contracts authorized – and regularly reviewed – by Richard Tauwhare, who took over as Head of Training from Christine Dharwarkar in 2002. Although most courses are held at the Old Admiralty Building a number are residential courses run at a hotel in Bray on the Thames or at the Ashridge Management and Research College near Berkhamsted.

While the main emphasis has been on core skills required as candidates progress to middle management and senior management appointments, an increasing number of programmes are geared to creating a sharpened awareness of factors in policy-making that were previously not given so much priority. One of the boasts of Robin Cook after four years as Foreign Secretary was that more than three hundred members of the Diplomatic Service had taken a one-day course on human rights with experts from NGOs such as Amnesty International and Justice. However, despite his commitment to put human rights at the forefront of policy, there were still reservations about the extent to which the programme had achieved its objectives.

A Human Rights Audit on the Foreign Office by Amnesty International stated: 'The key questions regarding the consistency with which foreign policy is applied – and whether it is driven by human rights concerns – rest on the relative importance given to trade or strategic interests as opposed to human rights, and whether the UK is prepared to criticise publicly its trade partners where they are responsible for human rights violations.' Amnesty International's conclusion was that in relation to specific states there was 'a mixed record on this count'. In its Human Rights Audit 2001 there was praise for the 'significant positive contributions' by the Foreign Office in East Timor, Kosovo and Sierra Leone, but concern was expressed about policies towards China and Saudi Arabia, with whom, it claimed, greater priority was given to 'business as usual' than to challenges over human rights failings.

Four courses have been introduced on global environmental issues to ensure that an awareness of them is incorporated into the considerations that arise in the implementation of political, consular, commercial and management policies. One two-day workshop called 'Civil Society, Corporate Governance and Environmental Ethics' provides guidance on practical environmental management in terms of energy and transport efficiency as well as waste reduction and recycling. Lectures by a member of the environmental department of Surrey University explain the implications of climate change and biodiversity loss.

Training is also given on how best to communicate environmental ideas in the implementation of British foreign policy objectives in other countries where environmental issues are not given such high priority.

As finance and economics play a progressively more important role in the work of diplomats, courses have been tailored to meet their requirements by lecturers from the London School of Economics. There are four short courses on international issues covering the role of the World Bank and the International Monetary Fund, emergency markets in eastern Europe and Asia, the economic aspects of the European Union's enlargement, and the British economy in global terms. At a more basic level, there is an introductory course for everyone on how the European Union works and how Whitehall deals with issues arising from the EU. Beyond that there is a four-day course on negotiating in the EU, teaching techniques on how to 'lobby, intervene, influence and work effectively with other interlocutors in the EU'. Training commercial officers to enhance export prospects for British industry is undertaken in courses lasting from five to ten days with visits to companies, major exporters and trade associations.

For young diplomats being posted abroad for the first time there is a comprehensive two-day course which can also be attended by their spouses or partners. Apart from learning what will be available in terms of accommodation, transport and medical facilities, the newly appointed diplomat will be briefed by the course instructor on 'how to recognise poor performance and be aware of bullying, loneliness and debt'. If that seems ominous for a first posting, worries can always be calmed by members of the Diplomatic Service Families Association, a team of twelve under a highly committed director, Emilie Salvesen, who have experience of handling problems about education, spouse employment and other issues such as long working hours with a great deal of understanding, based on their own experience in various posts. There is also a half-day course in personal safety awareness, offering advice on how to lessen the risk of being a victim of violent crime in a country where foreigners are a target.

Diplomats assigned as political officers abroad are given an intensive two-day course covering all aspects of the job, from obtaining and assessing information to organizing visits by ministers or delegations, and making the most of contacts at such routine events as embassy receptions for the Queen's birthday. The programme offers instruction on 'how you can draw out a source' as well as how to 'report on political developments, including reacting to unforeseen events' and explaining 'policy and lobbying including presenting information and influencing opinions (including press relations)'. But there is no attempt to prepare them for the wiles of journalists by introducing them to diplomatic correspondents or political editors working in the press gallery of the House of Commons, who may arrive with the Prime Minister on a visit to their embassy.

Farther up the ladder, those going to posts to become head of mission for the first time get a five-day programme introduced by the Director General Corporate Affairs which sets out the responsibilities involved in the role. It gives guidance on budgeting and financial controls, management of locally engaged staff, trade promotion, consular work with UK nationals, and the key elements of entry clearance in issuing and refusing visa applications. A three-day course is organized for those diplomats going abroad to be ambassadors for the first time. They are encouraged to bring their spouses or partners so that they will understand the aspects of the job particular to the country where they are going to live, and the areas in which they can provide special support in the fulfilment of the responsibilities of the head of mission.

To bring those diplomats who have been abroad for a number of years up to date with what has been happening back at home during their absence, there is a one-day course held in the training wing. It has sessions on the reforms resulting from the Foresight campaign, changes planned for the years ahead, pay and career development, and lectures on equal opportunities and employment law. They are instructed on the updating of information technology, and for those whose computer skills need improving there are refresher courses. Diplomats who have not attended a security course in the previous five years are expected to take the one-day home security programme, which instructs them on new security procedures and alerts them to the threat to the security of classified information through spying or leaks and the need for vigilance against subversion and terrorism.

Only recently has serious attention been paid to public diplomacy and the importance of having ambassadors skilled in presenting Britain's case to the press. Some heads of mission have won high praise as star performers with highly polished media skills on radio and television: Sir Nicholas Henderson in Washington during the Falklands War, Sir Ivor Roberts in Belgrade, Dublin and Rome, and Sir Michael Jay in eloquent French in Paris before he returned to London to become Permanent Under-Secretary of State. But training to ensure that others become as expert in projecting policies to journalists was not accorded much priority until a review of the programmes showed up the inadequacies. Now it is recognized that effective performances before the press and television in a foreign country greatly enhance Britain's standing abroad. Although the professional expertise of journalists remains largely untapped, and only two courses are available – a basic one-day introduction and a five-day course, both of which are intended primarily for those taking up posts as press officers at embassies – there are signs of greater urgency in training the new generation of ambassadors in media skills.

Another form of training for high-flyers takes place unannounced: second-ment to the private sector, where they can hone their skills in the international arena alongside those operating in a more competitive environment. Diplo-mats in mid-career are sent for a year or two with companies such as British Petroleum, Rank Xerox, Price Waterhouse, S. G. Warburg and Co., De La Rue and British Aerospace. Others are sent to the EU Commission or other govern-ment departments such as the Treasury and Trade and Industry. Occasionally there is an opportunity to take a year out for study and research at the Harvard Centre for International Affairs or the Royal Institute of International Affairs in London. Each year there are approximately two hundred members of the Foreign Office on secondment to the private sector, other government depart-ments or NGOs.

Training facilities are not confined to London-based diplomats. The bulky 168-page training programme made available to every member of the Diplomatic Service has a forty-page section on Distance Learning for those in overseas posts, which gives access to computer- and CD-based training, videos and a virtual learning resource centre. The video library, with over two hundred titles, has training programmes covering aspects of management, communi-cation and negotiating skills, teamwork techniques, persuasion by telephone and effective speaking and writing skills. Some of the most popular are *More Bloody Meetings* with John Cleese on chairing a meeting and controlling aggres-sion, *Straight Talking – the art of assertiveness* with John Cleese and Jennifer Saunders, and *Decisions, Decisions* with John Cleese and Prunella Scales. In the best BBC tradition some of the other videos, with titles such as *Phone Rage* and *Dealing with Aggression in the Public Sector*, carry the warning: 'Contains offensive language'.

It is very tempting for diplomats isolated from entertainment in spartan posts in central Asia to send back an order to London for some of the highly amusing videos from the John Cleese collection, such as *The Importance of Making Mistakes*, which illustrates the point that mistakes are a crucial element in the creative process, and *Humour is not a Luxury*, which demon-strates that humour can relieve stress and create the right perspective for motivating people. But these films are not intended to lighten the burden of a hardship post over a glass of malt whisky at sundown; they are meant as source material for an officer acting as a presenter at a group training session in an embassy and subsequently conducting a discussion on what has been learned. Any order must be authorized by the deputy head of mission, and arrives with the warning that as the videos cost around £1,000 posts will be required to pay if they are lost.

Not only is it forbidden for Distance Learning material to be handed on to other embassies in a country, it also cannot be passed on to other British posts in the region. However, the Foreign Office is ready under certain conditions to make British expertise available to other governments. There is an agreement with the French and German foreign ministries that they can send a few candidates each year to take management courses run in-house at the Old Admiralty Building. Sometimes courses are sent out to ministries – Thailand and South Africa being two recipients. The Cyprus Foreign Ministry asked for a course on drafting memoranda. In April 2003 a special programme was arranged allowing ten Afghan diplomats to attend lectures at the University of Birmingham and then gain work experience at the Foreign Office. To help the newly created foreign ministry in East Timor, a team went out to spend a month training those members of staff earmarked to become senior diplomats.

While there is widespread acknowledgement that the training in diplomatic skills is in a class of its own, the jewel in the Foreign Office's crown is the language training centre. Its official title, Diplomatic Service Language Centre, was changed to Language Group of FCO Services in October 2001 with the incorporation of translation and interpreter services, which accounted in 2001/2 for the translation of three million words in forty-four languages and the provision of interpreters on 380 days (in some instances several interpreters being engaged on the same day). Although Bismarck cautioned that 'too great a familiarity with a foreign tongue often provokes suspicion', the Foreign Office has always set great store by ambassadors being completely at ease in the language of the country in which they are serving – no matter what the language may be: French, Russian, Korean, Amharic or Tagalog. As a result, despite the perception that the British are poor linguists and prefer to raise their voices and speak slowly in English rather than attempt to recall some foreign vocabulary from their schooldays, Foreign Office diplomats in posts around the world have a reputation for speaking foreign languages with an elegance and fluency unmatched by those of any other nation. It may not come naturally and it is inevitably the outcome of years of hard work, but the reputation of British envoys as excellent linguists is regularly confirmed in every country where they are posted.

One of the proudest moments in the career of Sir James Craig, a masterly Arabic speaker, is often recalled at diplomatic receptions in Riyadh. When

Lord Carrington visited Saudi Arabia in November 1981, after a difficult period in relations following the furore over the television documentary *Death of a Princess*, he made four speeches that were translated sequentially paragraph by paragraph on each occasion by a different member of Ambassador Craig's staff. Prince Saud al-Faisal ibn Abdul Aziz al-Saud, the Foreign Minister, was so impressed by the impeccable Arabic used by the British diplomats that he made a point of extolling it afterwards in talking to his guests from other embassies.

An equally impressive feat of interpretation is frequently remembered in Djibouti, where a luncheon was held in January 1989 for Sir Geoffrey Howe after he nearly lost half his Foreign Office team when a rubber assault craft began to sink in a storm on their return from Paradise Island. The non-resident ambassador from neighbouring North Yemen, Mark Marshall, had assumed it was an informal occasion so no preparations were made for a speech by the Foreign Secretary. But relief at the rescue of the British diplomats from the sea prompted their host, Djibouti's Foreign Minister, Moumin Bahdon Farah, to go beyond a toast and deliver a long encomium in French on the importance of diplomacy in contributing to good relations between the two countries. Sir Geoffrey rose to the occasion with all the skill of an experienced barrister and a fund of amusing Welsh jokes, none of which would have been greeted so enthusiastically but for the instant interpretation by the then head of the Middle East Department, Sir Rob Young, who went on to become High Commissioner in India. It was a severe test since there was no text and the Foreign Secretary's impromptu remarks had some quirky pay-off quips.

The Foreign Office's reputation for having diplomats with an excellent command of French goes back a long time. It was a source of great satisfaction to Prime Minister Harold Wilson that he was able to confirm it when he went to Paris to meet President de Gaulle in January 1967, accompanied by Foreign Secretary George Brown, whose favourite French phrase to door-stepping journalists was *Pas de comment*. It was Wilson's good fortune to have with him his new private secretary, Sir Michael Palliser, recently seconded from the Foreign Office, who subsequently rose to become Permanent Under-Secretary. Sir Michael, whose wife was the daughter of the renowned Belgian statesman Paul-Henri Spaak, was a highly sophisticated bilingual diplomat accustomed to unravelling all the complexities of French political ploys.

When the British delegation entered the Elysée Palace the President's entourage was confident that his internationally acclaimed interpreter, Prince Andronikov, would easily outpoint his British rival in any test of accuracy. On these occasions the silent witnesses count the number of times one interpreter has to correct the other's version in translating the observations made to his own head of government. Wilson made no secret of his delight at the score, as Sir Michael had to make seven interventions to correct Prince Andronikov's translations into French of what the British Prime Minister had said compared with only two attempts by the prince to amend Sir Michael's translation of de Gaulle's remarks. However, the high esteem in which Sir Michael was held thereafter did not deter Prime Minister Margaret Thatcher from breaking with tradition fifteen years later and denying him the customary peerage at his retirement because of her outrage at what she regarded as the failure of the Foreign Office in general over Argentina's invasion of the Falkland Islands.

Nowhere is the Foreign Office held in greater esteem for the linguistic ability of its ambassadors and their diplomatic staff than in Moscow. Their reputation stands higher than that of any other foreign diplomats in the Russian capital. The tradition of excellence in the Russian language set by Sir Thomas (later Lord) Brimelow and Sir Curtis Keeble was impressively reaffirmed during the terrorist crisis at Moscow's Nord-Ost theatre in October 2002, when Chechen fighters held over seven hundred people hostage for three days until the Russian special forces stormed the building. There on the street was the fluent Russian-speaking ambassador Sir Roderic Lyne, questioning the Russian authorities about the British victims and helping to reunite a British family who had been separated in the exodus from the theatre.

Ever since 1856, when Lord Clarendon insisted on aspiring diplomats having 'a high qualifying standard in French', there has been an unshakeable conviction in the Foreign Office that members of the Diplomatic Service cannot represent their country effectively unless they are good linguists. Language training has been given increasing priority in the past decade. Ten years ago the Diplomatic Service Language Centre had a budget of £1 million to run courses in fifty-two languages. Currently, under its dynamic polymath director Dr Vanessa Davies, training has expanded by up to 40 per cent with provision for instruction in eighty-two languages. While the US State Department was struggling after the terrorist attacks on the World Trade Center and the Pentagon on 11 September 2001 to find diplomats with a knowledge of the languages of Afghanistan, Dr Davies already had several on a course studying Pashto as well as a course ready on Dari.

With a budget of £6 million – £2 million paid in languages allowances to successful students, £2 million for training in London and the remaining £2 million for training costs overseas – the centre deals with 1,000 people a year on anything from a half-day course to a two-year programme. In 2001/2 it provided over 65,000 training hours in sixty-three languages – courses in the

other nineteen languages not being taken up since there were no new postings to the countries where they were necessary – an increase of 8,000 hours
on the previous year. Half the staff of 150 are subcontracted from universities,
language schools and agencies to meet specific requirements for unusual
language skills. One proof of the success of the system is that 75 per cent of
all Britain's ambassadors are fluent in three or more languages. In order to
retain their command of a language – and the allowance paid for it – they have
refresher courses and tests (every four years) of their proficiency. Sometimes
they are sent to stay with a family in the country where they are going to serve,
with arrangements being made for them to study at an institution as well. As
Ambassador to France, Sir Ewen Fergusson kept his fluency in Amharic from
the days of his first posting to Addis Ababa in good working order in case he
found himself alongside an Ethiopian minister in Paris.

French has a special status at the centre, partly because of the requirements
for working in European Union institutions but also because there are over
three hundred 'speaker slots' – jobs for which fluency in French is essential
– to be filled continuously at three-year intervals as people are replaced on posting elsewhere. Spanish and German come closely behind French in priority.
In these, as in all languages taught at the centre, attainment is measured on
the national language standards. There are four levels: *survival*, which means
an ability, with basic grammar and vocabulary, to cope with conversation in
simple situations; *functional*, which requires a high level of accuracy in basic
grammar to handle straightforward work demands in giving and receiving
simple information; *operational*, which means the capacity to conduct substantive business with complex grammar constructions and vocabulary; and
extensive, which covers informal interpreting and negotiating with the breadth
of language of an educated national in the country. An extra classification has
crept in, a self-declared one styled 'native', which some candidates for posts
put on their CVs, but as Dr Davies is a stickler for proper professional standards
she insists that all linguistic competence must be verified by her experts.

There are regular trawls of newcomers to attract them to courses in 'hard
languages', usually with a high success rate. In recent years one in four of
the new entrants has opted for a gruelling study programme of twenty-five
hours with a tutor every week for up to two years. In 2002 there were nine
taking Mandarin, eight Arabic, six Japanese, three Russian, two Cantonese,
two Thai, and one each Bosnian, Burmese, Korean and Urdu. The attraction is
having an anchor for their career, getting early promotion, and becoming an
acknowledged expert in a region. After courses at either the School of Oriental
and African Studies or the School of Slavonic and Eastern European Studies

of London University, or at the University of Westminster, students are sent for training in the appropriate country. Those taking Arabic spend a year at universities in Cairo, Amman or Damascus; students of Mandarin go to Beijing University, those taking Cantonese to a university in Hong Kong for a year; students of Japanese go to a Foreign Office language school at Kamakura; Thai students spend up to ten months at the universities of Chiang Mai and Khon Kaen; Vietnamese students go to Hanoi National University; and Russian students have four months at the State Linguistic University in Moscow.

One of the consequences of the disintegration of the Soviet Union and the fragmentation of Yugoslavia was a sudden demand for language training to enable diplomats to operate effectively in the new states. It required provision at short notice of classes in Serbian, Bosnian, Croatian, Slovak, Slovene, Macedonian, Albanian and Kosovan Albanian, as well as courses in the languages of the Baltic states. Finding experienced teachers able to start classes immediately was not easy, but Dr Davies solved the problem by signing contracts with a company called SSEES – a joint venture between the School of Slavonic and Eastern European Studies and a private concern, Communicaid – to supply a team of teachers.

Even though English is widely spoken in Commonwealth countries it is much less predominant than hitherto in many nations because the new generation of the elite have not been educated in British schools and there is an increasing demand for national and ethnic identities to be recognized – which means a new emphasis on the local language. Mingling in the bazaars and markets in many countries, a diplomat needs to know the local language to assess the attitudes of the local people. In India some members of the Bharatiya Janata Party in the parliament, the Lok Sabha, refuse to speak in English, so there is a requirement for instruction in Urdu. Despite widespread use of English in Africa, diplomats going to Tanzania take courses in Swahili for six months and those taking up a post in Zimbabwe learn Shona.

For admission to the centre it is not enough to have an interest in learning a language as a hobby. Courses are either job related or geared to a specific requirement at a post, but they can also be taken on a part-time basis with sessions for an hour in the evening in Greek, Italian, Portuguese, Arabic, Chinese and Russian. Specialized courses are arranged on subjects such as Spanish culture, a critical analysis of newspaper texts in Chinese, political Russian, or how to read the nuances of a European Union telegram in French. Some are available in an intensive one-week course, others are fitted into an hour at lunchtime over a longer period.

Complete beginners in a language are given a minimum of ten weeks' tuition; a survival course takes at least eight weeks; and for functional and operational knowledge a minimum of five weeks. In preparation for certain language exams – French, German, Spanish, Russian, Arabic, Cantonese, Mandarin, Japanese, Korean and Thai – there are intensive courses of up to five days with sessions in the morning for the survival and functional levels or up to six hours a day for the operational and extensive levels. Although these languages attract the largest number of students there is always a demand for instruction in Turkish, Swedish and Finnish as well as some demand for rarer skills such as Malay, Ukrainian, Yoruba and Vietnamese. Facilities at the library and multimedia centre are impressive. There are over five thousand volumes in sixty-two languages on the shelves, a large video collection in thirty languages, interactive CD-ROMs in more than twenty languages at all levels, a vast supply of daily newspapers and magazines from many countries, individual audio laboratories, and access to word processors operational in sixty languages.

Diplomats have a good record for diligence as language students. Examination results show that in 2002 they achieved an average 85 per cent pass rate in both written operational Arabic and Japanese, while overall, in operational and extensive examinations, the pass rate is over 70 per cent. Rewards vary according to the language and the standards reached in it. There are five classes of language allowance with the four hardest – Cantonese, Mandarin, Japanese and Korean – in Class One, the next seventeen – difficult languages such as Uzbek, Arabic, Thai, Turkish and Azari – in Class Two, down to the eleven 'easiest' languages – all those of western Europe plus Afrikaans and Bislama, the form of pidgin English used as an official language in Vanuatu – in Class Five.

Allowances range from around £200 a year for functional French to £2,500 for an operational standard in Vietnamese, Kazakh or Amharic, up to the top scale of £4,250 a year for extensive command of Chinese, Korean or Japanese. Many diplomats have their salaries enhanced by three or four language allowances. The record is held by one member of the Diplomatic Service who receives allowances for twelve different languages. For that to be sustained the diplomat has to maintain the standards necessary to pass exams every four years, as that is the shelf-life set for qualification in each language. The fact that other specialist skills, though recognized as important, went unrewarded was a long-standing grievance among specialists working in London. Their discontent was acknowledged as justified in 2001 when allowances were awarded for special skills in accountancy, procurement and microeconomics.

Diplomats preparing for posting are encouraged to persuade their spouses to take language training so that they will be more at ease on arrival in a new country. Spouses are entitled to 100 hours of one-to-one instruction or 200 hours of teaching in class at the centre. As an added incentive to take the free tuition, spouses are also paid for reaching the specified standards. A spouse who is able to respond to a question at a French embassy reception by saying *'L'ambassadeur est mon mari'* will be entitled to an allowance of £137 for survival-standard French. If the spouse persists with language training an operational ability in Finnish would earn an annual allowance of £1,518, and with even greater persistence passing an examination in Turkish at extensive level could be worth £2,125.

So, equipped with a spread of expertise acquired from general training courses and a certain degree of fluency from passing written and oral examinations in one or more foreign languages, the aspiring mandarin is eager to move up the ladder in the Diplomatic Service. How fast and how far depends upon their having impressive appraisal forms and an ability to show the variety of talents required in order to be sent spiralling upward with postings and promotions.

FOUR

Spiralling Upward: Postings and Promotions

I was asked whether I had ever thought of Washington as a post. I replied that I had not, but as a matter of fact I would rather like to be sent to Persia. 'What, Persia?' said the Private Secretary, uncomprehendingly. 'Yes,' I replied. And half an hour later I got a chit saying that he had happily been able to arrange this. (I afterwards learnt that three other people had asked to be excused!) Lord Gladwyn on his first posting in 1924, *Memoirs*, 1972

There was a time when establishing a new embassy or diplomatic post took weeks, even months. Now it takes a plane ticket, a lap top and a dial tone – and maybe a diplomatic passport. We can hit the ground running. Gordon Smith, Canadian Deputy Foreign Minister, Wilton Park, 1998

LORD Salisbury, whose statue at the bottom of the Grand Staircase in the Foreign Office stands brooding over the diplomats making their way up to higher places, was always adamant on one point: 'I decide who goes where.' On that he brooked no interference, not even from Parliament. When he posted Charles Hardinge (later Lord Hardinge) to St Petersburg, promoting him over seventeen diplomats with more seniority, there were angry questions in Parliament. Lord Salisbury brushed his critics aside with lofty disdain, insisting that he knew his staff better than anyone else and he considered his choice of envoy to be the most capable person for the post. That was his prerogative as Foreign Secretary, he asserted.

This autocratic procedure for senior postings persisted for a century after Lord Salisbury. One of the most widely publicized instances was George Brown's treatment of Sir Con O'Neill, a leading mandarin of his era who had been chargé d'affaires in Peking and ambassador heading the British delegation to the European Communities. At the age of fifty-six in 1968, as a Deputy Under-Secretary, Sir Con made no secret of his desire to end his career with a posting as Ambassador to Germany. As a foreign secretary who did not like to be crossed, George Brown told Sir Con his next posting was to be head of the UK delegation negotiating to join the European Communities. So Sir Con did what he had done twice previously: he resigned. A generation later Pauline

Neville-Jones followed Sir Con's example when the Foreign Secretary declined to appoint her Ambassador to France.

The Foreign Secretary used to decide all the promotions to the 'Top Ten' appointments and leave the lesser 'plums' to be distributed by the Senior Selection Board, which usually had a junior minister sitting on it with the Permanent Under-Secretary and some of the Deputy Under-Secretaries. In theory, diplomats were consulted about the direction their careers were taking. They could set down their posting preferences for their next move – most were usually realistic enough to forgo joining the queue for Paris – and could discuss their choices and prospects with what was called the Personnel Operations Department. In practice they were often dispatched to a country where their political expertise or their language ability had no particular relevance. If there was a vacancy in Conakry or Kigali the personnel officer had to choose a replacement quickly without taking time to discuss with the candidate whether it was a post where he would enjoy working and his family would like living. In rare cases a posting could be declined, and if the reasons were convincing enough, for example on grounds of family health, then no serious setback to the diplomat's career would ensue.

Usually, there was no scope for argument and the decision of the personnel department was final. Not surprisingly the frustration and disillusionment of the victims of the system eventually set off alarm bells which the Foreign Office could not ignore. It called in management consultants Coopers and Lybrand Deloitte to conduct a wide-ranging investigation. The verdict shattered the calm in the corridors of power. Their report, issued in 1990 and based on the criticisms of over a thousand members of the Diplomatic Service, confirmed that the slump in morale and the shortcomings of the management system had become so serious as to undermine the effectiveness of foreign policy.

The most damaging revelation was the conclusion reached from assessing all the responses: 'There is a widespread belief that the Foreign Office–Diplomatic Service fails to provide all its staff with good careers and that more than half the sample population said they would leave the Service if a comparable job were available.' New entrants who joined with high hopes were disillusioned by what the report called 'the disparity between expectation and reality'. The lack of proper consultation about postings and promotion made staff feel that their careers were 'driven by decisions made in the dark by strangers'. The report exposed the failure in a sentence: 'There was for too many a "cloud of unknowing" over the whole process.' Its final warning was a clarion call for radical change: 'Something is clearly wrong in an organisation when its personnel service is found to be staffed by dedicated individuals working very hard over long hours and seeking to achieve high levels of fairness and objectivity in its process and when the recipients of that service have so little confidence in it.' It was an irrefutable argument for scrapping the Personnel Operations Department and making a fresh start with a modern management system.

At first the reforms were introduced piecemeal, but by the year 2000 the pattern of radical change had been established. Out went the dirigiste system of postings. The old structure of ninety-three grades and seventy different pay scales was scrapped. A flexible system aimed at creating a new environment of opportunities and rewards was put in place for all ranks in the Diplomatic Service. It opened the door for diplomats to choose where their career would take them under an open bidding system for postings. New entrants are given a gentle introduction to the new competitive arrangements: some forty junior posts are set aside by the Personnel Directorate so that newcomers are assured of an appointment matching either their first or second choices.

The posting system for Policy grades is called JESP – Job Evaluation Senior Posts – and there is a similar one for operational grades called JEGS – Job Evaluation General Service. Every senior appointment abroad in one of the 232 diplomatic missions in 190 countries, and every policy job at home in the Foreign Office departments, has a JESP score graded between 8 and 28. The highest score is for the Permanent Under-Secretary and Head of the Diplomatic Service, whose grading is the result of an assessment made by the Cabinet Office which determines the ranking of all permanent secretaries in all the Whitehall ministries. Next come the Top Ten in the Diplomatic Service – those traditionally called the Grade One ambassadors. Many assume that number one is Washington. Not so. It is UKREP, the ambassador heading the delegation to the European Union in Brussels, whose grade of 25 reflects the increasing involvement of the EU in the day-to-day administration of government business. Although the Anglo-American relationship is still close, the fact that it is not the 'Special Relationship' it once was right up until the end of the Cold War is attested by Washington having a JESP score one below UKREP at 24. The other eight plum jobs are Paris and Berlin at 23, Moscow and Delhi at 22, then Tokyo, NATO, New York and Beijing. When the embassy is due to change hands there is usually a review, as happened on Sir Christopher Hum's appointment to China in 2002 – at which time the JESP score stayed at 22.

The task of 'JESP-ing the jobs' – altogether approximately 450 – was undertaken in 2002 by Vivien Life as head of Management Consultancy Services in consultation with Peter Collecott, Director General Corporate Affairs, whose overall responsibility for administrative matters used to carry the Dickensian title of Chief Clerk until he took over. It is an exercise demanding scrupulously careful assessment – and diplomacy in its everyday sense – since the decisions affect salaries throughout the service. The six senior men in the Office with the title director general – formerly called deputy under-secretaries – are in the 20 to 22 bracket. Next are the directors with JESPs ranging from 15 to 20, along with thirty-two senior ambassadors such as those in Ottawa, Riyadh and Seoul. Jobs in the 13–15 range include the principal private secretary among three home posts and sixty-nine overseas, such as the ambassadors in Kuwait and Tripoli. Heads of department in London rank between JESP 8 and 12, with most at the upper end of the range. Overseas scores vary considerably from country to country: a deputy head of mission is at JESP 8 in Bucharest and Santiago, at JESP 9 in Lisbon and at JESP 10 in Helsinki. A head of mission – ambassador or high commissioner in a Commonwealth country – varies from JESP 8 in Port Moresby, 11 in Belize and 13 in Havana to 18 in Nairobi.

These variations are the result of the extent to which a number of factors are judged to be met in the criteria set for each appointment in a post. The first element in calculating a JESP score is management of people, not just in terms of numbers but also taking account of the potentially difficult circumstances in which management is required. Next is the accountability factor, not merely in a financial sense but in respect of the responsibilities for an important policy area such as running a big IT programme or for special projects for which directors are allocated large amounts of funds. The third factor is judgement – not always easy to assess since every ambassador is expected to have good judgement. But it has an important place in the reckoning when, for example, an ambassador is working in difficult circumstances in a capital with an unstable government or where an ambassador's opinion in the closed society in which he operates is the main source of guidance for any decisions taken on policy in London.

After these comes the hardest factor to quantify and to compare between one post and another: influence. For most ambassadors this is the basic yardstick of their standing in the country to which they are posted and of the esteem in which they are held by the government back home. A classic example – with an ironic ending – was the way Sir Peter Ramsbotham operated in Tehran, using his influence with the Shah of Iran to steady nerves in 1971 and secure defence equipment contracts when the British had pulled out their forces from east of Suez. He was rewarded by Sir Edward Heath with a posting to Washington, where his influence was envied by other envoys because of his contacts with Secretary of State Cyrus Vance, with whom he played tennis, and because of his network of soundings throughout America based on sending his staff to test opinion outside the capital. In the end it was not enough.

Sir Peter was dumped into the governorship of Bermuda, denigrated by the Downing Street spin doctors as 'an old fuddy-duddy', so that Foreign Secretary David Owen could put his friend Peter Jay, then Prime Minister Callaghan's son-in-law, into the Washington embassy in May 1977 to be alongside President Jimmy Carter.

Various considerations come into play in estimating influence. In some capitals the door to ministers who matter is readily open to the British envoy. In others it may take a lot of influential leverage to secure an early appointment. What influence achieves is also very relevant to the calculations. A diplomat could work like a Trojan in one country but not achieve what a laid-back counterpart in another country manages to do. The outcome of a hard day's work at the British embassy in Senegal may not be as important to the British economy as the same expenditure of influence and effort in Sweden. Nor is it always a calculation made in terms of influence with the government or the business leaders of a country. It could take account of an envoy's influence with the opponents of a government as well as with members of the ruling regime. Robin Christopher demonstrated his diplomatic skills in that respect as ambassador to Indonesia during the campaign that led to the breakaway of East Timor. His influence was acknowledged in September 1999 when he gave shelter at the embassy in Jakarta to Jose Xanana Gusmao as head of the National Timorese Resistance Council at a time when it was recognized that it was too dangerous for the independence leader to return to Dili. The key role Christopher played during these turbulent times in Indonesia resulted in his promotion to Ambassador in Argentina.

Another factor that enters the equation is a specialist one – professional competence – although this does not rear its head very often in an overseas post. It is applicable in legal situations where particular qualifications could play an important role in international negotiations. It could also apply to an appointment in London which requires professional qualifications as an accountant, architect or estate manager. Expertise in languages does not enter into the calculations because there are separate allowances for passing examinations at the language centre.

Reviews of the JESP scores are made every two years. They are undertaken in groups – for example, as all consuls general or all jobs with a JESP score of 16 and over. An individual diplomat at a post is not encouraged to write to London suggesting that his JESP be upgraded, although it may be reassessed if a director becomes convinced that a particular post has changed significantly. When a post faces a sudden increase in workload and a sustained period of extra responsibilities, as happened to the British High Commission in 2001 in

Zimbabwe amid the turbulence over white farms being taken over, there is a case for reviewing the JESP rating. However, when the increased workload is of short duration, as in the six months when the United Kingdom has its turn at the European Union presidency, there is no upgrading. Clearly, when a post's importance to Britain declines – perhaps because British business interests are switched elsewhere or political ties are weakened – the JESP score will drop down a notch – quietly, of course, to avoid giving offence to the government.

JESP-ing a newly created post is a difficult exercise. More hardship than usual in running a mission was expected in North Korea because Sir John Kerr, who visited Pyongyang to pave the way for the opening of diplomatic relations with the communist regime of the Eternal President, the deceased Kim Il Sung, had cast his expert eye over the sorts of problem to be faced. Nonetheless it proved to be a much tougher assignment than even an experienced Asia hand like the new ambassador Dr James Hoare, who was promoted from being Senior Principal Research Officer heading the Northern Asia and Pacific Group, anticipated on arrival in July 2001. He and his assistant had to be accommodated initially at the Koryo Hotel in the capital while work was being done at the mission premises, a dilapidated building in the Munsu Dong district which used to house the East German embassy. All that Ambassador Hoare had in his office were two laptop computers with no Internet facility. The promise of a satellite communication system was not fulfilled. At the outset it was a testing challenge of ingenuity in these circumstances to get a message to the Foreign Office in London. Finding the location of the government offices in Pyongyang required patient sleuthing since the Foreign Ministry does not disclose to foreign diplomats the addresses or telephone numbers of any government department except its protocol department. Even a visit to a concert necessitated an application to the Foreign Ministry.

Assessments of the difficulties in the new posts announced in 2001 in Chişinâu in Moldavia and Bishkek in Kyrgyzstan were not so complex to determine. Detailed information on which to base a JESP was provided by one of the directors who knew the countries. The upgrading of missions at Nagoya in Japan and Asmara in Eritrea from posts managed by locally engaged staff did not present many problems since there was local knowledge of the circumstances in which they operated. With the abandonment of the old inspectorate system under which Foreign Office assessors from London visited posts regularly, on-the-spot checks are now much less frequent. The new Management Consultant Services Unit makes visits to posts mainly when there is about to be a changeover and assesses with people in the job whether the JESP evaluation on paper matches the reality of the situation.

JESP scores are at the heart of the process for a diplomat making progress up the ladder to the upper echelons of the mandarinate. But before a member of the Diplomatic Service can play for the higher numbers in the bidding system there is one major hurdle to be crossed – the ADC, the test at the Assessment and Development Centre. Passing this examination opens the door to a bid for all the posts in the Senior Management Structure from Counsellor grade upwards. Until the ADC was introduced progression was slow. From second secretary to first secretary could take five years, and then there could be a further ten years before the big breakthrough to an appointment as counsellor. It could mean that a diplomat had to wait until between the age of thirty-five and forty before even the smaller plums of the service were within reach.

Now, a really bright newcomer can make the grade five years after joining the Foreign Office. If you are talented enough and prove it at the ADC test you can do it before reaching the age of thirty. The star performance that is held up for everyone else to emulate is that of Matthew Gould, who entered the Foreign Office after graduating from Cambridge in 1993. Following service as political officer in Manila and a period as speech writer to Robin Cook, he showed his brilliance by storming through the ADC test at the age of twenty-nine after only three years as a first secretary. At the other end of the scale the oldest successful candidate was a diplomat aged fifty-five.

The stated objective of the test, 'to bring on internal talent and promote excellence', is pursued at Wiston House, a sixteenth-century country mansion at Steyning in West Sussex, six miles north of Worthing, where the Wilton Park international conferences under the aegis of the Foreign Office are held. Instead of the academic atmosphere of conference discussions on issues such as conflict prevention in a setting reminiscent of a military officers' convalescent home, the ADC candidates face a gruelling mental assault course for two days. Usually there are two groups of six, split into threes, with some candidates in their mid- to late thirties eager to make the leap up the ladder and others in their fifties looking for a good ambassadorial post as their last job before retirement. Everything they say and do is closely monitored by scrutineers, one of whom is assigned to each candidate as a lead assessor.

There are three main elements: written exercises, individual role-playing tests, and a group exercise. Speed of response is the key to success in the written exercises. Unless a candidate has sharp reactions to a stream of questions and an ability to make snap judgements on a variety of unrelated subjects, a high score will be hard to achieve. Role-playing is done on a one-to-one basis with an actor trained to throw an unwary candidate off guard with a sudden switch of subject. Under close scrutiny of an assessor the scene is set for the role player to show his reactions in a situation such as this: 'It's your first day in a new job: when you arrive your boss is not there so you are required to take over with forty papers piled in the in-tray, a list of people who have telephoned, and a number of messages left with the secretary. You have to draw up a list of priorities and draft responses.' The next challenging role may be set up as follows: 'You return from a meeting to find personnel reports about three members of your staff and memoranda from different members of your staff: you have to assess the personnel situation and make recommendations on how to improve efficiency and restore harmony.' A third role-playing test may come in the form of being asked at short notice to do various tasks: 'Map out tactics for a UK delegation at international negotiations with letters to the Foreign Secretary from the Ministry of Defence, the Department of Trade and Industry and Amnesty International.' Each of these demands reasoned rapid reaction since such a simulated emergency situation is not something that can be prepared for by reading case records.

The toughest part comes at the end: the group exercise. It is a test of judgement and ingenuity in which the group is presented with a complex problem involving conflicting interests in a situation where the participants are not allowed to appoint a chairman. The key to success is avoiding giving the impression of trying too hard, demonstrating leadership by subtly steering the group in a particular direction without seeming to be arrogating to yourself the role of leader. As in the entrance exams at CISB the quickest on the draw shoots to the top, but whether the senior management structure is best filled by fast talkers remains to be seen. The assessors who compare their findings and make decisions would maintain that while quickness in thinking is an advantage it is not always the factor that tips the balance in judging a candidate. What ultimately determines success is whether the set standards are achieved in at least nine of the thirteen specified competencies being assessed. The gruelling nature of the tests was confirmed by the performances of the first 110 candidates at Wiston House, recorded over a number of years, when only four out of every ten passed – and most of them were in the younger age category.

Failure in any examination is inevitably depressing for the morale, never more so than for a forty-year-old first secretary anxious for a leap forward. It can be particularly hard for an older diplomat to take, seeing someone almost ten years younger stride through the test while he, with much more experience – and often with service in the sort of posts which in the Travellers' Club are called 'the salt mines', plus many good assessments in his annual appraisals – fails to impress enough during forty-eight hours at Wiston House. One consolation is that the failed candidate is not left on his own to work out what let him down. By going to the Personnel Directorate he can find out the competencies in which his marks were below standard. There are no courses run by the Training Division specifically tailored for candidates about to go to Wiston House – perhaps because it might give the impression that attending a course would automatically result in a good chance of promotion. But if an unsuccessful candidate goes to see Richard Tauwhare, the Head of Training, with the comments on his ADC test, he will be advised where improvements could be made. If it is a question of improving managerial and leadership qualities, the candidate can take a course at the Training Division. In some cases it could mean taking a special course at the London Business School or the Industrial Society.

Although the ADC test results are made known the day after the ordeal ends, the successful candidates are not instantly promoted. They have to wait until they are appointed to their next post. But it gives them the ammunition in the highly competitive bidding process to aim for a much higher place in the service. Before they start seeking a place in the sun, there is a special course for those who have just graduated through the ADC into the Senior Management Structure. The main emphasis is upon developing a person's capacity for strategic action and introducing the diplomat to the techniques of managing strategic organization. If the individual's career has not yet included any commercial work then that person is advised to take a special one-day training programme providing an insight into trade and investment promotion and giving an idea what is expected of a commercial counsellor by having a briefing session with industrialists and senior members of commercial companies.

Once equipped with more refined diplomatic skills from these training courses, aspiring mandarins are ready to enter the bidding for postings. It has been likened to a game of snakes and ladders – with the menace of the snakes not threatening to pull you down but just keep you on the same level for much longer. Surveying the JESP scores, some experienced players take the view that it is better to assess your prospects realistically and not aim to move up more than one or two points at a time. But for the more ambitious there is the incentive to model one's game plan on the adventurous leapfrog bid brought off by Denise Holt. At JESP 10, as Deputy Head of Mission at the British embassy in Dublin, she made a record leap of seven points to land the post of Director Personnel – a very large directorate comprising nine divisions with immense managerial responsibilities – against very fierce competition, and then went on to be promoted Ambassador to Mexico in 2002.

Young diplomats on their way up the ladder and preparing to bid for postings are usually seeking good moves either in D6, which is the grade of an established first secretary, or in D7, which is the grade of a more senior first secretary, often a deputy head of an important department. Competition in D6 is stiff since there are 601 officers in that grade with salaries ranging between £34,544 and £48,776. In D7 it is less so since there are 126 officers in that grade, their salaries ranging from £42,640 to £58,083. Those ready to bid for a move scan the list of forthcoming openings which are circulated in what are termed 'Windows'. For example, the June, September and November 2001 Window comprised a nine-page list of forty-nine jobs becoming vacant in these three months. Each job has a slot code and lists the grade, the date on which it becomes vacant, the title and location, the officer presently holding the job, and any language requirement. In most cases the posts are not to be filled for at least twelve months; sometimes it is eighteen months, and in the case of hard-language postings such as to China it is normally twenty-four months. The jobs on offer in this instance included some deputy head of mission appointments in Africa and South America.

At Senior Management Structure level the bidding system is the same but the prizes are much bigger. In theory the world is your oyster; only one prize is beyond the bidder's reach – that of the Permanent Under-Secretary, whose appointment is made by the Foreign Secretary, sometimes in consultation with the Prime Minister. In practice some of the plums are also in the gift of the Foreign Secretary or are the outcome of recommendations from what used to be described as the Magic Circle. At senior ambassador level you usually have enough friends at court to enable you to secure a posting to an important capital as the final appointment of your career. It may happen that a highly regarded ambassador is at home on mid-term leave and can be asked if a certain country would be an attractive proposition for his next posting – and if the response is enthusiastic the board will nominate that ambassador for the appointment.

Service at No. 10 Downing Street can be a springboard to the upper echelons of the Diplomatic Service when the Prime Minister's appreciation is marked by a much coveted posting. Sir Christopher Meyer's skill as a spokesman to the Foreign Secretary, and afterwards to the Prime Minister, helped to propel him to Bonn and then to Washington. His successor, Sir David Manning, who was appointed Ambassador to the USA in 2003, earned his promotion from working closely with Tony Blair as the Prime Minister's foreign affairs adviser during the Iraq crisis. Sir Roderic Lyne, who made his mark in the Private Office with Lord Carrington, was rewarded for his subsequent service with John Major at No. 10 Downing Street by being posted as UK Permanent Representative in Geneva and then upwards as Ambassador to Russia. The way Sir Nigel Sheinwald handled awkward issues as ambassador to the European Union so impressed Tony Blair that he took him into No. 10 Downing Street to succeed Sir David Manning as foreign affairs adviser, which earmarked him for subsequent promotion.

Without friends at court, a mid-career diplomat can receive advice and a sympathetic hearing from Alan Charlton, Director Personnel, or an assistant in his team, on options for his next posting. Knowing the likely strength of competition for various posts, an adviser can indicate where a candidate's particular skills would offer the best prospect of success. But it is still left entirely to the diplomat to choose the direction that he or she would like to take. The choice is made available in a regular priority telegram to all diplomatic missions with information on the posts for which diplomats are to be selected at the next three meetings of the selection boards – posts in the upper echelons of the service being decided by No. 1 Board, those posts with a JESP score of 8 to 12 coming before No. 2 Board. A diplomat who is a deputy head of mission or a head of department in London with a JESP score of 10 can bid for an upper-echelon job before No. 1 Board – not usually as high as JESP 17, as Denise Holt successfully did. But often a candidate who bids unsuccessfully for a JESP 13 post will be advised to lower his or her sights for a posting decided by No. 2 Board.

As there are more frequent vacancies in the JESP 8 to 12 range in the Senior Management Structure, there is a wider choice of posts coming up before No. 2 Boards. The jobs vary from consuls general or deputy heads of mission in a medium-sized embassy to ambassador in a small embassy or governor of a small dependent territory. Bids are required in writing and candidates have to state their case for being awarded the appointment succinctly – on one side of an A-4 sheet of paper. Someone seeking a move can bid for several posts at the same time but the application still has to be confined to a single sheet of paper in each case.

Candidates at the same JESP applying for a post with a JESP grade two points higher will not necessarily receive the same salary. There are nine different pay bands in the Senior Management Structure and a large range of salaries within each JESP bracket. A diplomat between JESP grades 9 to 12 could be earning between £53,534 and £87,598, while at the top end, between JESP 17 and 20, he could be getting anything from £77,635 to £116,904; between JESP 20 and 22 he could be in the range £92,696 to £131,276. The difference is due to increments for length of service and the accumulation of performance-related awards. These awards are worked out on a complex equity share system determining the amount of increment based on whether the diplomat's performance is judged to be outstanding, very good, good or just average – those who get a below-average appraisal get no increase. The range is substantial, from £1,000 for an average appraisal for a diplomat in Pay Band 1 at JESP 8 and £1,800 for the same appraisal in Pay Band 9 at JESP 20, to £3,965 in Pay Band 1 at JESP 8 to £7,137 in Pay Band 9 at JESP 20 for an outstanding appraisal.

Even when two posts have the same JESP score there can be wide variations in the perks that go with them. Apart from compensation for what is termed a hardship post with climatic problems – and there are 100 posts classified as hardship posts – there are considerable differences in the quality of life and accommodation, especially in Africa and Central Asia. In Mongolia the ambassador and his staff live in cramped accommodation in the embassy building at Ulaanbaatar, where the temperature rises above freezing for only four months of the year. Barbara Hay will never forget her first Christmas as Ambassador in Tashkent in 1995. Because of the pressure of work, making arrangements for a visit by the Foreign Secretary to Uzbekistan, she had to delay her celebrations for a week and then owing to a power cut, she sat in sub-zero temperatures cooking pieces of turkey on a Primus stove.

Standards of entertainment enjoyed by an ambassador also vary from post to post, and this affects the size of the allowance known as the *frais de représentation*. The luxury of the residence in Paris in the former town house of Pauline Bonaparte, just along the Rue du Faubourg St Honoré from the Elysée Palace, or of the residence at the Lutyens mansion in Massachusetts Avenue in Washington, is matched in few other capitals – only twenty-five of the Foreign Office's 3,900 properties around the world are historic houses. The top ten in the list of 250 posts accounted for almost 25 per cent of the total of £7,347,976 spent on hospitality in the financial year 2000/1. Heading that group in the six-figure bracket was the Paris embassy, where Sir Michael Jay in his last year spent £305,231 entertaining guests. Next among the big spenders was Our Man in Tokyo at £302,731, followed by New York at £267,024, Washington at £226,400, Brussels at £158,251, Moscow at £127,739, Hong Kong at £115,156 (which was £26,944 more than Sir Antony Galsworthy spent in Beijing), Buenos Aires at £105,381, and Seoul at £105,117.

In view of the Irish reputation for enjoying hospitality it is not surprising that the convivial Sir Ivor Roberts in Dublin had to spend more than Sir Rob Young in New Delhi – £61,465 compared with £56,153. Farther down the scale Our Man in Havana spent a modest £32,128 on hospitality, but that was double what his opposite numbers in La Paz and Johannesburg spent and three times the size of the entertaining bills in Algiers, Rangoon and Guatemala City. Among the most modest entertainers was Mark Pellew at the Holy See, with a hospitality bill of £7,758. At the bottom of the table was Dr James Hoare, who, in three months in the spartan North Korean capital of Pyongyang, had only rare opportunities to entertain, which cost a mere £335. Winning friends and influencing people is easier when you are a big fish in a big pool, such as is the case in Paris or Washington, where an invitation to dinner from the British ambassador is the most envied of all in diplomatic circles.

However, hospitality has its downside. Not only is it like running a five-star hotel – to the extent of an ambassador's wife having to iron a dress for a visiting lady minister during times of staff shortage – but entertaining on this scale involves an immense amount of work for the accountants, as all entertaining costs have to be itemized for the auditors. Hospitality offered by Sir Michael Jay in Paris from October 2000 to September 2001 involved him holding 453 functions attended by 12,145 guests. That amounted to 38 working breakfasts with 228 guests; 113 luncheons with 1,390 guests; 96 afternoon teas with 1,114 guests; 95 receptions with 7,119 guests; 111 dinners with 1,851 guests; and 443 overnight guests. In Washington during the same period the ambassador hosted 274 functions with a total of 8,500 guests: 21 working breakfasts with 187 guests; 94 luncheons with 731 guests; 63 afternoon teas with 1,217 guests; 31 receptions with 3,675 guests; 65 dinners with 2,551 guests; and 139 overnight guests.

In the league table for total expenditure by embassies, Washington comes top as the biggest spender. In the year 2001/2 its spending totalled £21,066,809.75, almost double that of the second in the table, Brussels, at £11,609,428.34. Third was New York at £11,529,733.70, followed by Tokyo (£10,588,946.82), Paris (£9,795,504.06), Berlin (£9,047,900.94), Hong Kong (£7,841,765.01), Beijing (£6,382,355.41), New Delhi (£6,183,510.50) and Moscow (£5,641,456.91). Among the surprising entries in the top twenty were Lima at number thirteen with £4,776,140.49 and Warsaw at number sixteen with £3,844,842.58.

Once the applications for postings are made, those seeking advancement to high office are left like papal candidates at the Vatican to wait for a signal. No matter how good a diplomat may be at presenting his qualities and talking his way into a job, he does not get a chance to do so because the selection board does not call candidates for interview. One of the principal reasons is the cost in terms of both time and money. The administration claims it would be disruptive at many missions if a diplomat were taken away from his job, say in Japan or Australia, and flown home for an interview at the Foreign Office. A candidate's merits are decided on paper. The decision is ultimately that of the chairman of the selection board – the disposition of senior mandarins being in the discretion of the No. 1 Board chairman, the Permanent Under-Secretary, that of the up-and-coming mandarins in that of No. 2 Board with the Director Personnel in the chair.

Sometimes there are up to twenty candidates for any one posting. They are winnowed down to a short list of three or four by the board after studying assessments of each candidate drawn up by retired ambassadors such as David Ridgway, former Ambassador to Cuba, and David Beattie, former Ambassador to Switzerland. The Personnel Directorate sends a large dossier on each applicant to the assessors – all the annual appraisals, lists of courses attended and language qualifications – and gives a deadline by which an up-to-date assessment must be available before the board meeting to discuss the suitability of the various candidates. The two-page form requires a judgement to be made on all listed competences – not by ticking off boxes for very good, good and fair but by means of a concise narrative, giving examples to illustrate performance in certain categories. By quoting specific commendations and sometimes letters of appreciation the assessment gives a detailed picture to the board of the special qualities of the candidate – for example, how he or she handled a difficult project in, say, Madrid, or how he or she coped under the pressure of extra work during the European Union presidency.

While the reforms were being introduced to eliminate the dissatisfaction resulting from the old authoritarian dirigiste system in 1999, a survey of 3,119 members of the Foreign Office indicated that there was a substantial amount of discontent to be overcome. While 77 per cent said they were proud to work for the FO and liked working for it, when questioned whether promotion was 'fair and objective' 55 per cent disagreed. When asked whether they were motivated by the performance-related pay system, 69 per cent said they were not. Almost as many – 64 per cent – did not think that the grading structure made the best use of the skills and potential of people in the service. Only 9 per cent considered that the strategic planning of personnel and resources was effectively carried out by the board.

One of the sources of discontent is that little consideration is given to the situation of the spouse of a diplomat who is bidding for a posting. Although the days of wives being required to knit woolly scarves for charity alongside the ambassador's wife are long gone, embassy wives are still expected to be enthusiastic members of 'the team'. Ironically, after a long battle to have the spouse removed from a diplomat's appraisal form, which used to rate her language ability and whether she was a good conversationalist at receptions, there are many in the Diplomatic Service Families' Association who want spouses restored to appraisal forms. If a spouse has a particular career or skill that could be developed in certain circumstances they would like due account

taken of this. The only occasion when a spouse's career is taken into consideration by the selection board is if both she and her husband are in the Diplomatic
Service and bidding for assignment to the same country – a situation which
occurs only rarely and then has to be carefully weighed because of the impact
upon confidentiality and holiday arrangements in the rest of the mission.

Discussions among diplomats in mid-career often highlight three controversial aspects of the new system: a suspicion of positive discrimination, the
demoralizing effect of what is termed MRS – Multiple Rejection Syndrome
– and the difficulty of filling less popular posts. A suspicion of bias towards
women candidates in the bidding system was aroused because of the target
set by the board of having 20 per cent of the Senior Management Structure occupied by women by the year 2005. Although this objective was introduced as a
means of compensating for the barriers that had slowed promotion for women
in the past, the Foreign Office Board strongly resents suggestions that there
is a lower standard set for women than for men. They insist that the bidding
system is based on merit, and the fact that more women are moving up the
ladder nowadays is testimony to their ability and the seriousness with which
they apply themselves to honing their skills. However, the rate of advancement
has been slower than the administration expected. In 1997 there were only
twenty-six women out of 450 in the Senior Management Structure – 5.8 per
cent. In 2002 there were fifty women out of 464 in the SMS – 10.8 per cent.

The problem of candidates being repeatedly rejected in their bids for advancement has proved to be harder to resolve. A succession of failures in the
bidding game is not only depressing for a diplomat in his mid-forties, it has
a demoralizing effect on spouses and family as well as a trickle-down impact
on the morale of others in the same department and applicants in the same
grade. One member of the Diplomatic Service Families' Association described
it as a very stressful experience: 'You support your husband and discuss what is
best for him, taking into account also the schooling prospects and the chances
of employment for yourself. You get all geared up when he makes his bid and
hope he will get the job. Then you hear it's not for us and you are back to square
one. You build up your hopes for the next bid and again this falls through.
When it happens a third time it is emotionally very draining.'

Repeated rejections can also affect the family's education. On a diplomat's
return from abroad the boarding-school allowance for children is continued
during a home posting but stops after five years. The pressure to get a posting so as not to lose the education allowance adds to the stress imposed on
the family.

Failures of apparently worthy candidates for jobs between JESP 10 and 12 up before No. 1 Selection Board created the suspicion in some quarters that it was not a level playing field. People had the impression that, with fewer diplomats bidding for posts in the upper echelons, those on No. 1 Board, being very senior members of the service, would know most of the applicants and find it difficult to avoid a certain degree of favouritism. A candidate who believed his good performance record would be emphasized by a member of the board under whom he had served was sometimes left with the suspicion that he was not successful in his bid because another candidate was better known and had a stronger advocate. It caused disgruntlement that a good performance record documented in a number of appraisals appeared to count for nothing when another candidate had influence inside the selection board.

A stratagem to stop morale plunging farther as a result of MRS was introduced by a device described by the Establishment as 'tilting the free market system back a little towards the dirigiste system'. Once a candidate has had his file on the agenda of the selection board on several occasions without any success, the administration notifies the next meeting of the board that a certain candidate has received three rejections. Officially, the administration would resent any implication that it was nobbling the selection board. But while very properly acknowledging that the ultimate decision rests entirely with the selection board, the Director General Corporate Affairs can utilize his long experience in 'nod and wink diplomacy' to impress upon it the consensus of the administration that, as a particular candidate's dossier has been appearing on the agenda for some time, it would be appropriate to recognize that his qualifications would be suitable for one of the postings under consideration. In this not so subtle way the impact of MRS has been at least partly corrected by some of the old-fashioned authoritarianism of the dirigiste days.

The third drawback of the bidding system is that it makes it much harder to fill the unattractive posts in the Diplomatic Service. With a free choice, young diplomats are much more likely to bid for a posting in Washington, Canberra or Madrid than be tempted to spend three years in a sweaty township in sub-Saharan Africa. The magnet of the opportunities offered by expertise in European Union affairs draws aspiring mandarins towards Brussels or a European department in London. There are many role models for them, having observed how the careers of Sir Michael Palliser and Sir John Kerr took them to be permanent under-secretaries after heading the UK delegation to the EU, and how Sir Stephen Wall, for many ministers their *éminence grise* in Brussels, was promoted to be the Cabinet Office supremo on European Union policy. Even though line managers advise young diplomats to move around the continents to acquire a broad-based portfolio of skills, there is a problem in 'selling' certain postings now that it is no longer possible to tell people that their next appointment will be in Central Asia whether they like it or not.

The difficulty in filling vacancies in certain countries is sometimes due to the stress that would be imposed on the spouse owing to the long hours the husband has to work and the conditions – climatic, social and environmental – in which they would have to live. There is concern at the divorce rate, which is high in the Diplomatic Service at all levels from junior first secretaries to senior members at deputy under-secretary grade. Of the welfare work of the Diplomatic Service Families' Association, 80 per cent is concerned with problems resulting from divorce. One of the first pieces of advice given by the DSFA to young couples going overseas on a first posting is to be aware of the risk of stress in their relationship.

Often a contributory factor in the problem of attracting applications for certain postings is the difficulty of finding suitable opportunities for a working spouse. The implications of the statistic that 65 per cent of parents in the UK are both employed are being increasingly reflected in the Diplomatic Service. Although an agreement with the Bolivian government in October 2001 raised the total of countries where British spouses can work to ninety-six there are still many postings where it is very hard for spouses with professional qualifications to find employment. Some have proved ingenious in overcoming the problems. One spouse in Tirana worked for a publishing house in London using her skills in IT, another in Amman undertook a Foreign Office project not directly connected with Jordan by communicating with people all over the world, and a third developed a thriving business as a hair stylist among expatriate wives in the diplomatic colony in Beijing. Nonetheless, the Diplomatic Service Families' Association believes that the Foreign Office could do more to help spouses, not by finding jobs for them but by providing a network through which to learn of opportunities.

Two recent innovations have gone some way, however, towards easing the difficulties faced by spouses. After intensive lobbying by the association, the Foreign Office instituted the Spouse Compensation Scheme, under which an allowance is paid to those overseas who can demonstrate that they want to work, have appropriate qualifications for it and either cannot find employment at all or are not able to get much work. The Foreign Office pays up to £2,300 a year to such spouses as compensation for loss of earnings. If the spouse earns more than £750 a month the allowance is reduced by 50 per cent. The payment can be used as a means of providing some extra cash on retirement. From April 2001 the regulations were changed to allow spouses of Crown servants to pay into a stakeholder pension when they are out of the country.

Another means of helping spouses was introduced by the DSFA Sponsorship Scheme, which the Foreign Office funds and the DSFA administers. Under the scheme a spouse can receive a one-off payment of £1,200 to acquire training in a ubiquitous skill – one that can be practised anywhere. The most popular is TEFL – Teaching English as a Foreign Language – which usually requires a four-week training course. Other options are computer training or Web design. If the courses for whatever skills are sought cost more than the allowance a spouse can still receive £1,200 towards the training fees. The scheme is available to partners as well as spouses, provided partners sign a declaration confirming that they have lived together for a year and that they intend to remain together for the foreseeable future. (Partners are also entitled to language training courses, medical coverage and subsidized travel and luggage transfer.)

When the hurdles to promotion are eventually overcome, the agonies of waiting are forgotten in the exhilaration of going to Buckingham Palace on being appointed to represent Her Majesty overseas. Watched by his or her spouse, the new envoy is escorted by the Permanent Under-Secretary into the presence of the Queen, whose visits round the world and regular reading of Foreign Office telegrams result in her having a greater understanding of the country in question than her newly accredited envoy – certainly in the case of Commonwealth countries, where her expertise is unrivalled. If anyone ever doubted the importance of her representative, the credentials she presents with a red royal seal confirm in the following emphatic terms that this envoy is a Very Important Person:

Elizabeth the Second, by the grace of God of the United Kingdom of Great Britain and Northern Ireland and Her other Realms and Territories Queen, Head of the Commonwealth, Defender of the Faith.

To all and singular to whom these Presents shall come, Greeting!

Whereas it appears to Us expedient to nominate some person of approved Wisdom, Loyalty, Diligence and Circumspection to represent Us in the Character of Our Ambassador Extraordinary and Plenipotentiary, Now Know Ye that We, reposing especial trust and confidence in the discretion and faithfulness of Our Trusty and Well-beloved Charles What's-his-name have nominated constituted and appointed, as We do by these Presents nominate, constitute and appoint him, the said Charles What's-his-name to be Our Ambassador Extraordinary and Plenipotentiary to Utopia aforesaid. Giving and granting to him in that character all power and authority to do and perform all acts, matters and things which may be desirable or necessary for the promotion of relations of friendship, good understanding and harmonious intercourse between Our Said Realm and Utopia and for the protection and furtherance of the interests confided to his care; by the diligent and discreet accomplishment of which acts, matters and things aforementioned he shall gain Our approval and show himself worthy of Our high confidence.

And We therefore request all those whom it may concern to receive and acknowledge Our said Charles What's-his-name as such Ambassador Extraordinary and Plenipotentiary as aforesaid, and freely communicate with him on all matters which may appertain to the objects of the high mission whereto he is hereby appointed.

Given at Our Court of St James's, the 31st day of December in the 50th year of Our Reign.

No wonder there is a spring in the step of the newly elevated mandarin on walking out of Buckingham Palace, armed with such a glowing mandate to represent Her Majesty and work with her ministers to promote and protect the interests of Britain wherever the Union Jack flies throughout the world.

FIVE

Mandarins and the Ministers

*The public impression of ministers bravely launching their own ideas
and arguments is carefully fostered by ministers themselves but is rarely
accurate.* Lord Hurd, *The Search for Peace*, 1997

*My officials are good, but I told them they were banned from calling me
'Minister' and they were to call me 'Peter'. They replied: 'Yes, Minister'.*
Peter Hain, August 2001

IMMEDIATELY Parliament is dissolved the Foreign Office braces itself for
a change of ministers – and sometimes a change in priorities and policies.
While the politicians go to the hustings for the general election campaign the
mandarins get ready to provide the material for instant briefings for the new
ministerial team to tide them over the first few weeks: a sort of child's guide
to the problems of the world, setting out themes on the basis of 'All you ought
to know about X'. One week before the result of the election is declared, the
Permanent Under-Secretary sends instructions to the directors general asking for briefs from the departments they supervise. The papers are assembled
traditionally in two bound bundles: one marked 'Blue', intended for Conservative ministers, the other marked 'Red' for Labour ministers. So far there has
not been any need for a bundle marked 'Yellow' for Liberal Democrats. With
the outcome of the election held on 7 June 2001 so obviously destined to be
a massive victory for Labour, no time was wasted in preparing briefs for a
bundle marked 'Blue'.

The guidelines for the briefing papers are determined by the party manifesto, even though they are usually couched in general terms. Foreign Office
departments are expected to translate party policy aspirations into a form
consistent with the practicalities of situations and any commitments undertaken in previous agreements with other governments. Overall, there may be
as many as twenty-five different briefs, but the Permanent Under-Secretary
enjoins his staff to ensure that they do not overwhelm the recipient with a
mountain of paper in the in-tray. Few incoming ministers have the appetite
that Sir Geoffrey Howe and David Owen displayed at the Foreign Office for

wading through vast quantities of documents, absorbing them with masterly precision and retaining an enormous amount of detail to use at a later date in negotiations. Even complex issues such as the matters under discussion at the European Union have to be compressed into précis form for the introductory period. Each supplier of briefings is required to identify six key matters whose essentials have to be grasped in the first week and summarize them in no more than two pages each.

Whether a new minister reads through every piece of paper in the bundle during his first weekend is a matter for his conscience – and his confidence in being able to fend off difficult questions from diplomatic correspondents at his first press conference. What he cannot afford to ignore is the additional document attached to the briefs: the list of engagements. In the case of Jack Straw, on his promotion from Home Secretary to Foreign Secretary after the general election on 7 June 2001, it was a whirlwind of commitments at conferences in Europe, with no time to indulge in his favourite weekend recreations of cooking puddings and watching Blackburn Rovers. No wonder that after less than forty-eight hours in the job, on arriving at a European Union ministerial meeting in Luxembourg, he was so confused that he said he was pleased to be in Brussels. Next he had a NATO summit and then the following day he flew to Gothenburg for a European Union summit.

It is on an occasion such as this that the expertise of the mandarins becomes the essential underpinning of a minister's negotiating stance. There is so much that is new in the issues and in the way the others round the table present their views that the newly appointed minister has to rely on the guidance of a mandarin. On the plane alongside Jack Straw, and in the corridors at the conferences, talking him through the various minefields in his diplomatic path, was Kim Darroch, then Director of EU Affairs, whose mastery of minute details of issues under negotiation resulted in his promotion to Director General Europe in 2003. From the outset Jack Straw was a complete contrast to Robin Cook, who behaved as if he knew it all from day one. Straw admitted that he was starting with a blank sheet on many issues and endeared himself to those mandarins who delight in making sure that every possible aspect of an issue is covered in briefing papers by saying: 'I'm a swot. I read all the stuff.'

It is not just a question of making sure that the minister gets the basic facts of a complicated issue presented to him in an easily digestible form. It is important that he remembers them when he is moving from one meeting to another in quick succession. The flow of appointments does not allow time for the mandarin to keep whispering in the minister's ear. In one week during which Jack Straw was plunged into substantial talks with one foreign minister

after another, his accompanying mandarin, Director General Peter West-
macott, provided an essential memory-jogger, like those which Sir Geoffrey
Howe, for all his remarkable powers of recall as a skilled barrister, insisted
on having at hand whenever he travelled. These memo slips, or clutch cards
as they were called in the Foreign Office, fitted neatly into a pocket, ready for
clandestine consultation, one for each meeting, with the main points to be
made listed as compressed reminders of the highlights from a briefing paper
that could run to forty pages.

When the first Labour government for eighteen years took office in 1997,
Robin Cook flicked through the briefs and set out his own strategic aims
to be achieved over five years. With the innovation of a mission statement to
'promote the national interests of the United Kingdom and to contribute to a
strong world community', he focused on four main targets:

> *Security*. We shall ensure the security of the United Kingdom and the Depend-
> ent Territories, and peace for our people, by promoting international stability,
> fostering our defence alliances and promoting arms control effectively.
>
> *Prosperity*. We shall make maximum use of our overseas posts to promote trade
> abroad and boost jobs at home.
>
> *Quality of Life*. We shall work with others to protect the world's environment
> and to counter the menace of drugs, terrorism and crime.
>
> *Mutual Respect*. We shall work through our international forums and bilateral
> relationships to spread the values of human rights, civil liberties and demo-
> cracy which we demand for ourselves.

To achieve his mission he acknowledged that he required 'the professionalism,
the expertise and the dedication' of the Foreign Office and invited it 'to join
us in working together to deliver these benefits for the British people'. But for
this partnership to work effectively Cook, like most foreign secretaries before
him, had to rely on the Foreign Office machine being kept well tuned to his
needs by the Permanent Under-Secretary. It was not always so. Lord Salisbury
kept his Permanent Under-Secretary, Sir Philip Currie, in the dark about his
dealings with other governments. He worked a lot from home, rarely coming
to the Foreign Office before lunch, and never bothered to consult his PUS on
any major issue of foreign policy. Nowadays the Foreign Secretary and his PUS
have to be constantly assessing the direction of policy-making in the shifting
circumstances of the times and adjusting the deployment of Foreign Office
resources to ensure that government policy is effectively implemented. That
requires a close working relationship and a bond of trust between the two

– a harmonious situation not always prevailing, however, in the corridors of power.

When James Callaghan arrived at the Foreign Office in March 1974, his first remarks to the Permanent Under-Secretary, Sir Thomas Brimelow, betrayed the suspicion of many in the Labour Party towards the Foreign Office: 'You know, we don't trust you' – an unusual misjudgement, since the PUS had been a member of the Fabian Society and on becoming a life peer on his retirement took the Labour whip in the Lords. It was only after the Cyprus crisis negotiations in Geneva in August 1974, when Callaghan realized how dependent he was on the expertise of mandarins such as Charles Wiggin and Alan Goodison, that he abandoned his suspicion of the Foreign Office and came to admire its professionalism.

Sir Michael Palliser had a difficult time as Permanent Under-Secretary during David Owen's regime, especially after what he regarded as a serious political mistake in appointing Peter Jay, then James Callaghan's son-in-law, as Ambassador to Washington. Nor was there much bonding between Anthony Crosland and the Foreign Office as he kept himself aloof from people and once rebuked his popular press secretary, 'Ham' Whyte, for intruding into his inner sanctum on the Royal Air Force VC-10 plane en route to the Far East with his wife: 'I want you to know that we are very private people.' A young first secretary, Richard Dales, who rose to be Ambassador in Sweden, was scathingly reprimanded when he deputized for Crosland, who was late in arriving for an official luncheon at the Foreign Secretary's residence at No. 1 Carlton Gardens. On his eventual arrival Crosland was furious to discover that Dales had served a glass of sherry to the visiting foreign minister. Not even waiting to ascertain whether the minister had actually asked for a sherry, Crosland cornered the hapless first secretary and crushingly observed: 'Never, never, never serve sherry in my presence or to my guests – it's only done in senior common rooms at Oxford.'

George Brown's relations with Sir Paul Gore-Booth as Permanent Under-Secretary were often strained but he established close ties with his next PUS, Sir Denis Greenhill, and insisted on having Sir Denis travel with him as his chief adviser. Although this practice was abandoned so that the Permanent Under-Secretary can 'mind the shop' while the Foreign Secretary travels, there has been a succession of close partnerships since then between mandarins and ministers. Having confidence in the Head of the Diplomatic Service to supervise the assessments of situations across the broad range of foreign policy is essential for a Foreign Secretary in these days of constant travelling. Although the Foreign Secretary can no longer afford to be out of the country for long periods, as Selwyn Lloyd was in 1959 when he stayed in Geneva for six weeks at the Big Four Conference on the two Germanys, he can sometimes be obliged to be attend meetings in other countries twice a week, and therefore needs to have trust in the judgement of the Permanent Under-Secretary in his absence.

Often that understanding is established in advance of entering government. It is the tradition that the Permanent Under-Secretary is authorized to have contacts – under recognized confidentiality restraints – with the opposition spokesman designated to be Foreign Secretary in the event of his party being successful at the general election. Thus Robin Cook had three lengthy meetings with PUS Sir John Coles prior to taking over at the Foreign Office in May 1997. Before the general election campaign that brought him to power, Tony Blair acknowledged the importance of taking soundings from mandarins by having separate meetings on foreign policy issues with Lord Renwick, former Ambassador in Washington and High Commissioner in South Africa, Sir David Hannay, former Ambassador at the United Nations, and Sir Michael Butler, former Ambassador to the European Union.

Except during parliamentary recesses, when foreign secretaries take the opportunity of extended visits overseas, there are regular meetings every week or ten days with the Permanent Under-Secretary, at which policy and administrative matters are discussed. Sir Malcolm Rifkind used to hold his own meetings on Tuesday and Thursday mornings with his junior ministers, his political adviser and spokesman – occasions which Sir John Coles also attended. John Major, in his brief ninety-three days at the Foreign Office in between being Chief Secretary and returning to the Treasury as Chancellor of the Exchequer, found it difficult to get to grips with the long briefing papers and had Sir David Gilmore travel to his home in Huntingdon before the Paris conference on Cambodia to explain the pitfalls to be avoided in discussing Hong Kong with the Chinese Foreign Minister, Qian Qichen. 'What I did not like was being asked to approve documents twenty times a day without having time to digest them and consider their impact upon policy,' he complained afterwards.

Despite some periods of disenchantment, ministers usually have a very close relationship with mandarins, none closer than that between the Foreign Secretary and his principal private secretary. It is often the case that the minister spends more time with him than with his own wife – they are together at meetings, at conferences, in planes and cars. In this situation proximity means power, and never was that more clearly demonstrated than when Murray MacLehose, a six-foot-two-inch Scot who towered over George Brown, was his imposing private secretary. Whenever he arrived at an embassy he would draw the British ambassador aside and convey this solemn warning: 'If you don't know it already, this man is an alcoholic. In the course of the next forty-eight hours he is bound to insult you, your wife, and probably everyone on your embassy staff. But you just have to live with it. There is no point in creating a fuss or resigning. It will achieve nothing. Just grin and bear it. He will be gone before the weekend and you can relax and pretend his visit never happened.'

His power – and his confidence that he could exercise it with impunity in an emergency – was confirmed on a Royal Air Force flight taking George Brown to Moscow in November 1966. After having his visit postponed twice because of bad weather, the Foreign Secretary was in no mood for further delays, regardless of the fog. When the pilot, John Evans, reported that air traffic control at Vnukovo airport had told him to change course and fly to Leningrad, as St Petersburg was then called, George Brown insisted: 'I am Her Majesty's Principal Secretary of State for Foreign Affairs and I decide what happens. I'm in charge – and that means in charge of navigation too. The whole future of peace in Vietnam depends on my getting down to talks in Moscow. Head down to Moscow – that's an order.' This was the moment when Murray MacLehose decided to intervene. He told the pilot: 'You are responsible for the safety of everyone aboard. Don't take any notice of what the Foreign Secretary is saying.' The pilot responded to MacLehose by changing course and heading for Leningrad. After landing he admitted: 'I wasn't intending to take any notice of Mr Brown anyway!'

Although MacLehose was frequently criticized – usually for trying to hide the hospitality tray of drinks – this incident ended without any rebuke. When George Brown left the Foreign Office he paid a glowing tribute to MacLehose in his memoirs, *In My Way*: 'He was to become one of those in the Foreign Office on whom I leaned most heavily. In my view he was one of the wisest of the middle generation in the Foreign Office and tremendously able, hard-working and sympathetic to the new world in which we were operating.' Private secretaries are hand picked and usually go to the top echelons of the Diplomatic Service. Murray MacLehose went on to be Governor of Hong Kong for eleven years and eventually became a peer. His successors also had distinguished careers: Sir Antony Acland, private secretary to Sir Alec Douglas-Home, became Permanent Under-Secretary and later Ambassador in Washington; Sir Ewen Fergusson, private secretary to David Owen, became Ambassador to France; Sir Roderic Lyne served with Lord Carrington and became Ambassador to Russia; Sir Anthony Galsworthy, private secretary to Sir Geoffrey Howe, became Ambassador to

China; Sherard Cowper-Coles, private secretary to Robin Cook, moved on to be Ambassador to Israel; Sir Stephen Wall, who served with David Owen, Sir Geoffrey Howe, John Major and Douglas Hurd, went on to be Ambassador to the European Union and later moved to the Cabinet Office as EU supremo.

As the record-holder for serving more foreign secretaries than anyone else – Anthony Eden, Ernest Bevin, Rab Butler, Patrick Gordon Walker and Michael Stewart – Sir Nicholas Henderson, who retired as Ambassador to France and was recalled three months later by Prime Minister Margaret Thatcher to become Ambassador in Washington, where he was a key figure during the Falklands War, rightly categorized private secretaries as 'the impresarios of Whitehall'. From what is quaintly termed 'the Private Office', where the private secretary holds sway alongside the famous room on the first floor looking out over St James's Park, everything in the day-to-day activity of the Foreign Secretary is organized and orchestrated – all the comings and goings, whom he sees and whom he puts off seeing, what he reads, whom he telephones, what he signs, what he puts off signing. It is aptly described by Nico Henderson in his fascinating volume of reminiscences, *The Private Office*, as 'the place where politics and diplomacy come together, Minister and the machine interlock, home and abroad meet; a clearing house for papers, a crossroads, a meeting-point, a bedlam. It is the most exciting room in the whole Foreign Office.' Ironically, adjacent to this buzzing nerve centre the painting above the door to the Foreign Secretary's office portrays a bare-breasted maiden with her right forefinger in admonishing mode at her lips, seated under a sign with one word on it: 'Silence'.

As the confidant of the Foreign Secretary, spending more time every day with him than anyone else – often more than eighteen hours a day – the private secretary is constantly exercising his judgement and discretion. He sifts through the flow of material to prune it down to the essential information the Foreign Secretary has to study and determines the order of priorities in terms of which material from inside the Foreign Office and from ambassadors abroad is to be read. As the same process of selection goes on during trips abroad, the private secretary has to ensure that the Foreign Secretary is constantly updated on developing situations and that he is instantly made aware of new moves under way anywhere in the world. Even at official dinners abroad he cannot relax, as David Owen's private secretary, Ewen Fergusson, realized on his first official visit to France at a dinner hosted by the French Foreign Minister, Louis de Guiringaud. No speech was scheduled for the occasion, but when his host rose to expatiate upon Anglo-French relations David Owen became anxious about what to say in reply. However, he need not have worried. When the private secretary passed the word that there was no speech prepared, the ambassador, Sir Nicholas Henderson, had everything in hand when the Foreign Secretary rose to speak. As David Owen admitted in his memoirs: 'Nico's fertile mind came to the rescue, frequently passing menu cards along to me with excellent suggestions of what I should say.'

The last duty of the private secretary before he leaves the Foreign Office at night is to decide which papers coming into the office towards the end of the day should be put into the overnight box for the Foreign Secretary to study in preparation for the following day. Here again he wields enormous power, and can have the final say by adding a comment about how good or bad any particular conclusions are. It is important for him to know not only what subjects are of interest to the Foreign Secretary but how much to put into the overnight box – in other words how much the incumbent can take. Lord Carrington was always chiding his Private Office not to burden him with what he called 'bumf'. John Grant had to be careful not to overload Robin Cook's overnight box. Whenever anyone mentioned Ernest Bevin having had five red boxes sent to him over a weekend, Robin Cook proudly proclaimed: 'I am happy to say that nobody has ever tried to present me with five red boxes.'

Sir Nicholas Henderson had a knack for finding out how foreign secretaries could be enticed to keep reading through the pile of papers in a red box, and disclosed: 'With Cook the lure was horses. So interlaced with the heavy papers on how to prevent proliferation or about qualified voting in the European Union Council of Ministers warm invitations were inserted to go racing.' Even if he often only skimmed through certain papers, Robin Cook had an extraordinarily retentive mind and often surprised his officials by dredging up details of a complicated issue months after reading his briefs. But he had limited interests, and it soon became known which regions failed to absorb his attention. He was not much concerned about events in Asia or the Pacific, even less so about Latin America – he did not make a bilateral visit to any Latin American country during his four years at the Foreign Office.

For his successor, Jack Straw, Private Secretary Simon McDonald had no qualms about giving him plenty to read as he had a voracious appetite for his boxes. However, there has long been concern about the workload imposed on ministers by the overnight boxes. Over fifty years ago Herbert Morrison complained in his memoirs: 'Under present-day conditions the burden on the Foreign Secretary is excessively heavy. Sometimes it was 2 a.m. and sometimes much later when I got to bed, the average being about 3 a.m. and I would be up again at 8 a.m. or thereabouts ... His excessively heavy work at the Foreign Office killed Ernest Bevin; and Mr Eden experienced grave illness during 1953.

If there is not to be a heavy sickness and mortality rate among our Foreign Secretaries something will have to be done.' Despite the warning, nothing has been done. The long working hours continue to make the job exhausting.

If the Foreign Secretary knows in advance that he will be going into deep water in a situation he will have made sure he has the expert on that particular problem accompanying him on his travels. But when there is a sudden unexpected development in another area requiring an urgent reaction from the Foreign Secretary and there is not time to consult the Foreign Office, he automatically takes soundings from the private secretary. As one of them once explained: 'You are the first person to say to the Secretary of State "Good idea" or "Bad idea" and that could be a crucial judgement on your part.' When there is sufficient time during an overseas trip for an opinion to be sought from the Foreign Office, it will come through the private secretary, and he is in the powerful position of being the last person whose advice is attached to the piece of paper set before the Foreign Secretary. Then, according to the experience of a former private secretary, 'if a submission comes in for the Secretary of State and you put a slip of paper on it saying "This is not the right policy for the following reasons ..." you have more chance than most to make him reconsider the advice and turn things round.' The outcome of that power was subtly put like this: 'You can edge the Secretary of State away from a precipice.'

It requires not only fine judgement but also a shrewd sense of balance. Knowing the Foreign Secretary's mind is one key element in being able to give an accurate interpretation of his likely views to senior mandarins in the Office. This is sometimes acquired in an almost casual manner when the private secretary is alone in a car with the Foreign Secretary and is sounded out on some issue that is not immediate but may have to be addressed after the current series of meetings. At the same time the private secretary has the responsibility of making sure that the assessments of the experts in the Office are properly weighed in the Foreign Secretary's mind. In this balancing act the private secretary's own contacts inside the Foreign Office, his awareness of the characteristics of the people making assessments and his familiarity with their hobby horses can add an important dimension to the way decisions are taken.

Another important function of the private secretary is that of note-taker at meetings with other foreign ministers. Writing up a concise report of the discussions, which has to be circulated immediately to other senior officials back at the Foreign Office, can be very demanding not only of his powers of recall but of his ingenuity. The dilemma was cleverly described in the lines of an anonymous versifier quoted in *The Unofficial Commonwealth* by John Chadwick:

> And now while the great ones depart to their dinner
> The Secretary sits, growing thinner and thinner,
> Racking his brains to record and report
> What he thinks they think
> That they ought to have thought.

A similar challenge was faced by Ewen Fergusson after a debriefing session with David Owen as they swam up and down in the swimming pool at the Prime Minister's residence at Chequers. When he went to his room to write his report he reached the conclusion that he left as a reminder to all private secretaries summoned to Chequers: 'Make sure your hands are dry and you have a notebook for any debriefing.'

Such a situation highlights one fundamental aspect of the relationship between mandarin and minister: a private secretary should never be thought to be 'winging it'. What he conveys must always be taken as the view of the Foreign Secretary with no embroidering. His position of trust – upwards to his minister and downwards to the Office – depends upon there not being any suspicion that he might be putting words into the mouth of the Foreign Secretary. He cannot afford to allow any private biases he may hold on controversial questions to colour the account he gives to others of the attitude being taken by the Foreign Secretary. A private secretary who gave the impression that the Foreign Secretary was perturbed by developments in country X, if it subsequently became known that the minister did not have a particular interest in the area as a whole, would devalue his position as an interpreter of ministerial views. Whenever an issue on which he cannot be 100 per cent sure of the Foreign Secretary's reaction arises, the only course for the private secretary to take is to avoid conveying an opinion until he has the opportunity to check with the minister. The golden rule for sustaining the relationship is that the private secretary's authority must never be doubted.

One corollary to this is that it is essential for the private secretary to keep himself – and, therefore, the Foreign Secretary too – up to speed with all the developments on the international scene. This used to be mainly a matter of keeping pace with the flow of telegrams, which rose from 2,000 a day in the Falklands crisis, after the Argentine invasion in April 1982, to 10,000 a day during the Gulf crisis, after Iraq's invasion of Kuwait in August 1990, and eventually to the record total of 15,153 one day during the British presidency of the European Union in 1998. Nowadays, with the ever increasing use of e-mails, there are fewer telegrams, but more varied sources of information to check. This means keeping in touch regularly with the Press Department, which has staff monitoring news agency reports and television bulletins.

The private secretary also relies on the spokesman to provide an assessment of the enquiries coming from newspaper correspondents which will indicate the front-page headlines the following day when the Foreign Secretary will be expected to have a comment ready for questions. In the days of daily three o'clock briefings to the inner circle of Fleet Street diplomatic correspondents, it was possible for spokesmen to deduce from the cut-and-thrust of questioning from *The Times*, the *Daily Mail* or the *Financial Times* what stories were being pursued which would require responses the next day from the Foreign Office. With the abandonment of afternoon briefings it is far more difficult for members of the Press Department to alert the Private Office to what may prove to be problems lying in wait for the Foreign Secretary in terms of the newspapers.

Equally important for the private secretary is a good network of contacts in Whitehall, enabling him to be aware of attitudes in other government departments which are likely to affect the position of the Foreign Secretary in Downing Street discussions on current issues. In the Cabinet power game such information is important in helping to maintain the authority of the Foreign Secretary. Insider knowledge gained by the private secretary from contacts in, for example, the Department of Trade and Industry or the Ministry of Defence could prove very helpful to the Foreign Secretary when there are differences of view over arms supplies in sensitive cases. Indications that the Treasury and the Department of International Development – where Secretary of State Clare Short often worked closely with Chancellor Gordon Brown in important initiatives on debt relief for the Heavily Indebted Poor Countries – could be making moves on globalization, on which issue they have sometimes out-manoeuvred the Global Issues Directorate at the Foreign Office, would usefully be signalled in advance by the private secretary. At one stage the Private Office network had the advantage of three Foreign Office trained mandarins in high places in Whitehall: Sir Kevin Tebbit as Permanent Secretary at the Ministry of Defence, Sir Francis Richards as Director of Government Communications Headquarters (GCHQ), and Sir David Wright as chief executive of British Trade International at the Department of Trade and Industry.

With the increasing involvement of the Prime Minister in international affairs – attending summits and regularly telephoning leaders in other capitals – it is incumbent upon the Private Office to be aware of what assessments are being made at No. 10 Downing Street. In situations where the Prime Minister does not use the normal official channels to launch initiatives, such as when Mrs Thatcher employed Lord Wolfson as an intermediary with Israel's Prime Minister, it is important that the Private Office keep in close touch with the Prime Minister's Office. During the latter period of Mrs Thatcher's premiership, when relations between her and Sir Geoffrey Howe deteriorated, Anthony Galsworthy as private secretary had extra responsibilities in keeping the link between the Foreign Office and No. 10 Downing Street from being seriously marginalized. There were times when he made as many as twenty telephone calls a day to Sir Charles Powell, the Prime Minister's influential Foreign Affairs Secretary, to ensure that the Foreign Office was kept in the loop on developments directed from No. 10. That was often difficult for the Private Office, even when Mrs Thatcher made Douglas Hurd her trusted Foreign Secretary. Sir Charles Powell would send a record of conversations Mrs Thatcher had with President George Bush in a sealed envelope to the Private Office for delivery unopened to the Foreign Secretary – no one else at the Foreign Office, not even the private secretary, was to be aware of the contents.

Although the influence of the Foreign Affairs Secretary at No. 10 diminished with the departure of Sir Charles Powell, his successors still enjoy a significant status on the international stage, which makes it imperative that the Private Office should have a close relationship with the Cabinet Office. In the early days of John Major's premiership he relied heavily on the razor-sharp mind of Stephen Wall, who had been his principal private secretary at the Foreign Office. Wall would hold detailed talks with Brent Scowcroft, the US National Security Adviser, sometimes three times a day, to pave the way for John Major to have strategic discussions by telephone with President Bush on the problems of the Kurds in Iraq. He ensured that the Private Office was quickly kept informed of the rapidly changing developments.

When Tony Blair embarked on his second term in Downing Street there was concern in the Foreign Office that the Office would be downgraded among allies as the Prime Minister began taking a more assertive role in the international arena over the Afghan crisis, following the terrorist attacks in New York and Washington on 11 September 2001. Like Mrs Thatcher, he preferred to use his own envoy, his tennis partner Lord Levy, a millionaire former pop music impresario with property in Israel, as an emissary to the Middle East to pave the way for talks with Prime Minister Ariel Sharon. Right from the outset there were anxieties inside the Foreign Office that Jack Straw – newly installed as Foreign Secretary, not having been involved in foreign affairs on the opposition benches and not yet familiar with the complexities of politics in the Middle East and the Muslim world – appeared to be sidelined at times.

The impression was created in some quarters that while Jack Straw was try-ing to catch up with other issues at the Foreign Office he was being bypassed on moves to resolve problems in Africa, where Clare Short's reputation as Min-ister for International Development gave her added authority. It appeared to be underlined when the peace signed by Uganda and Rwanda in London on 6 November 2001 was hailed as having been brokered by Clare Short with the personal backing of Tony Blair. The Prime Minister's commitment to a more constructive role in Africa was emphasized at his meeting in Downing Street with President Museveni of Uganda and President Paul Kagame of Rwanda, and was followed through by Clare Short edging them into resolving their dif-ferences in an agreement which Britain offered to monitor.

This suspicion of presidential-style diplomacy taking over from the tradi-tional expertise of the Foreign Office – sometimes without adequate advance preparations – was given credence by the ill-fated visit by Tony Blair to the Middle East in October 2001, when he was put in the humiliating position of being lectured by President Bashar al-Assad of Syria one day and by Prime Minister Ariel Sharon of Israel the next. It was widely recognized thereafter that if Tony Blair had spent more time consulting in advance with the Middle East experts in the Foreign Office he would have been warned against being trapped into a joint press conference orchestrated in such a way as to ensure that the Syrian leader scored telling points. This setback did not deter the Prime Minister from his globetrotting, which at times fuelled the suspicion in diplomatic circles that the Foreign Secretary was being consigned to a sup-porting role in the international drama. While President Bush kept his travel to a minimum, with one visit to China and the Far East, Prime Minister Blair had fifty-nine meetings with world leaders in the first sixty days of the Afghan crisis. Although he was also active in telephone diplomacy, with thirty-four calls to world leaders during this period, he clearly set great store by the value of his own face-to-face meetings, which involved making thirty-one flights and travelling 40,000 miles.

Blair continued his high-profile international role when the Kashmir crisis erupted in January 2002. Jack Straw appeared to be further marginalized as the Prime Minister flew to India and Pakistan in an attempt to calm the situation. This tendency towards a dominant presidential-style role was increasingly evid-ent during the Iraq crisis in 2002 and 2003, when Blair travelled to Moscow for talks with President Putin and kept in regular telephone contact with him. When Colin Powell, the US Secretary of State, appeared at times to have less influence at the White House than hawks such as Vice-President Dick Cheney and Defense Secretary Donald Rumsfeld, any dialogue Jack Straw had with

Washington was subsidiary to that of Tony Blair. At these times the Prime Minister's ability to present arguments in a way that would carry weight with President Bush meant that the Foreign Secretary was not regarded in Washington as having much clout. When Blair went for talks with President Bush at Camp David before and after the war in Iraq, Jack Straw was not involved.

Summit diplomacy has developed enormously in recent years, partly because of the nature of international crises and partly because heads of government can often enhance their reputation at home as well as abroad by being seen in an active role on the world stage – and do not like to miss an opportunity to do so. On EU and G8 occasions the Foreign Secretary is consigned to the role of a back-up member of the delegation, which inevitably gives rise to mutterings in Foreign Office corridors. The friction that sometimes arises, although it is never publicly acknowledged, is not a new feature of the Downing Street scene. As Sir Nicholas Henderson emphasized in *The Private Office*: 'A certain degree of irritation, actual or potential, between the Prime Minister and the Foreign Secretary is the normal law of Whitehall.' Despite having a close, friendly relationship with Lord Home, which some called 'the bonds of the grouse moor', Harold Macmillan candidly admitted: 'There is nothing so difficult or delicate in the management of government as the relations between the Prime Minister and the Foreign Secretary.'

How to preserve the cohesion between both sides of Downing Street in terms of the current buzz phrase 'joined-up government' has become an increasing preoccupation of the Private Office. This task was eased by Tony Blair's appointment of a senior mandarin, Sir David Manning, as foreign policy adviser to the Prime Minister. Having served in Warsaw, New Delhi, Paris and Moscow before becoming Ambassador to Israel and then to NATO, Sir David had also spent two years as a counsellor in the Cabinet Office, which gave him the experience of seeing the necessary linkage between initiatives taken on either side of Downing Street. He sustained the tradition of skilled advisers adding an extra dimension to the Prime Minister's thinking, which used to be provided in the Thatcher era by Sir Anthony Parsons, the UN ambassador at the time of the Falklands crisis, and subsequently by Sir Percy Cradock, former ambassador to China, who carried out the painstaking negotiations over Hong Kong.

Sir David Manning's appointment – and the succession of Sir Nigel Sheinwald, the EU ambassador, to his Cabinet role – underlined the value of ambassadorial experience at a time when ministers seemed to be short-circuiting the diplomatic system in direct telephone consultations with other governments. Nevertheless, there has been a steadily increasing belief in recent years that the importance of ambassadors has been greatly overrated now that events and opinions are conveyed instantly on screens worldwide. In many capitals the role of the ambassador has changed to such an extent that his status has also diminished. When Sir Derek Thomas, a key mandarin at the side of the Foreign Secretary on his travels as Political Director, went to Rome as ambassador, he did not get the sort of welcome given to one of his predecessors, Lord Rennell of Rodd (then Sir James Rodd), on his arrival there in 1908 for what was to be an eleven-year stay. Then the Italian Director of Protocol had the entire Cabinet headed by the Prime Minister parade at a reception at the British residence to pay their respects.

In those days, when ministers rarely travelled – Sir Edward Grey left the country only once in his eleven years as Foreign Secretary – the ambassador was the personification of the British government. However, despite the change in status there is still recognition in some capitals that the ambassador is an important figure in relations between two countries. This was acknowledged by the French government in saluting the significant role played in Anglo-French relations by Sir Michael Jay – politically, commercially and in terms of public diplomacy – when he left the British embassy on 22 September 2001 to take over from Sir John Kerr as Permanent Under-Secretary. Since he had arrived aboard a British destroyer to take up his post, Sir Michael was given the honour of travelling back to Portsmouth aboard the French warship *Germinal*. Another highly regarded British ambassador, David Ridgway, was given a rare tribute to a Western envoy by President Castro, who hosted a farewell lunch for him in Havana in June 2001 in recognition of his efforts in promoting British involvement in the exploration of Cuba's oil resources and other commercial interests between the two countries. On leaving the Diplomatic Service, ambassadors used to be invited into the Foreign Office for a farewell pat on the back from the Foreign Secretary. This was abandoned by Robin Cook, but when Jack Straw took over at the Foreign Office he introduced the courtesy of sending letters to retiring ambassadors thanking them for their service.

The main change in the role of the ambassador nowadays is that he is no longer the messenger, since the message has usually been conveyed already by the media. Inevitably, the days when ambassadors had power to negotiate and conclude agreements are gone. Ambassadors are still used to deliver formal protests, although ministers often prefer to convey the government's displeasure themselves, either by issuing statements or by carpeting the London envoy of the offending country. But the scope for influence still exists for ambassadors who have the skills and contacts to exercise it effectively – and sometimes in greater measure than ever before. As Lord Hurd, a member of the

Diplomatic Service long before he became Foreign Secretary, once observed: 'Professional diplomacy is needed to provide not facts and figures but the relationship between those facts and figures together with insights into the likely behaviour of those who take the resultant decisions.' After serving as private secretary to Attlee and Churchill and being African adviser to Macmillan, Sir David Hunt ended his career as head of mission in four capitals convinced of ambassadors' influence: 'For all the refinements of cyphers and systems of communications, more weight is given to their views and more left to their initiative.' He often quoted Jules Cambon's justification for the trust invested in an ambassador: 'The best instrument at the disposal of a government wishing to persuade another government will always remain "la parole d'un honnête homme".'

Despite the enthusiasm of prime ministers and foreign secretaries for direct contact by telephone – Robin Cook had a remarkably persuasive telephone technique and liked to use it especially with his European counterparts, in contrast to John Major, who was reluctant to have serious discussions by telephone – there are limitations to its usefulness. The time difference is one restraint; the language barrier another. Jack Straw used the telephone a lot for transatlantic consultations with US Secretary of State Colin Powell after his first visit to Washington, but was wary about engaging in serious discussions on the telephone with anyone he did not know well. He found it difficult to establish a good relationship on the telephone with someone unless there had previously been a face-to-face meeting.

Sometimes, however, a telephone call from No. 10 Downing Street could be a very effective way of overcoming resistance from a foreign leader to a policy that the Foreign Office was keen to implement. On occasions when the Foreign Office judged the time was ripe for the Prime Minister to intervene, it was arranged to set aside ten minutes from his schedule for the call to be made. It is described by mandarins winding down at the bar of the Travellers' Club as 'using the Prime Minister as a court card when playing a difficult hand'. A foreign head of government can be flattered that the British Prime Minister is prepared to take time on a busy day to make a call from London to outline a problem and explain how he would greatly value assistance.

Often the usefulness of an ambassador is measured by his distance from the Foreign Office in London. Ambassadors in capitals such as Beijing, Tokyo, Jakarta and Seoul, where ministerial visits are relatively rare – and planned in terms of hours rather than days – can make a significant difference to the considerations of a situation by the Foreign Secretary in London. Telephone diplomacy can sometimes produce quick answers for a minister in London, but is dangerous if both sides are not well versed in the nuances of each other's language, and the Foreign Secretary would never try to do business by telephone with governments in Saudi Arabia, Sudan, Colombia or Turkmenistan unless in dire emergency. There are times when telephone calls have to be made to the Kremlin, but the Foreign Secretary depends on a Russian-speaking ambassador such as Sir Roderic Lyne at tense times, such as during the Iraq crisis in 2002 and 2003, to handle sensitive matters and to make judgements based on his knowledge of the power game and the people playing it in various capacities.

When a foreign secretary travels to distant capitals he is dependent as much upon the insights of the ambassador as on the analysis by the Foreign Office's London experts of recent government speeches made in the country he is visiting. The ambassador's value is knowing what the President's hobby horses are, who is in favour with him, who is on the way out, who is likely to succeed if the President is edged out, which test drills for oil are going well, who is competing for new contracts, who is the economic guru in the background, or who could pull the plug on the economy if there are financial scandals. One of the major changes of the last few years is that the ambassador is expected to make that inside information – or at least the 90 per cent of it that is not classified intelligence – available to businessmen considering a major commercial involvement in the country, on the ground that the embassy should be customer friendly since it is the taxpayer who pays for its upkeep.

Companies rely on the expertise and influence of Arabic-speaking ambassadors to ease their path in countries such as Saudi Arabia, where Sir Patrick (later Lord) Wright was held in such esteem that British Aerospace did not deem it necessary to send their chief executive to Riyadh during Sir Patrick's eighteen months there before becoming Permanent Under-Secretary. They depended on his guidance and contacts – and secured a contract without a visit. Officially, 38 per cent of the Diplomatic Service's activity is concentrated on commercial work, helping British business. Sir Patrick always insisted that it was nearer 90 per cent, but this included devoting 50 per cent of his time to finding out enough to enable him to understand Saudi Arabia. Those who criticize the Diplomatic Service as being peopled by men in pinstriped trousers who are out of touch with 'the real world' and advocate hard-nosed businessmen to replace them as ambassadors ignore the length of time it takes to acquire a deep knowledge of the Arab world, its culture and conventions before they can play an effective role in commercial dealings. As few company executives have the time to become fluent in Arabic or Farsi, it is hard to see how they could make much of an impact in government circles in such capitals as Damascus, Riyadh or Tehran.

In terms of keeping in touch with 'the real world' it is almost as important in some countries for an ambassador to have good contacts with the
opposition as with those jockeying for position in the ruling party. This was
demonstrated during a visit by Sir Geoffrey Howe to Prague in April 1985,
when the clandestine activity of the embassy in nurturing contacts resulted
in a cloak-and-dagger boost to the opponents of the communist regime in
Charter 77. After the Czech authorities made it clear to Ambassador Stephen
Barrett that the Foreign Secretary could have no meetings with dissidents, he
pulled off a diplomatic coup by having the Czech-speaking officer on his staff,
Denis Keefe, organize a meeting at his home – not with the top leaders, as they
were under security surveillance, but with their deputies. While Sir Geoffrey
joined in carousing with his host, Foreign Minister Bohuslav Chnoupek, at the
Seven Angels wine bar, his Political Director, Sir Derek Thomas, slipped off
to rendezvous with the opposition, who included Ivan Havel, brother of the
dissident leader who became President. On rejoining his Foreign Secretary, Sir
Derek gave a thumbs-up and passed a discreet message which was assumed
to be 'mission accomplished' – in fact the note, it was subsequently revealed,
read: 'Doesn't the Gipsy fiddler remind you of Ernest Borgnine?', to which Sir
Geoffrey replied: 'Rather more like Nigel Lawson, I think.'

Especially valuable to a minister is the expertise of the China hands, those
members of the Diplomatic Service who are picked out, or pick themselves
out, early in their career to be lifelong experts in the culture, history, politics
and language of the country. What became known as Sir Geoffrey Howe's
Ming Vase diplomacy – the protracted, complex negotiations over eighteen
arduous months on the future of Hong Kong, seen as a priceless ornament
requiring extraordinarily careful handling to ensure its well-being on its return to China – would not have been successful but for the Foreign Secretary's
patient attention to detail and the gifted team of orientalists led by Sir Percy
Cradock. Even though Sir Percy and his fellow orientalists Dr David Wilson
and Anthony Galsworthy had long experience of puzzling over the nuances in
proposals made by the Chinese, there were many times when Foreign Minister Wu Xueqin kept them guessing – and that required immense reserves of
patience to work out appropriate responses.

Despite the weak bargaining position of the British government in the face
of the ineluctable deadline for the handover of Hong Kong at the expiry of
the lease, the delegation were determined to do everything to limit the future
interference of the Beijing government in Hong Kong's affairs under the One-
Country-Two-Systems formula. When they were warned that there would be
no meeting with the Chinese leader Deng Xiaoping to clinch the deal unless

Britain softened its position, the UK delegation countered with a hint that they would end their visit, with Beijing being blamed for the lack of success. After a night's reflection Foreign Minister Wu Xueqin reopened discussions by suggesting that the way forward was to be found in a Chinese proverb: 'You open the window and you see the mountain.' This left the Foreign Office orientalists flummoxed for a time. For all their experience in unravelling Chinese sayings, this one left them floundering until, with a few hints from the other side of the negotiating table, they got the message: 'Ignore the immediate obstacles and set out for the solution on the mountain top.' After smiles all round, Sir Geoffrey and Sir Percy went straight to the top, saw Deng Xiaoping, and agreed on a compromise solution.

An ability to make a well-informed judgement of which way the wind is blowing politically and economically in an important country such as Russia is demanded by ministers; they expect the expertise of the mandarins to provide it – and the record of doing so in recent years has impressed governments in Downing Street, both Conservative and Labour. When Sir Geoffrey Howe decided that it was time to open the door to a new relationship in Russia in the wake of the then imminent departure of the geriatric leaders Yuri Andropov and Konstantin Chernenko, he turned to his Russian expert Sir Nigel Broomfield for advice on the person to invite to London for a ground-breaking visit. It was a choice between Mikhail Gorbachev and the Leningrad party boss Grigory Romanov. The Broomfield decision to have Gorbachev, not Romanov, invited to Britain well before Chernenko's death ensured that Prime Minister Thatcher was the first Western leader to mark him out as 'the man to do business with'. Fifteen years later it was Foreign Office inside knowledge which picked out Vladimir Putin as the man of the future during the twilight period of Boris Yeltsin's regime, when other Western governments were looking to Yevgeni Primakov as the successor. Long before Putin was formally inaugurated as Russian President on 7 May 2000, Prime Minister Tony Blair went, on Foreign Office advice, to meet him in St Petersburg and spent a weekend establishing a new relationship of cooperation between Britain and Russia.

A similar sort of judgement, based upon the accumulated expertise in the Foreign Office of the factors that determine what eventually sways presidential elections in America, resulted in Downing Street not getting caught in the wrong camp in November 2000 when the results were eventually announced. At a time when many pundits in Whitehall were insisting it was inconceivable that Al Gore would not take over the mantle of President Clinton, the Foreign Office counselled caution. In a fifty-fifty situation, with George W. Bush so strongly backed, the Foreign Office advised the Prime Minister's 'special advisers' to steer clear of the Democrat campaign machine – no support for Al Gore, no favours for Clinton. There was much relief in the Prime Minister's entourage afterwards that they had heeded the Foreign Office counsel to keep their heads down and avoid opening relations with the new American administration on a sour note.

Where the combination of shrewd analysis, negotiating skill and the experience of facing off foreign governments is most valued in mandarins is in dealings with the European Union. With Sir Stephen Wall the expert on EU legislation in the Cabinet Office, John Grant in day-to-day negotiations in Brussels as EU ambassador, and Kim Darroch, Director General Europe, at the oreign Office, this triumvirate exercises immense influence. They are vital players in brainstorming sessions to assess all the intricate aspects of the European Union developments that will be discussed at Foreign Ministers' Councils or EU summits. Unlike Keith Vaz, who was responsible for European affairs in the first Blair government but did not immerse himself in the detailed debate and let most Brussels papers bypass him, Peter Hain adopted from the outset the role of unequivocal advocate of the European cause – his enthusiasm outstripping that of Jack Straw. He made it his priority to keep in close touch with the triumvirate and gobble up everything of relevance to British interests which emerged from the Brussels machine, the most intensive paper factory in the world. His successor, Denis MacShane, an equally enthusiastic Europhile, proved a glutton for EU documents too.

What the Foreign Office's European mandarins provide is not merely a running commentary on all the matters that will have an impact on the entire range of government business. Their knowledge of the way to obtain results in the highly competitive atmosphere of the European Union in Brussels or the United Nations Security Council in New York – know-how unrivalled anywhere else in Whitehall – gives the Foreign Office mandarins a pre-eminent influence in the formulation of the government's foreign policy, the decision-making process as it evolves, and the tactical implementation to see it through to a conclusion thereafter, as the following chapter reveals.

SIX

The Formulation of Foreign Policy

*The gulf between what is theoretically desirable and what is practically
attainable is so wide that it is sensible to concentrate almost exclusively
on the latter.* Lord Carrington, *Reflect on Things Past*, 1988

*Foreign policy is a mixture of the old and the new. We initiate but we also inherit
... We cannot legislate about the actions of other nations, we cannot wipe the slate
completely clean.* Lord Callaghan, *Time and Chance*, 1987

FOREIGN policy is like a long broad stream with many tributaries merging
into it at various points, sometimes creating turbulence on the surface, at
other times forming a strong undercurrent, on some occasions strengthening
the flow, and at other occasions adding obstacles that impede it. Measuring
the pace of the stream, assessing the ripples and alerting people to the necessary precautions to be taken to deal with the threat of any danger ahead, is
the first responsibility of the day for the Permanent Under-Secretary at the
meeting of mandarins convened in his room at 10.30 every morning. No matter what the challenge is or where a threat to British interests is posed, the
PUS knows that around his table in the ground-floor room exactly below that
of the Foreign Secretary are gathered all the principal sources of expertise in
the Foreign Office capable of meeting it.

This 'Gathering of All the Talents' began as a temporary stopgap measure
in October 1964 when Patrick Gordon Walker, who was appointed Foreign
Secretary after failing to get elected as Labour MP for Smethwick, had to spend
so much of his time campaigning in a by-election at Leyton that he was not
able to keep track of developments at the Foreign Office. The innovation was
introduced by the then Permanent Under-Secretary, Lord Caccia, so that a
report about the issues on the international agenda could be conveyed to
the Foreign Secretary at his engagements at the hustings answering voters'
questions on the domestic agenda. It was the duty of his private secretary, the
imperturbable Nicholas Henderson, to take his sheaf of notes from the PUS's
meeting and a clutch of telegrams for the minister to digest along with a plate

of spaghetti in a dreary room normally used for theatrical rehearsals at Leyton Town Hall. These briefings proved a waste of time for Patrick Gordon Walker as he failed to be re-elected and therefore was unable to deploy his talents on the evolving international scene as Foreign Secretary. But the system was recognized as such a useful way of bringing the collective wisdom of the Office together at the start of the day that it has continued ever since.

The Meeting – no one scurrying along the brown-tiled corridor to be on time for the opening of proceedings is ever asked which meeting he is going to attend since the summons by the PUS is the only one that matters at that hour – assembles between twenty-five and thirty people to assess what the day is likely to have in store for those concerned with looking after Britain's interests around the world. Traditionally the PUS used to sit in the middle of a long rectangular mahogany table, with his most senior colleagues, the directors general, around him while the lesser lights in the constellation took up their places behind them in the second row – all the directors who were not travelling abroad, the junior ministers' private secretaries, the Head of the Parliamentary Unit, the Head of Research Analysts, and the Head of the Press Department as the Foreign Secretary's spokesman. From the day Sir Michael Jay took over as PUS on 14 January 2002 all that changed. He took a chair at the top of the table and pulled the other seats back into a large semi-circle where people sat in no particular order and with no regard to rank. It transformed the formality of the occasion into a free-ranging debate conducted on the basis of who had the keenest insight rather than the greatest seniority.

Discussions are focused sharply on questions that are about to loom large on the diplomatic agenda, with priority assigned to any development already in the headlines of the morning newspapers or in reports on radio and television which may require the Foreign Secretary to make a statement later in the day. If there is a particular issue that seems likely to call for a wide range of expertise, the PUS asks those who will be involved in assessing it to stay behind for further discussion. Those who remain are the experts who will be the core of an ad hoc team to take the matter forward. There is no question of arguing over who should be the lead department, but the PUS will ensure that someone is acknowledged as heading the group. Thursday is the day for management matters, when the directors concerned give an update on staffing issues and the need for any reinforcements.

When there is not an urgent issue demanding attention the occasion is more of a freewheeling review in which the Permanent Under-Secretary solicits the latest reports about what is going on in various areas. He seeks to tease out opinions from around the circle rather than let the directors general hold sway. Directors and department heads are encouraged to speak up; since there is no formal record made there is no anxiety about losing face if the ideas they suggest do not command much support. By the same token, if someone stays silent and it is discovered later that a troublesome situation in his area has been gradually building up, the PUS will be quick to demand why the issue was not raised at the meeting. Unless there is a crisis the meeting is not allowed to overrun the allotted thirty minutes to prevent it becoming a debating society.

One of the main tributaries supplying the general flow of foreign policy is never openly mentioned at the Meeting but is often the most decisive aspect in the formulation of policy – the Intelligence Factor. On many occasions the shaping of policy is determined much more by the intelligence dimension than the political or ethical dimension. Responsibility for providing it is in the hands of the Chairman of the Joint Intelligence Committee, who operates from a secluded section of the Cabinet Office. The appointment is always held by a senior mandarin such as Sir Percy Cradock, Sir Rodric Braithwaite, Peter Ricketts or, in 2002, John Scarlett. It used to be thought that its importance would decline after the Cold War when the JIC enjoyed immense prestige as a result of its involvement with, among others, Oleg Gordievsky, the KGB officer who became a British agent in 1974 and provided valuable inside knowledge for eleven years until he came in from the cold. Instead, it has adapted its expertise to concentrate upon the new threats from the proliferation of nuclear know-how, the acquisition of chemical and biological weapons, international terrorism, drug trafficking and money laundering.

Intelligence assessments go first direct to the Prime Minister by tradition, since Winston Churchill gave the JIC enhanced status after its founding by Sir Maurice Hankey in 1936 and was its most enthusiastic customer. In view of their very sensitive nature they have a restricted circulation beyond the Prime Minister, the Foreign Secretary and the Permanent Under-Secretary, being seen only by certain Cabinet ministers such as the Chancellor of the Exchequer, the Defence Secretary, the Home Secretary, the Trade and Industry Secretary, the Northern Ireland Secretary and service chiefs. Outside Whitehall there is one very special recipient: the Queen. A copy – FYEO: 'For Your Eyes Only' – of the Weekly Summary of Current Intelligence is always carefully read by the Queen, as her prime ministers quickly realize in discussions of inter-national affairs at their regular meetings with the monarch.

Because of the number of red boxes with state papers sent to Chequers at weekends, highly classified intelligence documents used to be placed inside what were termed double covers: an inner envelope marked with a code for sensitive documents then enclosed in an outer envelope. But this system was changed during the first term of Harold Wilson's premiership, since when all sensitive material has been put in a separate blue box with a red stripe down the centre, which has come to be known in Downing Street as 'Old Stripey'. As the box stood out from the others it was usually the first to be opened and the most avidly read, since the contents were not included in any other material sent to the Prime Minister.

A broad range of specialist knowledge is assembled in the intelligence department of the Cabinet Office. The twenty analysts assessing the raw material are hand picked not just from the Foreign Office, MI5 and MI6 but also from other Whitehall departments including the Ministry of Defence, Customs and Excise and the Department of Trade and Industry. Each of the sixteen desk officers has expertise in a particular subject, and they work in teams of four. One was set up in 2001 to concentrate on the increasing amount of work related to drug trafficking and serious international crime. The teams are supervised by four deputy chiefs, who ensure exacting standards of quality control. They assess the continuous flow of raw material which is delivered to them in a variety of ways from British undercover intelligence agents, who are acknowledged in other capitals to be unrivalled.

A daily digest of the latest intelligence material is among the first papers read by the inner circle of ministers, with all the key information compressed on to one page. This has never been treated as merely routine reading material by its recipients. After the terrorist attacks in New York and Washington on 11 September 2001, the fast-moving events of the Afghan crisis made each updated intelligence analysis top-priority reading. As Professor Peter Hennessy stressed in his volume on intelligence entitled *The Secret State*, after Black Tuesday 'Intelligence moved to a position of centrality which it had not occupied since the most perilous moments of the Cold War.' Prime Minister Tony Blair set great store by JIC assessments from the outset of the Afghan crisis and eagerly assimilated them when they landed on his desk.

There were times when the expertise of the British agents who were gathering intelligence in the area gave him the edge over President George W. Bush as American Central Intelligence Agency resources were not so extensive in Pakistan. Blair had the added advantage of having at his disposal two exceptional members of the Diplomatic Service with a profound understanding of the area and its key players: Hilary Synnott, High Commissioner in Pakistan, and Stephen Evans, who had served in Islamabad and had been seconded in 1996 to the United Nations Special Mission to Afghanistan. A gifted linguist, Stephen Evans, was sent to Kabul within days of the Taliban being ousted. In recognition of their services, Synnott was knighted and Evans awarded the CMG in the Queen's Afghanistan Honours List.

In normal times, however, it can sometimes take three weeks to have threat assessments compiled and approved by the JIC when it is a matter of examining a situation that has security implications beyond the next six months. But when there is a call for an urgent risk assessment on a suddenly emerging problem in a country such as Macedonia, it can be done in forty-eight hours or less. The end product is not, however, presented as a policy recommendation to ministers. The JIC insists that its value depends upon its objectivity. If the JIC were thought to be partisan in recommending a particular policy there would be a risk that it would be suspected of choosing material that suited a specific interpretation. At the same time it recognizes an obligation to draw attention to the implications of the government implementing a particular policy by pointing out that there could be a serious threat to British interests.

Direct guidance is provided when the Foreign Secretary or the Prime Minister requires an up-to-date analysis of the security situation in, for example, a Middle East country in advance of a meeting with an Arab leader or the Israeli Prime Minister. This could take the form of a meeting with other experts, a formal JIC assessment paper, or merely providing some raw intelligence material to be absorbed as part of the briefing for receiving a Middle East visitor. Each major development gleaned from an intelligence agent, an embassy or a news flash on television is instantly assessed by the Chairman of the JIC and his team and a first reading of the situation is conveyed immediately to No. 10 and the Foreign Office. It could be the start of a hectic process of analysing every aspect of the evolving crisis, weighing its impact on Britain's interests, and supplying assessments three or four times a day. It was the JIC to which Tony Blair turned in September 2002 when he required a dossier to be drawn up assessing the dangers that could be posed by Iraq's arsenal, including the prospect of weapons of mass destruction. But while the assessment came from the JIC it was the Prime Minister, with the assistance of his Foreign Affairs Adviser, then Sir David Manning, who drafted the document's political and military conclusions.

Significantly, one unique legacy of the so-called special relationship, so carefully nurtured by Prime Minister Thatcher with President Ronald Reagan before being finally consigned to the history books at the end of the Cold War, remains: the Anglo-American intelligence connection. It has stayed very close since the gold mine of material provided by Oleg Gordievsky, which was made available to the Central Intelligence Agency, was acknowledged to be of inestimable value in briefing the American team for the Reagan–Gorbachev summits. The JIC Chairman meets American intelligence chiefs every month, either in London or Washington. The trust between the UK and US intelligence commands is in a class of its own: no other country enjoys such close cooperation with either partner. However, it has never been absolutely total, for example in cases where there is a situation of supreme importance for national security. Gordievsky's 'turning' as a double agent for the SIS, when he was recruited from the KGB in Copenhagen in 1974, was not disclosed to the Americans at the time. Only four people in Downing Street were in the know: Prime Minister Margaret Thatcher, Foreign Secretary Sir Geoffrey Howe, the PUS, Sir Antony Acland, and the Head of Intelligence, Sir Antony Duff. CIA Director William Casey was kept in the dark about the source of all the Kremlin secrets he received from the JIC until after Gordievsky came in from the cold in a daring escape from Moscow in 1985.

Every Wednesday afternoon, when the main weekly intelligence meeting in the Cabinet Office is convened by the JIC Chairman, the Americans occupy a special place alongside the British intelligence chiefs. Although they are not involved in discussing every paper, since some are of interest only to the UK, for example matters concerning Northern Ireland, the Americans participate fully and usually provide some elaboration of assessments from their own sources. The Canadians and Australians also attend these meetings but play a less active role. New Zealanders have been excluded ever since the Americans refused to sit down with them after they banned nuclear vessels from their waters. The bond with the Americans is such that they come together frequently with their British counterparts and discuss every aspect of the material coming from all sorts of clandestine sources. They often bring classified documents from Washington and compare notes on the evaluation of situations that are open to different interpretations. British intelligence chiefs do not sit in with the Americans in Washington since there is no equivalent of the JIC in the US administration. However, while they do not participate in the actual evolution of American assessments, the detailed conclusions are made available to the JIC – and not to any other Western intelligence organization.

Significantly, what is not admitted publicly is that Britain's openness with the Americans on all intelligence matters is unique. It does not extend to the UK's European partners, who are not invited to any JIC meetings. Despite all the aspirations towards achieving a Common Foreign and Security Policy in the European Union, the JIC does not share intelligence assessments with any other European government. If questions were ever asked, the answer would be that no European Union partner has adequate security arrangements in place to allow it to receive from British Intelligence, and to keep safe, even quite lowly classified assessments. This means that the European Union's High Representative for foreign policy, Javier Solana, has to operate without access to the intelligence information that is vital for well-informed assessments of situations in the Balkans and the Middle East. Even when he acquires staff with the necessary intelligence expertise, the UK intelligence network will not hand over to European partners all that they give to the Americans. The JIC is emphatic: raw intelligence material will not be provided.

British intelligence chiefs do not disguise their doubts about the professionalism of the EU in security matters. 'Police cooperation is one thing – intelligence cooperation requires a lot more depth of commitment than is to be found within the EU,' one former professional explained. Although the JIC keeps in touch regularly with individual countries such as France and Germany, the exchanges with their intelligence authorities are not on anything like the level of confidentiality that exists between it and its American counterparts. Even Lord Robertson as NATO Secretary-General did not see the sort of documents that used to be circulated to him in Cabinet when he was Secretary of State for Defence. Papers sent to NATO partners on matters concerning Russia or the Balkans are evaluations and judgements scaled down, without the highly sensitive material seen by the Americans at the JIC weekly meetings.

Much of the highly sensitive material is derived from a source unmatched anywhere outside the United States: GCHQ – the Government Communications Headquarters – universally recognized as the leading exponent of global signals intelligence (Sigint), intercepting secret information circulating round the world. In a state-of-the-art technology centre nicknamed the Doughnut, from the shape of the building in Cheltenham where they moved in 2003, some 7,000 experts with fluency in sixty-seven languages eavesdrop on confidential communications and analyse their potential threat to international security. Its function has been described by Prime Minister Blair as crucial: '[it] forewarns us of threats to our national security, helps the Government to promote international stability, provides support and protection for our forces, contributes to our economic health and strengthens our efforts against terrorism and serious crime'. The importance of its role was underlined by the fact that the choice of Dr David Pepper as Director of GCHQ, taking over from Sir Francis Richards in April 2003 after a long career in operational intelligence work, was an appointment made with the approval of the Prime Minister.

Although it was not officially acknowledged to exist until it was formally avowed to Parliament in 1983, its intelligence operations stem from the Government Code and Cipher School set up in 1919 with twenty-five cryptologists and thirty operators at Bletchley Park in Buckinghamshire, and brought under the aegis of the Foreign Office in 1922. After its successes in the Second World War with the creation of Colossus, the world's first electronic computer, and the breaking of the Germans' Enigma code, it was established as GCHQ in 1946 and moved to Cheltenham in 1952. The value of its authoritative analyses was quickly recognized by the US government, which finalized an agreement with the British government in 1947 enabling the vast wealth of important information gathered to be shared exclusively between GCHQ and the National Security Agency.

Despite the priority given to the work of the Joint Intelligence Committee, there is constant concern about the challenge facing the experts of reading the signals correctly and alerting the government to the imminence of danger. If reminders were needed, the scrutineers of signals have only to recall Prime Minister Thatcher's statement only six weeks before Argentina invaded the Falkland Islands on 2 April 1982: 'Our judgement is that the presence of the Royal Marines garrison ... is sufficient deterrent against possible aggression.' Again, in August 1990 when there was a stream of intelligence reports on large-scale Iraqi troop movements to the Kuwait border, the Downing Street assessment was that President Saddam Hussein was in no position after the massive casualties and economic drain of the eight-year war with Iran to embark upon invasion.

For all the Foreign Office expertise on the Muslim world, the terrorist threat from al-Qaeda was not properly assessed despite one very percipient observation from the Permanent Under-Secretary, Sir John Kerr, which went largely unnoticed when he told the Commons Foreign Affairs Committee on 24 April 2001 – five months before the attacks on the World Trade Center and the Pentagon – 'I also worry about the threat of Afghan-based terrorism.' After the terrorist attacks at Kuta beach in Bali in October 2002 there was criticism of the Foreign Office for not having issued the appropriate warnings from the Central Intelligence Agency. And following the Iraq war criticism of the justification for military action which arose during the Hutton Inquiry and deliberations by the Commons Intelligence and Security Committee centred on the way intelligence assessments were made and presented. As Peter Preston observed in the *Guardian* on 15 September 2003: 'The bleak truth, as detailed by the Intelligence and Security Committee, is of duff stuff from Iraq (and 9/11) passing up the line without the hard questioning it needed.'

As a result of reviewing the frequently levelled complaint that the Foreign Office is good at responding to crises but on occasion has been less successful at thinking strategically about future challenges and anticipating problems ahead, Sir John Kerr's successor, Sir Michael Jay, embarked on a radical reorganization of the Foreign Office by scrapping the Policy Planning Department and creating a Directorate for Strategy and Innovation. Under Simon Fraser, a high-flyer who served with Sir Michael at the British embassy in Paris, the DSI was charged with marshalling all the resources of the FO coherently in order to control the flow of the foreign policy stream. Its mandate, set out on its establishment in September 2002, is to ensure that the Foreign Secretary and the Foreign Office Board are provided with 'fresh, strategic thinking on current, long-term and cross-cutting issues, and to make an influential contribution to policy formulation'.

One of the DSI's first tasks was what some cynical observers at the Travellers' Club described as 'bringing the FO up to date with the "vision thing"', obeying Tony Blair's instruction to all Whitehall ministries to focus on 'the Big Picture'. Sir Michael Jay gave Simon Fraser the task of drawing up a ten-year Strategic Plan setting out the long-term direction for the conduct of policy, its priority areas and the required structure to make the best use of the FO's resources. There was a deadline of twelve months for him and his project leader, Susan Hyland, renowned as 'one of the sharpest intellects in the Office', to produce their vision for approval by the Strategic Plan Governance. As part of this unprecedented exercise in assessing the objectives of British foreign policy, with an attention to detail not usually considered feasible on such a scale, a vast conference of ambassadors was convened by the Permanent Under-Secretary.

Over 150 heads of mission – 104 ambassadors in foreign capitals, forty-six high commissioners in Commonwealth countries, and various senior envoys such as the ambassador at the United Nations in New York, the UK Permanent Representative to the European Union, and the ambassador to NATO – gathered for a two-day conference at the Queen Elizabeth II Conference Centre in London in January 2003. With senior officials from other Whitehall departments and leading figures from business and the City also in attendance, they were addressed by the Prime Minister and the Foreign Secretary before dividing up into working groups under the supervision of the Permanent Under-Secretary. The final version of the Strategic Plan emerging from the DSI after further months of work had to be hammered out by eighteen decision-makers: the Foreign Secretary, his junior ministers, the Permanent Under-Secretary, the chief executive of British Trade International, the FO directors general, the FO Legal Adviser, the Director of Resources, the Director Strategy and Innovation, and the Foreign Secretary's two special advisers. The sixty-two-page document, published as Cm 6052 in December 2003 under the title 'UK International Priorities: A Strategy for the FCO', sought to perform an intricate balancing act between Britain's long-standing close ties with the USA and Downing Street's aspirations to be at the heart of Europe as a leading player in the European Union alongside France and Germany. But while stressing that 'strengthening our influence within the EU will be one of our highest priorities', there was no disguising the fact that there was a higher priority when the document went on to state: *'Our relationship with the US will continue to be the UK's most important individual relationship and a vital asset. It will be essential to achieving many of our objectives, especially in ensuring our security'* (author's emphasis).

Although the Commonwealth was accorded little more relevance than that of a 'valuable informal group', the document acknowledged that managing relations with Islamic countries would be one of the most strategic challenges in the next decade and beyond. At the same time domestic pressures on foreign policy were reflected in an emphasis on the need to protect the UK from illegal immigration, drug trafficking and international crime. In his intoduction Foreign Secretary Jack Straw trod warily around United Nations involvement, with an eye to the reluctance of the Americans to give the organization an enlarged say, when he stated: 'We shall need to be ready to use all the instruments we have – aid, advice, training, pressure and, if appropriate, military force – to protect ourselves and others from harm. And we shall need to agree in the UN the principles on which such action will be based.' One could almost hear the diplomats at the Quai d'Orsay quote back Hamlet: 'Ay, there's the rub.' Its reception here was not exactly euphoric. For some sceptics it smacked too much of a blend of wish list and public relations exercise on a grander scale than the original FO promotion in Robin Cook's mission statement, introduced with the flourish of a company prospectus on a new issue to attract shareholders.

To deal with policy-making in the shorter term a completely new structure was introduced. Ever since a separate Planning Department was created in 1964 it had drawn on the talents of a succession of rising stars such as Sir Michael Palliser, who became PUS, and others who went on to hold senior posts, such as Pauline Neville-Jones, Robert Cooper, George Walden and Sir David Gore-Booth. But after three decades, despite earning plaudits for the way it intervened with NGOs on issues such as conflict diamonds in Angola (as will be shown in Chapter 8), its main output – sometimes as many as four position papers a month – appeared to ministers as 'worthy' but often 'disconnected from the here and now'. There was often criticism that the planners were apt to focus their attention on peripheral matters, resulting in their being termed 'the Blue Sky Department'. It was recognized that policy and the resources needed to implement it effectively had to be treated in a joined-up strategic way. In the broad stream of policy-making it had become evident in the course of Foresight's exploration of how the system was not working properly that at the very top there was no firm strategic grip on the issues and the manner in which the organization tackled them. Too often policy recommendations were made without a realistic assessment of the resources they required.

This situation was highlighted by the existence of two boards at the top which met separately: the Board of Management and the Policy Advisory Board. One examined matters in terms of administration and management, the other analysed problems purely in an intellectual frame of policy options. Sir Michael Jay dissolved both and installed a new joint board for joined-up decision-making. It has ten members: the Permanent Under-Secretary and six senior officials, two non-executive members from the private sector, and the Group Chief Executive of British Trade International. Instead of one unit, the Policy Planning Department, dealing with policy, and a subsidiary one in the Resources Planning Department serving the Board of Management, an integrated unit for the new board was created in the Directorate for Strategy and Innovation with a high-powered staff of twenty-five. Nonetheless, although any downgrading of prepared policy initiatives was denied categorically by the new regime, it soon became apparent that in the new set-up the provision of policy options for possible future challenges had been scaled down.

While the number two from the Policy Planning Department, Nick Kay, who made his reputation as a shrewd analyst at the British embassy in Cuba, was appointed Deputy Director of DSI, responsible for coordinating all work on planning themes to ensure a smooth transition, since he left to become Deputy Head of Mission in Madrid only one substantive issue has normally been presented at meetings of the new board, which take place eleven times a year. Usually it is an issue of prime importance which has to be carefully thought through in advance, such as the presentation made in October 2002 on the theme 'Europe 2005', which examined the issues involved with the expansion of the European Union and the evolvement of NATO in an enlarged role. In this radical readjustment of priorities on policy-making, justification for the scaling down of position papers was exemplified by the need to concentrate the activity of the planning staff at the DSI on urgently assessing strategic options during the various phases of the Iraq crisis over President Saddam Hussein's possession of weapons of mass destruction. This preoccupation did not, however, include any involvement of the DSI in the preparation of the government's much-criticized fifty-five-page dossier entitled *Iraq's Weapons of Mass Destruction*, presented by Tony Blair on 25 September 2002 as a case for action against Saddam Hussein.

In a move to strengthen the flow of ideas into this mainstream element of policy-making a new forum for discussion was created with the establishment of a Directors' Committee. This brings together all the senior officials with hands-on involvement supervising the running of all the departments covering areas such as the Middle East, Europe, and Asia and the Pacific, Africa and the Commonwealth, as well as functional aspects such as the European Union, Drugs and International Crime, Overseas Trade and International Security. Policy papers prepared in the DSI for the board's consideration go first to the Directors' Committee, where observations and amendments can be added. On their way down from the board the decisions on the papers are discussed in the Directors' Committee to determine how best they can be taken forward on the ground. To ensure close liaison between the board and the Director's Committee there is a joint secretariat, initially headed by Andrew Key, who earned his spurs as liaison secretary with the Board of Management handling the Foresight proposals. He handed over in February 2003 to a rising star, Wasim Mir, an outstanding graduate from the London School of Economics.

Overseeing all the assessment of priorities for the allocation of resources, a new top-level body came into existence in September 2002: the Finance and Strategy Group. It stemmed from the experiences of Jack Straw's first visit to China in July 2002 when he discussed global issues with President Jiang Jemin. He had never been as far east before and was deeply struck by the immensity of the country and its potential to exert a huge influence well beyond its own region. On his return Straw decided that he and his ministers needed to play a larger role in strategic resource decisions. Until then ministers had been not more than marginally engaged in the allocation of the Foreign Office budget and discussions about where resources should be focused. These questions had been left to senior officials and the Permanent Under-Secretary as the chief accounting officer for the Foreign Office to the National Audit Office.

Straw made it clear that neither he nor his ministers wished to become bogged down in details such as whether an extra consulate should be opened in Spain or whether more locally engaged officers could ease the workload of the diplomatic staff. But there was a strong case for their greater involvement in determining, for example, how Asia could be given more attention and whether there should be a refocusing of resources with less priority on Africa and more on eastern Europe. So the Finance and Strategy Group was inaugurated, meeting once a month with the Foreign Secretary, his four junior ministers and the board with an agenda initially often concerned with tackling the squeeze on running costs as a result of the Treasury's curbs in the spending round. On major questions of policy, when a position paper is agreed by the board and submitted to the Foreign Secretary, there may be a discussion in the Finance and Strategy Group to assess the cost of pursuing the policy and the amount of resources – human and material – required to implement it.

This increased political input into the mainstream of policy-making was symptomatic of the changes introduced as the Labour government consolidated its command of administration after the buffeting experienced by Robin Cook in the first term. From the outset Jack Straw gave his junior ministers much more freedom to become involved in policy discussions than Robin Cook had. Robin Cook had a limited interest in forward-looking policy and rarely let any of his junior ministers become involved in it. In the shake-up after the general election in 2001 Denis MacShane, an MP with a sharp analytical mind honed during his days as a journalist, was encouraged to take a close interest in the evolution of policy. On his promotion to succeed Peter Hain as Minister for Europe he became even more involved on policy issues, resulting in regular consultations with Simon Fraser at the DSI. As Minister of State, Baroness Symons, a former General Secretary of First Division Civil Servants, covers British Trade International and North America as well as answering to the FO in the House of Lords. Denis MacShane's successor as a junior minister, Bill Rammell, needed no prodding to pitch into policy discussions as chairman of the Labour Movement for Europe. Mike O'Brien established his commitment to the Middle East peace process and was licensed by Jack Straw to embark on fact-finding visits to sound out attitudes towards the 'road map' for an Israeli–Palestine settlement produced by the quartet of the USA, the EU, the UN and Russia.

Even more significant is the greatly increased scope for political influence on the evolution of policy enjoyed by the two special advisers on the Foreign Secretary's staff. In Conservative administrations the activities of special advisers were mainly concentrated on keeping the Foreign Secretary aware of the possible political repercussions among backbench MPs and constituency activists of the development of certain policies. There was a tradition of making a sharp distinction between the official role and the party political interests of the Foreign Secretary. When Lord Carrington was lambasted by the right-wing Monday Club at Harrogate for 'selling out the settlers' during the Rhodesian independence negotiations in 1979, he was on his own. Strict impartiality was maintained by the then Foreign Office News Department in not even issuing diplomatic correspondents with the speech made by the Foreign Secretary in a *tour d'horizon* at the Conservative Party conference. Not so under the New Labour government. When Jack Straw addressed the Labour Party conference at Blackpool in September 2002 his speech was immediately available on the Foreign Office website.

Not only were there two places reserved for Straw's special advisers, Dr

Michael Williams and Ed Owen, at the decision-makers' meetings of the Strategic Plan Governance alongside ministers and senior Foreign Office officials, but their elevated role gave them direct access to the DSI and its policy planners. From the outset Simon Fraser realized that the special advisers had an important role to play in feeding ideas to Jack Straw, who trusted their judgement and appreciated their role in assessing the political impact discussions in the Office, particularly when his daily engagements and foreign travel did not give him enough time to study the constant flow of submissions. They also take part in a monthly meeting the Foreign Secretary holds on short-term strategy as well as attending his weekly meetings with all the Foreign Office ministers.

Another innovation was the widening of the trawl for new ideas on policy within the Foreign Office and posts abroad by the creation of Policy Net, which evoked in the corridors of the Foreign Office the catchphrase 'Thinking with 1,000 brains'. Taking advantage of state-of-the-art information technology, the DSI seeks the views of diplomatic staff around the world. In a follow-through on the initiatives of the Young Turks, the DSI took up their cause with the mantra 'We are the champions of Foresight'. Some of the themes from position papers and other topics under discussion have been distributed on the Foreign Office net for comments, with the aim of enabling the entire staff, including locally engaged personnel, to have an input into the mainstream of policy. The system seeks to tap into knowledge and experience gained not merely from people's current posts but from their recollections of how problems were tackled in previous posts. Valuable contributions on the question of conflict prevention came from ideas sent from Tirana and a locally engaged staff member at Chiang Mai in Thailand.

This new flexibility has been applied to another important tributary to the flow of policy: the Research Analysts department, whose origins go back to 1943 when it was a key part of the Foreign Office reforms introduced by Anthony Eden, who appointed Professor Arnold Toynbee as its head. Since then the department has been greatly enhanced and become the envy of many Western foreign ministries because there is nothing comparable to it in any other capital. As Richard Lavers, its head until he left to become Ambassador to Guatemala in November 2001, aptly put it: 'It is an intellectual powerhouse, staffed by dedicated, highly intelligent people who are among this country's most prominent experts in their specialist fields.' The analysts are an essential buttress against short-termism in policy-making since they have the capacity to set issues in their proper historical context and provide facts and figures from previous challenging situations. Departments seeking to carry weight with their proposals make sure that the relevant analyst sees the draft of submissions before they are finalized. Lavers explains it shrewdly: 'It is not simply a question of a safety net to prevent errors which can arise through ignorance of certain facts. Rather it concerns the vital nuance, the shaded judgement.'

The resources that the Head of Research Analysts has at his disposal are impressive: nine research groups, each with six analysts, supplemented by a support staff making a total of eighty experienced officials, the largest department dealing with political affairs. Eight of the groups cover geographic areas. The remaining one embraces a wide range of global responsibilities: the United Nations and other international organizations, human rights, environmental issues, and conflict prevention. Analysts are recruited as full members of the Diplomatic Service, largely from academe and usually with two degrees. When vacancies are announced there are often hundreds of applicants. The one-time popular conception of them as semi-detached scholars engaged in leisurely discussions in the cloisters before producing elegant dissertations on an esoteric theme has long since been abandoned, as they are nowadays required to provide concise submissions at short notice on the background to a sudden crisis.

Following the Cabinet Office Scrutiny of 1993, research groups are not housed in a remote eyrie at the back of the Foreign Office but are located alongside their main client geographic departments. This makes the daily interchange on developments between departments and analysts much easier. The proximity has produced a closer interactive relationship and means that analysts, by being readily available for instant consultation, can be the first to highlight a new development in a situation and bring its significance to the notice of policy-makers. This integration into the policy-making process has been accelerated by having the Head of Research Analysts, Simon Buckle, report directly to Simon Fraser, the Director of Strategy and Innovation.

Although they have the value of being more or less permanent fixtures in the Foreign Office, and thereby provide the continuity that most departments lack because of the postings system dispersing staff every three or four years, analysts are sometimes given the chance to deploy their expertise in the field. Such was the case when Dr James Hoare was sent to Korea to head the new embassy in Pyongyang. Normally it is their close contact with the recognized authorities in specialist subjects in universities which gives their constantly available advice added value. While they are updating their expertise by attending hundreds of conferences in the UK and abroad, thereby producing streams of fresh information feeding back into the databank at the Foreign Office, the research analysts organize some seventy seminars every year, sometimes on their own, at other times in partnership with academic institutions such as the Middle East Centre at Durham and the School of Slavonic and East European Studies.

Like the assessors working in the Joint Intelligence Committee, the research analysts set great store on being recognized as policy neutral. In the best tradition of the Toynbee era they insist that they do not make policy but acknowledge that the depth of information they supply can have a strong influence on the decisions taken. They absolve themselves from responsibility by asserting that while they set out elements to be taken into consideration it is up to the policy-makers to decide what to deduce from them. Unlike other members of the Diplomatic Service, however, the research analysts are able to take sabbaticals to undertake research. Publication of books or articles in learned journals is regarded as beneficial to work in the department since it enlarges the analysts' experience of problems in their specialist field and thus could benefit subsequent research projects in the Foreign Office.

At all stages, from its conception to its delivery, the flow of foreign policy is heavily dependent on one particularly important tributary, which glides along silently out of the limelight: the legal dimension. The Legal Adviser, Sir Michael Wood, with a staff of twenty lawyers in London, three in Brussels, two at the UN in New York and one in Geneva, has the responsibility of ensuring that actions taken by the Foreign Office are in accordance with national and international law – a very exacting requirement since they are not always easy to interpret. Departments have a lawyer assigned to them who follows their work closely and advises them on the legal implications of what they are contemplating. Human rights issues keep the lawyers very busy. Disarmament proposals have always entailed a heavy workload, as did the campaign for an International Criminal Code, which was vigorously driven by Robin Cook. A long-established rule requires that a submission being sent to the Foreign Secretary must carry a note confirming that any legal aspects have been cleared with the Legal Adviser. The government's Ministerial Code lays down the circumstances in which ministries must have the blessing of the Attorney General before proceeding. It is up to the Legal Adviser, in casting his eye over policy areas, to intervene without waiting to be asked for an opinion in order to point out the dangers of pursuing a certain line of action if he thinks it may infringe the government's legal obligations.

One of the most carefully planned legal operations was that undertaken to secure a trial of the two Libyans accused of causing the deaths of 270 people in the bombing of PanAm Flight 103 over Lockerbie in December 1988. When Robin Cook became Foreign Secretary nine years later he was determined to end the stalemate and made it a priority issue for the then Legal Adviser, Sir

Franklin Berman, to tackle. This resulted in many behind-the-scenes moves at the United Nations, in Libya and in South Africa where President Nelson Mandela took on the role of a go-between with President Muammar Qaddafi, all of which culminated in a UN report confirming that the accused could receive a fair trial under the Scottish judicial process. Every intricate step on the way to the trial opening at Camp Zeist in the Netherlands under Scots law on 3 May 2000, and ending with the verdict on 31 January 2001, was assessed by Sir Franklin Berman with the Foreign Secretary, who in turn devoted a lot of his time to discussing each phase with Lord Hardie, the Lord Advocate.

Another tributary whose strength was greatly increased immediately Robin Cook took over at the Foreign Office is the ethical dimension. Some of the advocates of moral values being accorded greater weight in policy gave the impression that ethics were accorded a place in foreign policy only on the arrival of New Labour. Morality in politics, is, however, as old as party manifestos, if only at times as a matter of lip-service to impress an audience, whether at the hustings or at the United Nations General Assembly. Its place in foreign policy was neatly put by Douglas Hurd as 'somewhere between Gladstone and the saloon bar'. As his shadow, in a valedictory to Robin Cook as Foreign Secretary in the debate on the Queen's Speech on 20 June 2001, Francis Maude put it bluntly: 'The idea that a foreign policy has a dimension that is ethical and everything else can be unethical is absurd. At its best Britain has always pursued an ethical foreign policy and it should not be necessary to brag about it.'

Right from the outset, however, Cook defied his critics, whose scorn resulted in a *Daily Telegraph* headline the next day, 'Cook to lead the Foreign Office on moral crusade', and showed he was embarking upon more than rhetoric. In pledging to put 'human rights at the heart of our foreign policy', he also promised to publish an annual report on 'our work promoting human rights abroad' – something that no other foreign secretary had done. Until the early 1990s human rights matters were handled by two officials in the United Nations Department. Under the new impetus from Cook a large Human Rights Department was established with a staff of twenty diplomats and an innovative activist from Amnesty International, Harriet Ware-Austin, appointed as policy adviser.

The department is divided into three parts: a United Nations section for lobbying at the General Assembly, covering South-East Asia, Latin America and the Caribbean, and working on the death penalty issue; a section dealing with the Organization for Security and Cooperation in Europe, the Council of Europe, and efforts to end torture, child abuse and maltreatment of women; and a Public Policy and Projects Unit, which distributes funding of £7 million a year. More than five hundred projects have been funded in ninety countries since 1997, not all of them popular with the host government. In 2001 they included funding the exhumation of graves in Guatemala for legal investigations and help for the Truth Commission enquiring into the Fujimori regime in Peru. The largest amount allocated to any one country went to China, where, apart from projects on women's rights and civil education, funding was given to Beijing University for investigations into the judicial process and police station procedures. Funding was also provided for the appointment of a human rights adviser in the British embassy in Manila, Dan Painter, a former member of Amnesty International who worked with the UN Commission on Human Rights. Other advisers have been sent to Kiev – to cover Moldova, Romania and Ukraine – and to Nepal. Five countries where funding of over £100,000 has been allocated are inspected each year to ensure that projects are being fully carried out.

Another scheme operating successfully out of the headlines to promote training in respect for human rights and the protection of civil liberties was set up under the title ASSIST – Assistance to Support Stability with In-Service Training – in April 1998. It is administered partly by the Foreign Office's geographical directorates and by the Security Policy Department, which had a total budget of £6,823,279 for the financial year 2000/1 and funded over 180 projects in more than sixty-five countries. These included sending six British instructors to run a two-week course in human rights for thirty police officers in Brazil, promoting penal reform by introducing community service in Latvia, courses run by West Mercia Constabulary to train officers in the United Arab Emirates in the sensitive handling of rape cases, and seconding a Chief Constable for six months to Indonesia to create a new code of ethics for the police service. The scheme also provided £1 million for English-language training, funding for British Military Advisory Training Teams in Africa, peacekeeping training for Chinese officers, and courses in disaster management.

The problem of giving human rights such a high profile lies in the fact that it exposes the Foreign Secretary to accusations of either inconsistency or hypocrisy when the objective of an ethical dimension appears to be marginalized in the handling of export licences for arms and in dealing with human rights abuses in major countries. Robin Cook was put in the dock publicly and in Parliament on several occasions charged with double standards. While he tried to defend the decision not to revoke licences for the sale of 'trainer' Hawk aircraft to Indonesia on the grounds that they were for external defence, he failed to convince those who protested about arms sales to a regime beating up demonstrators with equipment 'made in Britain'. He had similar problems over equating the supply of arms to Zimbabwe and Morocco with the commitment to spreading human rights values.

The difficulty for any foreign secretary is that he has to be mindful of the economic aspects of arms sales as well as the morality of the purposes to which they are put. His Cabinet colleague at the Department of Trade and Industry will not let him forget that over half a million jobs in the United Kingdom are dependent on Britain remaining among the world's top arms exporters. The Chancellor of the Exchequer, while warning the Heavily Indebted Poor Countries that their debt burdens would not be eased if they allow the savings from debt servicing to be used to buy weapons, does not let the Foreign Secretary ignore the fact that arms sales account for vast export earnings – once, in 1997, in excess of £4 billion a year. Most of the time the dilemma of steering a course between economic interest and principles is resolved in a fudge that rarely comes under the public spotlight.

There are times when these hidden tensions surface and create the embarrassment of what the Foreign Office euphemistically terms '*un mauvais quart d'heure*'. One such occasion occurred in April 1996 when the Saudi Arabian government expressed its concern at the campaign against it organized by an exile in Britain, physicist Dr Mohamed al-Masari. Home Secretary Michael Howard responded by issuing a deportation order for al-Masari to be expelled to the Caribbean island of Dominica. He said al-Masari's presence threatened arms contracts and 70,000 jobs – the £20-billion al-Yamanah deal and a Vickers deal for tanks worth £900 million. Relations were strained after al-Masari won his appeal against the deportation order. Another embarrassing episode concerning aid and trade erupted with the disclosure of the scandal over the £417-million Pergau dam in Malaysia in 1993, when it was revealed that the Conservative government had linked aid to the sale of British arms. Some of the controversy over where to draw the line between principles and national interest was removed by the Labour government abolishing the controversial Aid and Trade Provision in 1997, but loopholes remained through the acceptance that in certain circumstances bilateral aid could be tied to looser conditions.

The pitfalls of the arms trade, even when the intention is to 'help the goodies', were driven home to the Labour government in May 1998 when Robin Cook and his Minister of State, Tony Lloyd, were in the dock over the 'Arms for Africa' affair. Moves to restore a stable regime in Sierra Leone under President Ahmad Tejan Kabbah after he had been overthrown by a military coup ten months previously, by supplying arms, may have sounded like a good idea at the time. One problem was that the weapons shipped from Bulgaria in a $10-million contract with the London-based security firm Sandline arrived too late to be used to oust the rebels. Even more seriously, the intervention was held in some quarters to have contravened a United Nations Security Council embargo which, ironically, had been drafted in the Foreign Office. Although Prime Minister Tony Blair tried to dismiss it all as 'hoo-ha', since the Foreign Office had been acting correctly in seeking to instal the legitimate government, it left ministers and officials appearing naive and negligent, if not deceitful, in treading through the minefield of African politics.

Balancing the need for good diplomatic and trade relations with China, especially in view of the Anglo-Chinese agreement on Hong Kong for 'one country, two systems', with a commitment to hold all governments to account on human rights has proved to be a difficult tightrope act for foreign secretaries. Robin Cook's visit to China in January 1998 engulfed him in criticism for resorting to 'quiet diplomacy' and not raising any of the individual human rights cases on his list during his talks with Foreign Minister Qian Qichen. After eighteen years in prison, the human rights campaigner Wei Jingsheng, whom Robin Cook declined to meet, was critical of the Foreign Secretary for leaving 'the victims of China's human rights abuses in the lurch'.

The dilemma for Cook, who chose to raise the dissidents' cases at a lower government level and tread a careful path between row and kow-tow, was starkly set out when he told the Foreign Affairs Committee: 'The prime consideration of British foreign policy in relation to China must be because we have a duty of care to the six million residents of Hong Kong.' There was a similar dilemma for the government in its attitude to the fierce conflict between the Russians and the Chechnyans. Because there were political reasons for having some sort of partnership between Russia and NATO, as well as for persuading Russia to accept the enlargement of NATO with eastern European countries, critical comments in Downing Street were muted about the Russians bombing Grozny.

Despite a commitment under the charter signed in November 1999 at the Istanbul summit of the Organization for Security and Cooperation in Europe, attended by Russia among the fifty-five nations present, that conflicts in one state are the concern of all, there was no disposition to take Russia to task over its action in Chechnya. Although Sweden's ambassador to Moscow, Sven Hirdman, asserted in May 2001, when his country held the presidency of the European Union, that the EU had evidence of serious human rights violations in Argun, near Grozny, no attempt was made to invoke the charter commitment as President Putin was being fêted by Prime Minister Blair as someone the West could do business with. Menzies Campbell, the Liberal Democrat foreign affairs spokesman, voiced the dismay of many others when he insisted in the House of Commons on 20 June 2001: 'It would have been possible to engage with Putin on issues of common importance such as European security while saying all the time: "As long as your record on human rights in Chechnya is so abysmal, you cannot expect to receive all the benefits of full engagement." To some extent the Government sold that pass.'

In succeeding to this tightrope role Jack Straw took a lower profile while asserting in the Foreign Office Annual Report on Human Rights in 2001 that they remained 'at the heart of our foreign policy'. In justifying the military campaign against Afghanistan in an article in the *Observer* on 18 November he stated: 'Engaging with global problems is both a moral duty and a practical imperative.' Nonetheless, while acknowledging in the annual report that there was much unfinished business requiring responses from governments and recognizing that 'it might mean talking to other countries about their treatment of minorities', there was no sign of a more robust approach to China. During Hu Jintao's visit to Britain as Vice-President in October 2001, human rights organizations criticized the decision to have him discreetly ushered in and out of Downing Street by a side entrance to shield him from the Free Tibet campaigners standing in protest in Whitehall. Although the human rights abuses in Burma and Rwanda have been vigorously condemned, for a long time Foreign Office ministers confined themselves to platitudes over the violence against farmers in Zimbabwe when their land was invaded by President Mugabe's supporters. It strengthened suspicions that the easy targets get the big stick while the big powers and those that present a political problem are handled cautiously with a 'constructive dialogue' on human rights issues.

Another large tributary affecting the flow of foreign policy is the European factor. Almost every major issue confronting the government has a European dimension – from terrorism to asylum, drugs to the environment, agriculture to fishing, conflict prevention to peacekeeping, investment to banking, defence to plane-making, crime to climate change, transport to shipping, and so on. The old division between home affairs and foreign affairs is gone; the overlap means constant interchange between departments. All Whitehall ministries have to be concerned about what goes on in Brussels and keep in touch with the vast outpourings of documents on regulations.

Because of the increasing importance of the European dimension in policy-making throughout Whitehall, Sir Michael Jay decided in 2003 to promote the dynamic Foreign Office expert on all matters European, Kim Darroch, to Director General Europe, with a seat on the new Foreign Office Board. This ensured a direct input of authoritative analysis on European economic, political and security issues into the formulation of policy at board level. The extra weight given to European factors was reflected in the strengthened team assembled in support of Kim Darroch – a directorate led by Dominick Chilcott with three assistant directors. It enabled the Foreign Secretary to have readily accessible up-to-the minute detail on all EU developments whenever he faced questions in Parliament or had to appear before the Foreign Affairs Committee.

The interaction on European issues between various ministries is demonstrated by the fact that more than half the civil servants working at 10 Avenue d'Auderghem in the Office of the United Kingdom Permanent Representative to the European Union (UKREP) are from departments in Whitehall other than the Foreign Office. They are all high-flyers in one ministry or another, but the person in authority at the top is the ambassador from the Foreign Office, always a very senior mandarin as the roll-call shows: Sir Michael Butler from 1979, Sir David Hannay from 1985, Sir John Kerr from 1990, Sir Stephen Wall from 1995, Sir Nigel Sheinwald from 2000, and John Grant from 2003. Playing the lead role requires Britain's EU ambassador to have all the strands of the negotiations under his control and be able to play off pressures on one side with compromises on another. The detailed knowledge accumulated day after day and often late into the night at Brussels gives him the sort of expertise that a minister with so many other matters distracting his attention does not have the opportunity to acquire. Often it is a matter of lateral thinking in making links between unrelated dossiers.

The quaintise (an American term widely used at the EU, meaning 'cunning stratagem') – as if taken from the pages of Machiavelli's treatise on statecraft, *Il Principe* – is graphically described by a former member of the Brussels mafia:

> You sit there hour after hour through the night in Brussels and you listen to the delegate opposite you droning on about the Widgets Directive and you realize that the point he is making is crucially important otherwise he would not be returning to it over and over again. So you flick through your papers and read the Whitehall notes on widgets. Next morning you telephone the department in London dealing with widgets and discover that although we are against the directive it is not a life-or-death issue. That afternoon at the ECOFIN [Economic and Financial Council] meeting a tax question comes up for discussion which is a red-hot matter for the Treasury – and there opposite you is the delegate who was steamed up about the Widgets Directive.
>
> In true Machiavellian style you corner him at the coffee break and ask: 'How important is the Widgets Directive to you?' When he confirms it is really important and you are convinced that he is not bluffing – that is a vital judgement – you then say '*Mon cher collègue*, how important is the tax question

to you?' When he shrugs his shoulders and says: 'Thank you for asking. What an interesting idea', then lo and behold he gives way on the tax question and the Treasury thinks you will be turning water into wine for an encore. In return you find a way of modifying the British stand on widgets which brings enormous relief to the delegate sitting opposite you. At the end of the day – as must be done every day even if the meetings do not finish until well after midnight – you report to London on the day's business and they just cannot understand how you solved their problem so brilliantly.

In day-to-day dealings with the European Union it is essential to have mandarins who are well versed in the arcane art of EU horse-trading, euphemistically called negotiations, and almost equally important that they are experienced in 'Eurospeak', the special devious language used in the corridors of power in Brussels. Britain's trio of mandarins experienced in such black arts has a key player at the sharp end: John Grant, the Ambassador to the European Union who is always alongside the Foreign Secretary in Brussels, acting as the eyes and the ears of the Foreign Secretary in his absence. Having twice previously served in Brussels, John Grant had all the requisite skills for presenting the government's case, a talent honed from his days as a much respected briefer in the News Department and subsequently spokesman at UKREP. His ability to react with finesse to a sudden change in a situation was demonstrated to colleagues many times when he was the principal private secretary to the Foreign Secretary during the prickly period of Robin Cook's tenure of the office. In Brussels John Grant is in direct contact many times a day with the Cabinet Office, where Sir Stephen Wall, a former EU ambassador, makes sure that each development is in accord with what the Prime Minister and Chancellor of the Exchequer regard as essential for Britain's interests, that any changes will be acceptable to the various ministries affected by them, and that wherever necessary preparations can be made for any amendments to British law. The third member of the trio is the Director General Europe, Kim Darroch, making sure that the external and internal implications of economic and institutional developments such as EU enlargement are consonant with Britain's policy objectives. Overseeing their work from a general political and security perspective is the Political Director General, John Sawers, who keeps in frequent contact with his opposite numbers in other capitals, sometimes as many as twelve times a day with, for example, his French colleague in times of crisis.

Decisions on foreign policy are rarely taken in Cabinet. It is given a weekly report of foreign affairs generally and European Union matters by the Foreign Secretary, but this is largely a *tour d'horizon* just to keep them up to date. A review in greater depth takes place in the Cabinet committee that deals exclusively with European business, EDOP – Defence and Overseas Policy (Europe Subcommittee). This meets about eight or nine times a year under the chairmanship of the Foreign Secretary and may be attended by the ambassador from Brussels in case questions from ministers on the complexities of an issue require the detailed knowledge of an expert. Before each meeting the Director General Europe briefs the Foreign Secretary on every major item on the agenda with an assessment of how they should be tackled, along the lines of 'This is what we think our objectives should be; this is what is probably negotiable and eventually attainable; this is where the other EU members are coming from on this issue; and here is the best advice on the tactics of getting from this situation to the outcome which most closely meets our objectives.'

This process of assessing how to achieve objectives is intensified before each negotiating session. Preparations usually begin every Friday when the British ambassador flies from Brussels to London for planning sessions, but at times of crisis he may be called over on Tuesdays or Thursday as well. In between those visits, if an issue involves several ministries there is a video conference set up at the Cabinet Office linking UKREP with the others round the table. As one veteran of these sessions explained: 'It is no use saying the solution is to push from A to B because more often than not some other EU member is blocking the road. You have to devise alternative routes, usually you need four, so that if obstacles are thrust in your way you can get where you want to be in the end.' Where it requires great finesse is when the issue comes up for discussion under the rubric of the EU's Social Chapter. Ministers are then warned: 'There is no veto. It is subject to majority voting. So the tactics have to be directed at seeking the best deal possible, which in the circumstances is X plus Y.' As politicians accustomed to compromise, ministers are realistic enough to recognize their limited options and usually give the go-ahead for this deal with the proviso to their negotiating team to seek an extension on timing while trying to squeeze a little more on one paragraph and yielding a little less on another. Thereafter, it is up to the ambassador to go back to Brussels and play it by ear at the hard grind at the negotiating table. Ministers in London cannot have the detailed knowledge of the nuances of the negotiations, which depend at times on an ability to read the body language of the other EU members and assess whether their poker hand would be strong enough if it came to putting their cards on the table.

Where major political decisions are required on what is termed the Big Picture, the Cabinet is usually left to rubber-stamp the conclusions reached by the three grandees of Downing Street: the Prime Minister, the Chancellor of the Exchequer and the Foreign Secretary. It is that trio which largely decides the government's position on key matters such as joining the single currency. But short of these crucial stages in Britain's relationship with Europe, the everyday stepping stones are to a great extent determined by the European mandarins working closely with the Foreign Secretary. The first eighteen months of the Cook era were beset with difficulties, but thereafter he established a relatively good understanding with those officials whom he trusted. While they in turn rarely warmed to him, they came to respect him as a shrewd politician with a remarkable mind – some described him as a flawed genius.

Robin Cook was very fast at absorbing European matters in which he was interested and following the thread of a complex argument in Brussels. Although not an easy partner in tackling problems in the way that Jack Straw proved to be, he had astute political judgement in assessing what would command support in an international forum and what would face trouble. Officials admired his exceptional talent for dealing with his fellow EU foreign ministers, either on the telephone or cajoling them round the table in Brussels, where it would be unusual for them to take a decision that they knew would cause him problems back at Westminster.

Provided the general line of policy is cleared with the Foreign Secretary and the Cabinet Office, the European Directorate in the Foreign Office is capable at times of wielding immense influence in the formulation of policy because of its ability to coordinate the requirements of the other Whitehall departments and its experience in devising ways of countering other European delegations when they deploy obstacles and delaying mechanisms liable to affect British interests. While the ultimate bargaining may take place behind closed doors, either with foreign ministers or heads of government, all the guidelines for choosing certain options and the costs that each would incur are usually carefully set out in advance by UKREP and the European Directorate.

The experience may be traumatic for a new minister plunged into this EU whirlpool. Even for a veteran like Douglas Hurd, who had been a diplomat for fourteen years in Beijing, New York and Rome, and served with two prime ministers, Margaret Thatcher and John Major, it was often an ordeal, as he acknowledged afterwards in *The Search for Peace*:

> I used to fly to Brussels on a Sunday afternoon in advance of an EU Council meeting on Monday, so that over a delegation supper on Sunday night I could go through carefully all the items on the agenda with our experts on the spot. The next day I would spend 12 hours, perhaps a good deal more, imprisoned in the Council building, as the Presidency tried to make progress on one item after another, reserving the trickiest for informal discussion over lunch. Over

the meal ministers, deprived of their advisers, could be driven to concentrate on what they really wanted, forgetting the finer points in their written briefs. One had to eat, speak, listen and remember, all at the same time. They were testing occasions, sometimes enjoyable, sometimes thoroughly depressing.

At EU summits, when it comes to the communiqués it is the expertise of the political directors, who know their EU partners' hobby horses and can play one off against the other, which can be crucial in securing a form of words that makes the most of the good points from Britain's perspective and plays down the negative side. These presentational skills make life a lot easier when the Foreign Secretary has to explain the outcome of negotiations in the House of Commons.

In keeping with his much vaunted claim to be eager to play a key role at the heart of Europe, Foreign Office ministers appointed by Tony Blair have stressed the importance of always seeking to coordinate policy with their European partners. The mandarins have shown themselves much less sanguine about making a reality of the professed aim of the Common Foreign and Security Policy, however. While it is recognized in the Foreign Office that it is impor-tant to avoid policies at variance with those of EU partners wherever possible, the idea of having a consensus on a single foreign policy is usually dismissed by British diplomats as an objective often inconsistent with transatlantic coordination. Athough urged by ministers to pursue such a goal, they rate its achievement as a politician's pipe dream.

How exasperatingly beyond the reach of the European Union this objective remains was shown when ministers met in Luxembourg on 15 April 2002 to work out a collective position on the incursions of the Israeli army into the Palestinian cities following the suicide attacks by Muslim extremists. Most members, headed by France and Spain, backed the United Nations Commis-sion for Human Rights resolution passed in Geneva by forty votes to five, con-demning Israel for 'mass killings' of Palestinians in the Jenin refugee camp. But Britain, Germany and Italy closed ranks with the United States in refusing to single out the Israelis for such criticism and declined to endorse the verdict of the UNCHR resolution.

There used to be a tradition of Anglo-French cooperation on the Middle East dating from the days of the Sykes–Picot Agreement in 1916, but the crisis of February 2003 over intervention in Iraq exposed the vast gulf that opens up between the two nations at times. Tony Blair's call for Europe to stand united with the United States was affirmed in an eight-nation declaration. It was not shown to either President Chirac or Chancellor Schroeder because of the reluctance of the French and German leaders to agree to military action against Saddam Hussein without giving more time for United Nations weapon inspections. This gulf was widened when the French and Germans blocked a decision in Nato for contingency planning to enhance Turkey's defence with Patriot missiles in preparation for war with Iraq.

While British policy was aligned with that of President Bush, the French and Germans devised a totally different approach in their Mirage Project to enlarge the weapons inspection system with a threefold increase of UN inspectors on the ground and an aerial search with French reconnaissance jet planes and German drones. The Blair government's dismissal of the scheme, as brusque as that by the Bush administration, caused widespread misgivings in the country, including among many in the Labour Party, whose anxiety the former Cabinet minister Lord Thomson summed up by stating it was a pity that the Franco-German initiative did not 'come from the European Union as a whole with our Prime Minister at the heart of it'.

The deep cross-Channel divide over European aspirations for a Common Foreign and Security Policy was made glaringly obvious when Jack Straw tabled a resolution at the UN Security Council on 7 March 2003 giving Iraq until 17 March to comply fully with the obligations set out in UN Security Council Resolution 1441. While Tony Blair immediately engaged in intensive diplomatic activity, telephoning other members of the Security Council for support, the French Foreign Minister, Dominique de Villepin, flew to Africa to persuade the governments of Angola, Guinea and Cameroon to block what President Chirac condemned as the 'rush to war' resolution drawn up by Britain and the United States.

After the follow-up resolution was withdrawn at the Security Council in face of a threatened French veto, and the Anglo-American assault was launched against Iraq, those in Downing Street who peddled the idea that the rift between London and Paris would be quickly healed were proved false prophets. At the first EU summit in Brussels after the war the *entente* was far from *cordiale*. President Chirac rejected attempts to justify military intervention after the event and insisted: 'France will not accept a UN resolution that legalizes military action and gives to the belligerents, the Americans and the English, the right to administer Iraq.' While Tony Blair struggled to keep the door open for improving policy coordination with the pledge 'We will need to have a period of reflection as to why these differences exist and how we overcome them', there was no one volunteering to be an honest broker between Britain and France. Germany's Chancellor Schroeder was blunt: 'It is not my role.'

On other matters where the British government previously sought support from its EU partners, in dealing with crises in Zimbabwe and Sierra Leone their response ranged from half-hearted to blatantly indifferent. This was highlighted in February 2003 when President Chirac invited President Robert Mugabe to Paris for a Franco-African summit regardless of strong British objections based on the agreed ban on travel for ministers of the Zimbabwe government as a result of its lamentable human rights record. When the French government took action in Africa by sending troops to Abidjan to shore up the Ivory Coast regime they did not consult Downing Street.

British government policy on European defence is shaped by Foreign Office mandarins much more than by staff at the Ministry of Defence. Sir Emyr Jones Parry, in his time as Political Director, was co-author in 1998 of the St Malo Declaration which paved the way for Europe's rapid reaction force with the commitment: 'Europe needs strengthened armed forces that can react rapidly to the new risks and which are supported by a strong and competitive European defence industry and technology.' When Sir David Manning was moved from Nato ambassador to become Foreign Policy Adviser to Prime Minister Blair, it was Sir Emyr Jones Parry who succeeded him in Brussels. There, it is the Foreign Office's ambassador and his deputy, surrounded by brasshats of all sorts from admirals and group captains to brigadiers, who exercise the dominant influence in the policy-making process on meeting the challenges in the Balkans. Then twice a year – in the spring in a member country, in December at NATO headquarters at Evere outside Brussels – foreign ministers, with their Foreign Office experts at their side, review the politico-military problems facing the Alliance. The disposition and deployment of NATO forces is a matter on which the Ministry of Defence naturally has a large input, but the ultimate decisions are made by the Foreign Secretary in consultation with the ambassador to NATO, who is in day-to-day discussions with Alliance partners on situations as they develop.

On many occasions – especially at times of crisis – one tributary second only to the European factor in its importance to the flow of policy is the United Nations dimension. Because of the United Kingdom's major role as one of the five Permanent Members of the UN Security Council, the shaping of British foreign policy often has to take account of its impact at the United Nations and the likelihood of its securing widespread support there. Heads of mission there have always been among the top four in the Diplomatic Service, mandarins such as Sir Anthony Parsons from 1979 to 1982, followed by Sir John Thomson, Sir Crispin Tickell, Sir David Hannay, Sir John Weston, Sir Jeremy Greenstock and, in 2003, Sir Emyr Jones Parry. The mission's significance is underlined by the fact that the number two has the rank of an ambassador and the vast staff includes six counsellors as well as five first secretaries handling economic matters. The United Nations 'branch office' in Geneva is headed by a senior ambassador and has nine first secretaries covering a wide spectrum of UN activity.

The importance of a highly skilled diplomat heading Britain's UN mission has been demonstrated many times, never more effectively than when Sir Anthony Parsons began at dawn on the eve of Argentina's invasion of the Falklands to round up his fellow ambassadors at the UN Security Council to align them in support of Britain. His expertise in drafting resolutions quickly was exemplified when he secured the requisite minimum of nine Security Council members at short notice to agree to have an emergency meeting convened on 'a matter of grave concern'. His skill was again demonstrated when he drafted a further resolution – without waiting to have it authorized by the Foreign Office in London – calling for the withdrawal of Argentine forces without tying the hands of the United Kingdom by preventing it from sending a task force, which was passed as UN Security Resolution 502 when he persuaded the Russians to abstain.

Knowing how to use Britain's influence to its fullest at the United Nations was also shown to be a great asset in the hands of Sir Jeremy Greenstock. His draft of a resolution in May 2000 threatening sanctions if Eritrea and Ethiopia did not stop fighting paved the way for an end to the conflict, which cost tens of thousands of lives. Later that year he was the prime mover in securing Security Council agreement to establish an international tribunal for Sierra Leone to put on trial the rebel leader Foday Sankoh. Britain's campaign against conflict diamonds was boosted in February 2001 by the UN mission winning support for sanctions against Liberia for selling guns in exchange for diamonds from Sierra Leone rebels. But it is not just a matter of behind-the-scenes moves in the air-conditioned lobbies of the United Nations building. It was Sir Jeremy Greenstock heading a delegation of five UN ambassadors to Dili in September 1999 which exposed the plight of the refugees and led to the effective intervention of UN peacekeepers and eventual independence for East Timor from Indonesia.

Sir Jeremy's skill as a draughtsman played a vital role in the arduous search for a formula for the UN Security Council resolution on sending weapons inspectors back to Iraq. His back-stage diplomacy was crucial during the prolonged struggle among the five Permanent Members for a strengthened Security Council resolution in September 2002 on the mandate for tackling the crisis over Iraq's weapons of mass destruction. The terms on which the UN weapons inspectors were to return to Iraq caused serious differences between the United States and France, as well as a succession of hurdles raised by Russia, and called for skilled diplomatic persistence by Sir Jeremy in following through the interventions of Tony Blair, edging compromises out of President Bush and manoeuvring to sell them to President Chirac of France and President Putin of Russia. No one was sure what the outcome would be until the last session on 8 November 2002 when Resolution 1441 was passed unanimously to the surprise of many UN delegations. But a much more serious challenge came over the British-sponsored follow-up resolution setting a 'final deadline' of 17 March for compliance by Iraq. The opposition to it proved that there are limits to consensus-building by diplomacy.

These interventions demonstrated the increasing importance of one particular tributary in the policy flow when traditional diplomacy is not enough: the 'presidential one', emanating not from the White House but from No. 10 Downing Street. Its evolving significance began in the wake of Argentina's invasion of the Falkland Islands when Prime Minister Margaret Thatcher became disillusioned with the Foreign Office and treated Francis Pym, who took over as Foreign Secretary on the resignation of Lord Carrington, with ill-concealed contempt. Her scathing dismissal of the Foreign Office as an institution 'where compromise and negotiation were ends in themselves' was used in her memoirs as justification for having Charles Powell, her trusted foreign affairs adviser, at her side as she played an ever more dominant role in the policy decision-making process. Prime Minister Tony Blair, who made no secret of his admiration for Mrs Thatcher's ability to stamp her authority in the international arena, steadily enhanced his reputation as an interventionist in foreign policy matters from the time he won a second term with a massive majority which resulted in the term 'presidential' entering the Westminster political lexicon.

His swift response to the terrorist attacks of 11 September 2001 established from the outset that many of the determinant elements in the flow of policy during the Afghan crisis would come from the Prime Minister's side of Downing Street, not that of the new Foreign Secretary, Jack Straw. This required the Foreign Office mandarins to couch their advice with circumspection, since Blair set his priority from 12 September onwards as being 'shoulder to shoulder' with President George Bush regardless of any reservations about the gung-ho American crusade against terrorism wherever it was to be found, in Iraq, Somalia, the Yemen or Sudan. His whirlwind tours of far-flung capitals to garner support for the campaign – highlighted in the previous chapter – led to his impetuous promise to commit 6,000 British troops to 'stabilize Afghanistan' at a time when calmer heads in the Foreign Office were advocating a more cautious approach. Heeding this advice would have spared Blair the embarrassment of having to stand the British force down a week later because the US command made it clear that they were running the campaign and did not want them.

Nonetheless, No. 10 Downing Street continued to take the lead in the international arena, leaving the Foreign Office in a secondary role when the Iraq crisis followed the intervention in Afghanistan. It was Blair, not Straw, who produced the dossier on Iraq's weapons of mass destruction, and it was the Prime Minister who played the dominant role in mediating between his European Union partners and the White House over how to bring pressure to bear on President Saddam Hussein. While Straw kept in close touch over the Iraq crisis with his Russian opposite number, Igor Ivanov, it was Blair who played the major role in trying to bring President Putin on side for UN Security Council Resolution 1441 when he went for a long session of talks at the Russian leader's dacha outside Moscow in October 2002. Although Straw tabled the follow-up resolution on 7 March 2003 it was clearly dictated by Blair, as was inadvertently admitted by Ambassador Sir Jeremy Greenstock in a hurried television interview while the Security Council was still sitting when he referred in a Freudian slip to 'the Prime Minister's resolution'.

Blair's closeness to President Bush, cemented by his instant support on 11 September 2001, gave him access to the White House that no other member of the Western alliance could achieve. He could also claim that his public support for President Bush at a time when France and Germany were distancing themselves from what they regarded as a 'rush to war' against Iraq enabled him to argue successfully at his Washington summit on 30 January 2003 for further recourse to the UN Security Council, even though both leaders insisted that Saddam Hussein was already in breach of the obligations set out in UN Security Council Resolution 1441.

The course of the war in Iraq and its aftermath were directed at summit level between President Bush and Prime Minister Blair. Any doubts about the standing of Tony Blair in Washington were answered by the readiness of President Bush to travel to Northern Ireland for a summit with him at Hillsborough Castle on 8 April 2003 when they started planning the role of the coalition forces in the reconstruction of Iraq. If he needed to justify such a dominant personal involvement in foreign affairs, Blair could quote the authority of Walter Bagehot, who upheld the global role played by Sir Robert Peel in a biographical study written in 1856: 'He cannot consult with the Secretary of State for Foreign Affairs, and exercise the influence which he ought to have with respect to the conduct of foreign affairs, unless he is master of everything of real importance passing in that department.'

Such mastery was essential at meetings of the War Cabinet to enable the Prime Minister to balance the competing expertise of the inner circle making decisions over the crises first in the 'war against terrorism' after the events of 11 September 2001 and then in dealing with President Saddam Hussein over the perceived threat from his weapons of mass destruction. Blair had to have considerable command of detail to deal with decisions being reached round the table by those attending the War Cabinet: John Prescott, Deputy Prime Minister, Jack Straw, Foreign Secretary, Geoff Hoon, Defence Secretary, Gordon Brown, Chancellor, John Reid, Leader of the House of Commons, David Blunkett, Home Secretary, Clare Short, International Development Secretary, plus the officials – Rear Admiral Sir Michael Boyce, Chief of the Defence Staff, John Scarlett, Chairman of JIC, Sir David Manning, Foreign Policy Adviser, Jonathan Powell, Chief of Staff at No. 10, and Alastair Campbell, Director of Communications. His ability to keep pace with the rapidly changing military situation of the war in Iraq was a major factor in sustaining his dominant authority.

However, irrespective of which side of Downing Street takes command in planning how to deal with political challenges facing Britain, a lot of time is spent reacting instantly to unforeseen events. As Henry Kissinger observed in his book *Diplomacy*, the luxury of cool, calm study that academics enjoy is not for those who have to deal with foreign policy on a day-to-day basis: 'The analyst can choose which problem to study, whereas the statesman's problems are imposed on him. The analyst can allot whatever time is necessary to come to a clear conclusion; the overwhelming challenge to the statesman is the pressure of time. The analyst runs no risk. If his conclusions are wrong, he can write another treatise. The statesman is permitted only one guess; his mistakes are irretrievable.'

Quick thinking is required whenever there is an eruption in the smooth flow of foreign policy, especially if British lives are stake as they were when Britons were held hostage by rebels in the Yemen in December 1998, or when British soldiers were taken prisoner by a gang of West Side Boys in Sierra Leone in August 2000. Political judgements have to be made when there is a coup, such as happened when General Pervez Musharraf seized power in Pakistan in October 1999 or when George Speight took control of Fiji in May 2000. When there is a massive international crisis, such as over the Gulf War in 1990, the Iraq war in 2003 or the terrorist attacks on 11 September 2001 in New York and Washington, the capacity to react effectively is a crucial test of diplomatic, military and policy planning skills.

As far as its own role was concerned, the Foreign Office demonstrated the value of its emphasis on professionalism in the latter crisis. The seven-room Crisis Management Centre, the bunker in the basement of the Office, was opened at once, with Stephen Wright, the Director General for Defence and Intelligence, in charge of the round-the-clock operations. Supervising the assessments were William Ehrman, the Director for Security, and Stephen Evans, the Afghanistan expert subsequently sent to Kabul. Expertise was assembled from the departments dealing with counter-terrorism, security, defence, South Asia, research, intelligence, and consular matters for round-up meetings morning and evening, as well as emergency consultations through-out the day and night. The Permanent Under-Secretary briefed the Foreign Secretary at 8 a.m. and went with him at 8.30 to the twice-weekly War Cabinet meetings held by the Prime Minister at No. 10 Downing Street. When Jack Straw was out of the country the PUS took Stephen Wright with him to the sessions of the War Cabinet. In preparation for Tony Blair's visit by Concorde to Washington for talks with President George W. Bush in November 2001, the PUS assembled a sheaf of detailed briefing papers on all aspects of the Afghanistan situation. When the Taliban were driven out of Kabul it was the PUS who decided on the mandate for Stephen Evans in taking over the role of special envoy there.

Events requiring the coordination of international intervention on a large scale, such as a flood disaster in Mozambique, hurricanes in the Caribbean or civil wars in Africa displacing hundreds of thousands of people as refugees, bring many outside elements into the decision-making process. The govern-ment, and especially the Foreign Office, comes under strong pressure for instant responses from Parliament, the media, NGOs, lobby groups and think tanks. Advice pours into Whitehall. How to take it, when to take it, how much to accept and how much to reject, requires a fine sense of political judgement, since those calling for action do not bear the consequences that those who carry it out are obliged to face. When so much is at stake it is appropriate to examine exactly how much attention is paid to those seeking to influence foreign policy from outside the corridors of power in Downing Street.

SEVEN

Parliament and Foreign Policy

The unkind truth is that now Parliament is no longer at the centre of national life. Matthew Parris, *The Times*, 20 December 2001

The main arena of political debate is now the broadcasting studio, not the floor of the House of Commons. Peter Riddell, *Politics and the Media*, 1998

UNTIL the terrorist attacks of 11 September 2001 in New York and Washington the attention given in Parliament to the conduct of foreign affairs had been steadily declining. Apart from during events of grave international consequence over the last two decades, such as the Falklands War and the Gulf War, and the continual agonizing over relations with the European Union, the amount of time devoted to foreign affairs had been seriously scaled down. From the end of the Second World War up to the mid-1960s the House of Commons spent about 10 per cent of its time on international matters. Thereafter, until the Afghan crisis in 2001, it slumped to an average of a little over 5 per cent of its time. Only one in ten adjournment debates, where the subject is chosen by backbenchers, was on a foreign affairs issue. Less than 1 per cent of the matters raised in oral questions in the House of Commons was about foreign affairs. A full day's debate on foreign affairs used to be a major parliamentary occasion with an opening *tour d'horizon* by the Foreign Secretary followed by a critique from the opposition's shadow minister, which set the scene for a lively scrutiny by MPs of Britain's place and performance on the world stage. However, by the beginning of the twenty-first century the conduct of foreign policy had become a matter of such diminished priority in Parliament that the opposition did not use any of its twenty Supply Debates in the year 2000 for foreign affairs.

The massacre of innocent civilians in New York's Trade Center changed priorities and the perspective of Parliament on foreign affairs. In the first month after the attack on 11 September 2001 the House of Commons debated international terrorism and its consequences at length on four occasions. Since then the focus on foreign affairs has been sharpened. The scrutiny of what

Britain's foreign policy is intended to achieve and what in fact it has done to protect and promote the best interests of the country and its citizens has been more closely targeted on what matters. It was the decision to go to war with Iraq which brought Parliament right into the centre of the policy-making process for the first time since the Suez crisis in 1956. Substantive debates resulting in a rebellion of 139 Labour MPs on 18 March 2003 brought home to the government the need to take Parliament more into account.

In theory, the legislature in a parliamentary democracy is the paramount authority in determining how every aspect of the affairs of the state is conducted. It is Parliament which passes laws, which holds the executive to account, and which is the principal forum for debating all the issues of importance to the nation. In foreign affairs there is little requirement for legislation except for bills such as those concerning citizenship in overseas territories and the ratification of international treaties such as that dealing with the enlargement of the European Union. Foreign Office ministers are intended, like their Cabinet colleagues with domestic portfolios, to be accountable to Parliament, but they cannot be held totally responsible when their freedom of action in the international arena is circumscribed by the actions of other states. As Sir Percy Cradock observed in his book *In Pursuit of British Interests*: 'Much foreign policy is bound to be reactive. Britain is only one of many actors on the stage. Many overseas events are unpredictable or have not been predicted.' Nonetheless, the Foreign Office and its ministers have come to acknowledge to a much greater degree than ever before that they must take account of what Parliament, its members and their constituents are prepared to accept in the way the role of Britain in the world is handled.

As a result there has been a significant expansion of the Foreign Office department that deals directly with the concerns of Parliament. The Parliamentary Relations Unit was established at the initiative of Sir Geoffrey Howe soon after he became Foreign Secretary in 1983 because he realized, as he admitted in his memoirs, that the Foreign Office 'did not enjoy a high reputation with Press or Parliament'. However, the managerial mandarins did not share Sir Geoffrey's concern at that time and the unit became little more than a postbox for parliamentary questions to the Foreign Secretary. It was Sir John Kerr who upgraded the unit, which became the Parliamentary Relations and Devolution Department in 2000 – taking over the Devolved Administrations Department handling the interests of Scotland and Wales. Expanded to a staff of twelve under Mark Hutton, well versed in the way Parliament works as someone seconded from the House of Commons Clerks, the department achieved a much higher profile, a process continued by another eager modernizer from the House of Commons Clerks, Matthew Hamlyn, who took over in September 2001.

Its purpose has been to improve the service of the Foreign Office to MPs and their committees by endeavouring to have answers made as full as possible instead of the former practice of divulging as little as possible. When all questions tabled in the House of Commons and the Lords for an oral or written answer are distributed to the relevant departments in the Foreign Office, these departments receive guidance on parliamentary requirements. As an experienced parliamentarian Jack Straw insisted that the Parliamentary Relations and Devolution Department should see all drafts and policy submissions to ministers so that they may suggest to desk officers how answers can be improved. As well as alerting diplomats to the parliamentary aspects of an issue which may have been overlooked, Matthew Hamlyn's staff have the responsibility of ensuring that the necessary background is added on an 'if asked' basis to cope with any supplementaries from MPs.

The preparation of answers includes enquiring from a minister's private office what style of presentation is required. One minister, who did not like to be seen in the House of Commons wearing spectacles when the television cameras were focused on him, insisted on having a large type size for his briefing notes. Nonetheless, he became very popular because he also insisted that his answers had to be succinctly written and, wherever possible, no more than one sentence long. The various departments drafting answers are notified of those MPs who are likely to be interested in what Foreign Office ministers say on sensitive issues such as human rights, Arab–Israeli questions or Cyprus. Although it is denied that a list of 'awkward questioners' is kept, there is always a pool of knowledge in the FO on which MPs have expertise on certain topics and are likely to press hard for answers. Wherever there are foreign affairs matters before either the Commons or the Lords, in the chamber or in committee rooms, the Parliamentary Relations and Devolution Department keeps a close watch on the possible consequences for the Foreign Office. Attention is focused on three main areas in which Parliament aims to make an impact on the conduct of foreign policy: debates in the chambers of both Houses; questions written and oral in both Houses, as well as Prime Minister's Questions; sessions of select committees and reports of their inquiries in both Houses.

The tradition of big foreign affairs debates in the Commons gripping the attention of the nation is a rarity nowadays. Wide-ranging reviews of Britain's foreign policy usually only take place in the debate on the Address following the Queen's Speech which opens each session of Parliament when the Foreign Secretary launches the second part after the opening debate begun by the Prime Minister. Although it is not an occasion for new ideas on foreign policy to be set out, the debate on the Address on 22 June 2001, which began with Jack Straw's first speech as Foreign Secretary in the Commons, was an opportunity for Parliament to gauge what changes of emphasis there might be from the days of Robin Cook and a chance for the Foreign Office to assess from probing interventions in the debate where Parliament was looking for change. While Straw ranged over European Union issues, the Middle East and Africa, there was ample scope for a large number of other concerns to be raised in the five-hour debate, which was wound up by Defence Secretary Geoff Hoon. But the debate was so diffuse that, as often happens, the opportunity for serious cross-examination was squandered.

In-depth debate frequently occurs on European issues as they are guaranteed to arouse passion because of the deep gulf between the government and the opposition. Concern over issues such as the future of Gibraltar or Sierra Leone provokes debates, as also has been the case with the violence in Zimbabwe following the Land Acquisition Act in April 2000, which enabled white-owned farms to be taken over by President Mugabe's government without compensation. Although there has been little evidence of these debates causing a shift in foreign policy, the cumulative expression of anxiety in Parliament has made it more difficult for the government to be evasive and shelter behind 'quiet constructive diplomacy'. When this concern in the Commons is taken up in the House of Lords, where former foreign secretaries can weigh in with their authority, it can add significantly to the pressure on the Foreign Office.

Despite the cynical characterization of the upper chamber as 'an eventide home for fuddy-duddies', the quality of debate in the House of Lords has often demonstrated the vast reservoir of knowledge and direct experience of members who can challenge positions taken in the Foreign Office. By the device of 'moving for papers' it is possible to initiate a wide-ranging debate on the international situation, as Lord Carrington did on 12 January 2000. For six hours there was what the late Lord Longford called 'a feast of oratory' such as is rarely heard now in the Commons. With over thirty speakers, including four former foreign secretaries, four former Cabinet ministers and a former Head of the Diplomatic Service, the debate began with Lord Carrington's concern at what he termed 'grave mistakes' made by the Western powers in Bosnia and Kosovo triggered by the premature recognition of Slovenia and Croatia. It ranged over many other questions with equal intensity, such as the Middle East crisis, Nato, the reform of the United Nations Security Council, the role of the Commonwealth, the Caribbean, plus a memorable illustration of African diplomacy in an account by Baroness Park of an incident during her days in the Diplomatic Service when she rescued a soldier from an angry mob in the Congo and was subsequently rewarded by him opening the entrance to a ferry to let her escort a group of British subjects to safety.

Another typical example was the debate on Zimbabwe on 12 December 2001, which was opened by Baroness Park with a ringing indictment of President Mugabe: 'One man with his corrupt associates has created a black hole of starvation, violence, lawlessness, corruption and destruction.' Among others adding their wealth of experience to the call for action were Lord Carrington, the Rt Revd Roy Williamson, Bishop of Southwark, who had been a missionary in Zambia, Lord Hughes and Lord Redesdale, who had been election observers in South Africa. Yet, despite all the authority behind the observations brought to the attention of Baroness Amos as the Minister for Africa, the experts in the Lords were not able to secure any commitment for resolute action by the government since it was unwilling to force a showdown with President Mugabe before the Commonwealth Heads of Government meeting in Brisbane.

Early Day Motions are used as a means of alerting the Foreign Office to issues causing concern on the backbenches of the Commons. Backbenchers are limited to speaking for no more than ten minutes on their motion and realize that there is little likelihood of it leading to a debate. Sometimes a motion is tabled to highlight issues such as the Cyprus problem, which is appreciated by constituents of Cypriot origin, or to express sympathy for the victims of terrorism in India, which will impress voters in constituencies where there are families with Indian connections. Backbenchers, anxious to make an impact, try to persuade a large number of fellow MPs to add their signatures to a motion, which may not carry much weight inside the Foreign Office but may gain them useful publicity in local newspapers to stand them in good stead at a general election. Most of the Early Day Motions are on domestic matters, but between 1997 and 2001 backbenchers succeeded in raising forty issues concerning the United States, twenty-three on Cyprus and twenty-three on India.

Tabling questions – oral and written – is recognized as a means of registering an awareness in the Foreign Office of a matter that MPs consider is not receiving the attention it deserves. Each year there are usually nine foreign affairs question-time sessions which are fitted into the Commons schedule between 2.30 and 3.30 p.m. in rotation with those of the other government departments. In 2001 a total of 41,366 questions on foreign and domestic issues were tabled by the 659 MPs. The cost of providing answers was officially put at over £5 million. Some MPs are tireless in tabling questions across the entire political spectrum, with Norman Baker, Liberal Democrat MP for Lewes, top of the persistent questioners at 3,319 tabled between 1997 and 2001. Hot on his heels was John Bercow, Conservative MP for Buckingham and then shadow Chief Secretary of the Treasury, who tabled 2,619 between June 2001 and January 2002, which was 6 per cent of all questions asked.

Part of the reason for this total was his campaign 'to expose government waste'. Since the average cost of answering a written question is £129 and an oral question £299 his questioning is estimated to have cost in excess of £300,000. John Bercow's concern about days lost through sickness at the Foreign Office elicited the pledge from junior minister Ben Bradshaw on 12 December 2001 that the Foreign Office was fulfilling its commitment to reduce days lost from eight days per staff member per year in 1998 to 5.6 days in 2003. Many MPs coming across situations in their travels abroad often use Question Time to prod the government into action, as Michael Connarty, Labour MP for Falkirk East, did on 23 January 2001 on returning from Palestine when he asked the Foreign Secretary to take up the matter of 'the imprisonment of 53 young people who would not be in prison if Israel implemented the United Nations Convention on the Rights of the Child'.

Campaigns on human rights issues can be given widespread public support by means of persistent questioning in Parliament. MPs keep the spotlight on the plight of victims of oppression such as Aung San Suu Kyi, the Nobel Peace Prize winner who was held under house arrest for nineteen months in Myanmar (Burma), and Gedhun Choekyi Nyima, the boy kept isolated by the Chinese since 1995 after being named as the eleventh Panchen Lama by the Dalai Lama. One of the most successful at arousing the public conscience to put pressure on the government has been Jeremy Corbyn, Labour MP for Islington North, who used Question Time as part of his campaign for Augusto Pinochet to be brought to justice during the sixteenth months when the Chilean dictator was held in Britain. His activity inside the Commons boosted support throughout the country for the Chile Campaign for Human Rights. Although Pinochet was allowed to return to Chile in March 2000 by Jack Straw as Home Secretary on the grounds that the dictator was medically unfit to stand trial, pressure was maintained on him subsequently as Foreign Secretary to keep raising the issue of the progress of proceedings in Santiago with the government of Chile.

Yet however well intentioned and determined MPs are at Question Time, the results are often meagre. Where MPs have the best prospects of exerting some influence, small though it sometimes turns out to be, is in the scrutiny of the select committees, most of which were created in 1979 to establish a greater degree of accountability in the conduct of government business. As well as having parliamentary clerks to organize the sessions, the committees have the right to appoint special advisers, 'either to supply information which is not readily available or to elucidate matters of complexity within the committee's order of reference'. Under the provisions of their establishment, select committees have powers to 'send for persons, papers and records'. Only one, the Committee on Standards and Privileges, can order the attendance of a Member of Parliament, but in the words of the parliamentary explanation, 'While a Committee cannot insist on Members attending one of its meetings, Ministers will normally accept an invitation to give evidence.'

For the first twenty-three years of the select committee system one MP remained exempt from that requirement: the Prime Minister. Tony Blair maintained that there was no reason to depart from the long-standing convention that prime ministers did not submit themselves to an interrogation by select committees – the last serving prime minister to appear before a parliamentary committee being Neville Chamberlain when he was questioned about the Secrets Act in 1938. However, to head off mounting criticism of his aloofness from Parliament and his tendency towards a presidential style in government, Blair broke with tradition and announced on 26 April 2002 that he would appear twice a year before the Liaison Committee, which incorporates all select committee chairmen under the chairmanship of Alan Williams, Labour MP for Swansea West. The change, which Mr Williams admitted came 'out of the blue', provided for sessions to be held in public and covered by television with the Prime Minister facing questions on foreign affairs as well as domestic issues. To enable the Prime Minister to brief himself it was agreed that there should be an agenda set in advance so that he would know the subjects to be raised. Thereafter only one barrier remained: Blair still refused to allow his special advisers to be questioned by select committees.

Four committees concern themselves with Foreign Office matters: the Public Accounts Committee, the Intelligence and Security Committee, the European Scrutiny Committee (one in the Commons, a similar one in the Lords) and the Foreign Affairs Committee. Like every other Whitehall ministry, the Foreign Office has to be prepared to justify its expenditure to the Public Accounts Committee, which carries out investigations on the evidence of the National Audit Office. It is not just a question of ensuring that there is no financial irregularity. It is focused on value for money in the way the resource budget – £1,651 million for 2003/4 – is spent. Their investigations extend beyond the Diplomatic Service to the way funds given by the Foreign Office are used – £291 million to the BBC World Service and £167 million to the British Council in the year 2003/4. It is inevitable that questions are raised about the need for such elegant properties as embassies, especially when the book value of the Foreign Office estates in 2002 was calculated to be £1.6 billion. So far, however, the Foreign Office has fended off criticism directed mainly at the cost of the Paris and Washington embassy buildings, which are in their different ways admired by influential foreigners as showpieces of the best of British and as such attract interest in events held there. Nonetheless, the Foreign Office has not been slow to take advantage of spiralling land values. It made a large amount of money by selling part of the garden at the colonial-style high commissioner's residence of Eden Hall in Singapore in 2001, which the much respected Sir Hamilton Whyte had lovingly cultivated in the mid-1980s. The British consul-general's residence on New York's Fifth Avenue was sold for £15 million and a substantial profit was made by disposing of the property in Dublin, where the land had a high development value, and moving Sir Ivor Roberts to a much more attractive house. Sir John Kerr was proud of one record at the end of his career in January 2002, that of being the first Permanent Under-Secretary since the Second World War to have avoided any cuts in Foreign Office expenditure. Moreover, he succeeded in prising more money out of the Treasury in 1998 and in 2000.

One committee avoids the limelight: the Intelligence and Security Committee. It does not hold public hearings and usually keeps its findings secret – except for its report on 15 September 2003 on the Iraq war. It is also unique in that its members are personally chosen by the Prime Minister and their reports are sent to him with a copy to the Foreign Secretary. To chair the committee Prime Minister Blair selected Ann Taylor, former member of the Cabinet as Leader of the House of Commons and subsequently Chief Whip, who admitted to the Commons in the debate on the Address to the Queen's Speech on 22 June 2001 that foreign affairs was 'not an area in which I specialize'. Seven other MPs were chosen for the committee: James Arbuthnot (Cons. Norwich), Kevin Barron (Lab. Rother Valley), Alan Beith (Lib Dem. Berwick-on-Tweed), Alan Howarth (Lab. Newport East), Michael Mates (Cons. Hampshire East), Joyce Quin (Lab. Gateshead East and Washington West), Gavin Strang (Lab. Edinburgh East and Musselburgh), and one life peer, Lord Archer of Sandwell (Lab.).

The Chairman of the Joint Intelligence Committee usually appears before the committee twice a year, when members may ask about administration, policy or budgetary matters, but they are not allowed to enquire about intelligence operations taking place in any particular country. Because the committee's remit covers security at home and abroad, the Home Secretary as well as the Foreign Secretary appear before it. The intelligence chiefs of MI5 and MI6 can also be summoned, but they do not disclose details of any current investigations being undertaken. The committee can ask for an assessment of the security situation in a country where British troops are involved, such as Sierra Leone, but no secret documents are made available. It was the Intelligence and Security Committee to which Jack Straw, under pressure from MPs, assigned investigations into the way warnings about the possibility of terrorist attacks were handled prior to the bombings in Bali in October 2002, thus avoiding public hearings. The government evaded demands for a public inquiry into events leading to the Iraq war and left it to the Intelligence and Security Committee, but subsequently was obliged to order a judicial inquiry into the death of the weapons expert Dr David Kelly which, under Lord Hutton, ranged far more widely than Tony Blair anticipated.

The oldest committee in the Commons, and the most technical, is the European Scrutiny Committee, which came into being in 1974 following the accession of Britain to the EEC. With sixteen members under the chairmanship of James Hood, Labour MP for Clydesdale and a former miners' leader, it has a staff of fourteen – the largest of any select committee. Its members are not chosen like those of other departmental select committees but are put forward on a government motion after consultations. The committee has the power to scrutinize all European documents, assess their political and legal importance and recommend which of them may merit detailed consideration in the House of Commons. This results in approximately 1,300 EU documents a year being analysed by the committee, which reports on 500 to 600 which it judges to be important and recommends about thirty for further debate. As its mandate under the House's Standing Order 143 covers 'any document which is published for submission to the European Council, the Council or the European Central Bank', the committee can range over Green Papers, White Papers, Commission reports and even draft recommendations still to be endorsed by the Council.

Its mandate is not just financial supervision under its authority to check on the development of Economic and Monetary Union. It can use Article (*iv*) of the Standing Order authorizing scrutiny of 'any proposal for a common strategy, joint action or common position' to assess all developments concerning the Common Foreign and Security Policy. Under that rubric the committee can question the Chief of the Defence Staff as well as the Defence Secretary. The committee can bring within its purview any legal or institutional developments that could have implications for Parliament. With that remit it can take soundings from Sir Stephen Wall, the kingpin of the Cabinet Office on EU directives, or John Sawers, Director General, Political, at the Foreign Office.

At each meeting of the committee, which is convened at 4 p.m. every

Wednesday that Parliament is in session, members deal with about forty items of business: EU documents and responses from ministers. Its recommendations for more detailed examination go to one of the three European standing committees – Committee B, which covers the Foreign Office, the Treasury, the Department of International Development, the Home Office and the Lord Chancellor's Office. There, a Foreign Office minister can be asked to appear and answer questions without advance notification of the subject for up to ninety minutes, not just from the thirteen members of the committee but from any MP – sessions are open to all MPs although they are not allowed to propose a motion or vote.

The Scrutiny Committee can decide that an EU document is of such importance that it should be tagged to a motion in the Commons. Thereafter it will appear in the order paper below the motion for debate. Another method is a direct recommendation for a document to be debated in the Commons – a practice that occurs about three times a session. With a Scrutiny Reserve Resolution it is necessary for the House to give clearance for a document that is recommended for debate. Under the Votes and Proceedings Resolution of the House of Commons of 17 November 1998, 'No Minister of the Crown should give agreement in the Council or in the European Council to any proposal in the European Community for European Community legislation or for common strategy, joint action or common position ... which is still subject to scrutiny or which is awaiting consideration by the House.' Strictly interpreted, these provisions give Parliament widespread powers to examine every aspect of the conduct of foreign policy in the European Union.

In parallel with the Commons Scrutiny Committee, the Lords has its own Select Committee on the European Union, which complements the work in the Commons rather than competing with it. Unlike the committee chairpersons in the Commons, the chairman of the European Union Committee in the Lords, Lord Brabazon of Tara, is salaried. Alongside him sit twenty members, many of whom have had held senior positions in government, such as former Chancellor of the Exchequer Lord Lamont of Berwick. They are distributed among six subcommittees, two of which concern the Foreign Office: Subcommittee A, dealing with economic and financial affairs, trade and external relations, and Subcommittee C, which is concerned with the Common Foreign and Security Policy. A further group of fifty peers is co-opted, including former members of the Diplomatic Service such as Lord Hannay, Lord Powell, Lord Wright and Lord Wilson. Their investigations go into much greater detail than those of the Commons committee and last much longer. While the Commons committee reports on some five hundred documents a year – some of them within a week – the Lords committee rarely handles more than twenty documents a year.

By far the greatest potential for parliamentary influence on foreign policy is to be found in the Foreign Affairs Committee. It not only commands great respect in the House of Commons for its scrupulously non-partisan approach to every issue investigated, but its zeal in preserving its independence has made it impervious to any pressure from government. At times its very robustness has unnerved ministers and made Foreign Office officials squirm in their chairs with embarrassment under inquisitorial questioning. Right from the start it has had high-calibre MPs as chairmen: first Sir Anthony Kershaw, former junior Foreign Office and Defence Minister from 1979 to 1987, followed by David Howell, former Energy Secretary and Transport Secretary from 1987 to 1997, and then Donald Anderson, a former member of the Diplomatic Service and a barrister who was opposition spokesman on foreign affairs for nine years.

That Donald Anderson shone as an excellent and independent-minded chairman was acknowledged immediately the Labour government was re-elected in June 2001. They decided he was too good and too independent and dismissed him, along with another member of the awkward squad, Gwyneth Dunwoody, who chaired the Select Committee on Transport. It provoked outrage on both sides of the House that the new chief whip, Hilary Armstrong, had behaved in such a crass way to two of the most respected backbenchers. Motions by two former ministers, Labour's Frank Field and the Conservative Douglas Hogg, and an interview in *The Times* by former Speaker Baroness Boothroyd, boosted the backbench rebellion. It was doubly embarrassing for Robin Cook as the new Leader of the House after being given a rough ride in select committee sessions as Foreign Secretary. Despite attempts to avoid a humiliating defeat by promising changes under his proposed modernization plans for Parliament, the rebellion proceeded to a vote, resulting in a crushing victory on 16 July by 301 votes to 232 for the resolution to reinstate Donald Anderson – with a drop of almost two hundred in Labour's 'reliable' 412-strong vote – and a similarly emphatic vote to restore Gwyneth Dunwoody.

It proved the case for a more democratic selection system instead of it being used by whips to create compliant committees. Under the headline 'Revolting Peasants' in the independent parliamentary journal *The House Magazine* in October 2001, Donald Anderson recorded the lesson for the government without any bitterness: 'There is no doubting the significance of that vote: it brought home to the Government that there are limits to its powers, that it must take the views of Parliament into account.' When he asserted that it was 'surely wrong in principle that the government selects those whose job it is to scrutinise them', he was echoing advice from the thirty-three-member Commons Liaison Committee which went unheeded by the Blair government in March 2000. Then the Liaison Committee called for changes for all twelve select committees with the observation: 'We believe that the nomination of members to committees is not satisfactory. It is too much in control of the whips.' It urged changes to the system which would ensure that 'members are not kept off committees nor removed from them on account of their views'.

Once restored, Donald Anderson reasserted the Foreign Affairs Committee's independent stand on scrutinizing the foreign policy issues facing the government and his practice of seeking consensus by a democratic decision-making process among his team of ten MPs – six Labour, three Conservative and one Liberal Democrat. The choice of issues to be investigated is determined by putting the first six suggested topics to members so that they can rank them in order of priority. They have learned by experience not to examine too large an issue. The first investigation under Donald Anderson's chairmanship set up in July 1997 was into human rights. They split into three groups, one travelling to Kenya, Uganda and Nigeria, the second to the Middle East, and a third to the Far East, which was limited to Thailand and the Philippines after the Burmese authorities in Myanmar turned them down. The process proved too time-consuming, taking almost a year. Thereafter, it was decided to have a session on human rights after the Foreign Office issues its annual report.

Normally the Foreign Affairs Committee travels as a team, but inside a country they may move around in groups to save time, as they did in China, when some went to Shanghai and others to Canton and Hong Kong. When the committee went to Russia to see the workings of Foreign Office missions they all examined the situation in Moscow and then some went to St Petersburg, others to Ekaterinburg. The travel budget is settled by bidding, along with other select committees, for an allowance from an overall allocation set by the House of Commons Commission, which is composed of MPs and chaired by the Speaker. The Foreign Affairs Committee usually gets more than most – £123,436 in 2001/2 – because its work involves it in more travelling than the others. This budget covered two EU visits – one to Brussels, the other to Madrid as Spain held the presidency – two to the USA, one to Turkey and one to Cyprus. Each visit has to be costed in advance and its budget is separately negotiated. The financial bargaining is a reflection of the turf war which has become more intense in recent years as the European committees – Commons and Lords – and to a lesser extent the Intelligence and Security Committee as well as the Defence Committee extend their range of activity into areas previously considered the exclusive concern of the Foreign Affairs Committee. Two issues have attracted attention from competing committees: the Common Foreign and Security Policy (CFSP) and the preparatory convention for the Inter Governmental Conference (IGC) to shape the future of the European Union after enlargement to twenty-five members in May 2004.

Not only does the Commons European Scrutiny Committee take an increasingly active interest in the CFSP but the Lords moved on to the issue quickly with a report in July 2000 six months after the subcommittee was established to examine it. Its conclusion that what was needed was 'military capabilities not symbolism' so that the European nations 'do more to contribute to peace and stability' was reached after visiting Brussels for talks with Nato leaders and the EU Commissioner Christopher Patten, as well as ten sessions to take oral evidence from sixteen people, including General Klaus Naumann from Germany. In a way emboldened by having its remit extended to include the CFSP, the Commons Scrutiny Committee also staked a claim to a place in the British delegation to the convention leading up to the IGC – a place which the Foreign Affairs Committee has always regarded as its by right. The Scrutiny Committee now sends members to each EU country that takes up the presidency in the six-month rotation so that they can assess what action programme is planned and what effect it could have on Britain. It had its team in Madrid before the Foreign Affairs Committee flew there in January 2002 to go over the same ground with the same Spanish government officials. The Scrutiny Committee also extended its travels to assess possible problems created by applicant states for EU membership, visiting Cyprus in November 2002. This rivalry causes resentment not only in the Foreign Affairs Committee but also at the British embassies where arrangements have to be duplicated. 'It results in MP fatigue,' as one ambassador observed after a previous double round of delegations.

The Foreign Affairs Committee has a legitimate grievance since it is concerned with the entire range of Foreign Office activity, authorized under Standing Order 10 to 'examine the expenditure, administration and policy of the Foreign and Commonwealth Office and associated bodies'. It is dismayed that the turf war has arisen because the European committees have moved from being steeped in the processes – studying the nuts and bolts of EU moves in the context of how they might affect United Kingdom legislation – into assessing policies and their possible implications. The Foreign Affairs Committee maintains that it has a right to know what the policy of the Foreign Secretary will be towards forthcoming issues on the agenda of European Councils. As a result the Foreign Secretary usually submits himself to cross-examination by the Foreign

Affairs Committee, as Jack Straw did on 10 December 2002 in advance of the Copenhagen summit on enlargement.

For the European Council at Laeken in December 2001 the usual Foreign Office memorandum on the agenda for the committee to study beforehand was a substantial document of twelve pages. On that occasion Straw was accompanied by Director General Stephen Wright and by Kim Darroch, then European Union Director, so that they could respond to detailed questions on some of the ten major summit items, which ranged from Afghanistan to the future of Europe, enlargement, defence, and Galileo, the proposed satellite navigation system. By arrangement the committee had a short opening session on President Mugabe's suppression of opposition in Zimbabwe, but the Foreign Secretary fended off any commitment to action on the ground that the situation was to be reviewed shortly by the Commonwealth Ministerial Action Group. It was followed by a separate session with the Foreign Secretary on the Foreign Policy Aspects of the War Against Terrorism, for which his experts had prepared a thirty-point document updating its previous memorandum.

The turf war with the Intelligence and Security Committee has generated problems that are more difficult to resolve because of it being the Prime Minister's creation. After the first debate in the Commons on the events of 11 September 2001 the chairmen of five select committees met to discuss how they should deal with the problem and resolved that their clerks should keep in touch to reduce the overlap in their work to a minimum. The Intelligence and Security Committee remained aloof as they have a special input on terrorism and were aware that the Foreign Secretary would be more forthcoming to them than to the Foreign Affairs Committee. This was no surprise to the latter, as it had highlighted its concern in a survey of its work published in December 2000, stating: 'The Foreign Affairs Committee must have access to the requisite intelligence and security information and to officials of the Intelligence services where this is germane to its own inquiries. This issue arose in relation to our inquiries into Sierra Leone and Kosovo, but it is an issue which may arise in any of our inquiries. The Committee attaches great importance to an assurance given by Douglas Hurd, then Foreign Secretary, that the Intelligence and Security Committee would not "truncate in any way the existing responsibilities of the Committee".' Its limitations were exposed in the investigations following the Iraq war. It rankled that the Intelligence and Security Committee was able to question John Scarlett, Chairman of the Joint Intelligence Committee, and Sir Richard Dearlove, chief of SIS (MI6), when the Foreign Affairs Committee was denied that opportunity.

Where the Foreign Affairs Committee has a unique role is in providing an informal forum for an important foreign leader or opposition delegation which might be difficult to fit into the government programme of formal visits. One of the most significant of these was in 1983 when the Foreign Office astutely selected Mikhail Gorbachev as 'the man most likely to succeed' the ailing President Konstantyin Chernenko, but could not send a note to the Kremlin saying 'We would like to invite your number three to visit Britain as we think he has a big future.' Instead the invitation was sent by Sir Anthony Kershaw as Chairman of the Foreign Affairs Committee to Mikhail Gorbachev as Head of the Foreign Relations Committee of the Supreme Soviet. With subsequent private assurances that there would be long sessions with the Prime Minister at Downing Street, Gorbachev used the visit to establish his credentials in the West – and Mrs Thatcher was able to begin building a special relationship with the man she 'could do business with'.

A stream of VIPs have been given a semi-official forum by the committee, such as President Abdurrahman Wahid of Indonesia, Prime Minister Viktor Orban of Hungary, the Serbian Prime Minister Zoran Djindjic, Kenyan opposition leader Michael Kijana Wamalwa, and a delegation from the Russian Duma. These informal sessions, which were held on 139 occasions between May 1997 and December 2000, are different from the normal evidence-taking meetings in one important aspect: television cameras, journalists and members of the public are not present. When the visit of Yugoslav President Vojislav Kostunica had to be rearranged because it coincided with other Downing Street commitments it was the Foreign Affairs Committee which give him a forum and invited members of the Defence Committee and members of the International Development Committee to attend and ask him questions. However, when the Foreign Office presented a list of seven officials they wanted to be present no invitations were given because the committee, as part of the legislature, did not want to be seen as ready to do the bidding of the Foreign Office as if it were part of the executive. For the same reason of preserving the committee's independence, Donald Anderson as chairman declined an invitation from Jack Straw to attend his Monday morning meetings with all the junior ministers, even though committee members welcomed the Foreign Secretary's cooperative attitude compared with that of Robin Cook, whom some MPs regarded at times as abrasive to the point of being provocative in his dealings with the committee.

Where the Foreign Affairs Committee has always been eager to influence the Foreign Office is over its dealings on behalf of small territories living in the shadow of a large neighbour. This was never more clearly demonstrated than in the long investigation in the mid-1990s entitled 'Relations between the United Kingdom and China in the period up to and beyond 1997', when the committee reflected the widespread concern in the country about the prospects of Hong Kong after the handover to China. The committee took up many issues, such as the dilemma of non-ethnic Chinese without British citizenship and the attempt of Governor Chris Patten to make Hong Kong's electoral system fairer and more democratic. There was a striking contrast in the evidence-taking sessions between the sympathetic probing of Chris Patten, Sir David Ford, the High Commissioner, and Michael Sze, Secretary for Constitutional Affairs, and the stern grilling of the old China hands, former ambassadors Sir Percy Cradock, Sir Alan Donald and Sir Richard Evans. Members of the committee drove home the point that the central issue was not the interests of China and Britain but those of the people of Hong Kong as 'our clients'. In the end the hundreds of pages of evidence and memoranda in the committee reports may not have shifted policy in Beijing towards Hong Kong one centimetre, but they served notice that the world would be closely watching Beijing's fifty-year commitment to 'one country, two systems' in the former colony.

The committee's concern about honouring commitments has been shown in the way it has repeatedly focused on the government's obligations to the people of Gibraltar in discussions between British and Spanish ministers. The committee took its stand on the 1969 Order-in-Council on the constitution of Gibraltar, stating: 'Her Majesty's Government will never enter into any arrangements under which the people of Gibraltar would pass under the sovereignty of another state against their freely and democratically expressed wishes.' One of the harshest admonitions of the Foreign Secretary resulted from an inquiry undertaken when there was alarm in Gibraltar over an agreement aiming to resolve the problem by June 2002 following a meeting between British and Spanish ministers. After evidence-taking sessions with Peter Caruana, the Chief Minister, and Peter Hain, then Foreign Office Minister of State, the committee delivered a stern rebuke in its report of 7 November 2002 – ironically coinciding with a referendum in Gibraltar which rejected any sharing of sovereignty with Spain by 17,900 votes to 187, almost a 99 per cent rejection. It severely criticized Foreign Office Ministers for not disclosing that joint sovereignty was under discussion with the Spanish government as 'a serious failure in their accountability obligations to this Committee and to Parliament'. Lambasting Jack Straw for describing the Gibraltar government's decision to hold a referendum as 'eccentric', the committee stated: 'We think that in British Overseas Territories it is of great importance that democratic expressions of view should take place when territories themselves so determine.' The committee's strongest condemnation was reserved for its pronouncement on the actual negotiations: 'We conclude that the Government was wrong to

negotiate joint sovereignty, when it must have been known that there was no
prospect whatsoever that any agreement on the future of Gibraltar which included joint sovereignty could be made acceptable to the people of Gibraltar,
and when the outcome is likely to be the worst of both worlds – the dashing
of raised expectations in Spain, and a complete loss of trust in the British
Government by the people of Gibraltar.'

If there was any doubt about the ability of the Foreign Affairs Committee
to call the Foreign Office to account, that perception was dispelled emphatic-
ally in the inquiry into the controversial 'arms to Africa' scandal in 1998 over
contracts by the British company Sandline International to supply weapons
assigned to help restore President Ahmed Tejan Kabbah to power in Sierra
Leone after his overthrow in May 1997. It resulted in a torrent of criticism
engulfing Robin Cook for hypocrisy over his proclamation of an ethical dimension in foreign policy, especially after Sandline insisted that its activities in
Sierra Leone were undertaken 'with the full prior knowledge and approval of
Her Majesty's Government'. The catalogue of bungling at various levels made
it impossible for either the Foreign Secretary or Sir John Kerr, the Permanent
Under-Secretary, to escape unscathed from the wrath of the Foreign Affairs
Committee.

Sir John Kerr had to suffer the embarrassment of returning to the committee after a gruelling ninety-minute inquisition to retract a statement to
the effect that he thought Foreign Office Minister Tony Lloyd had been told
about a customs investigation in the brief prepared for use in a Commons
debate on 12 March 1998. The Permanent Under-Secretary did his best to
exonerate Robin Cook, saying the Foreign Secretary had a massive workload,
that he should not be expected to react to 'every cough' and 'it was not the
sort of business the Foreign Secretary should immediately be bothered with'.
Sir John covered gallantly for his Foreign Secretary with the assertion: 'I was
confident that these guys who work in the Foreign Office will have got it right.'
Robin Cook was also obliged to amend a statement he made to the House of
Commons on 12 May to the effect that no intelligence reports about Sandline's
activities had been received at the Foreign Office. His retraction came in the
form of a written reply on 19 May confirming that five such intelligence reports
had been received between 8 October 1997 and 10 March 1998.

The verdict of the Foreign Affairs Committee in its report on 9 February
1999 was the most scathing it has ever published, condemning the Foreign
Office for an 'appalling failure' to brief ministers properly. Sir John Kerr was
criticized for having 'failed in his duty to ministers' by withholding information about a customs investigation, others for being either guilty of 'at best

political naivety' or 'contempt of their duties'. The relations between British High Commissioner Peter Penfold, who had accompanied President Kabbah into exile in Guinea, and Sandline were held to be 'open to criticism'. Robin Cook was also accused of trying to obstruct the inquiry, particularly by not allowing the Director of M16 to be questioned by the committee. As a result, the committee's report said it was time for 'a more mature attitude' towards the committee, which should have access to security documents and intelligence officers.

Its conclusions were blunt: 'The Sandline affair gave us cause for concern about the relationship between Ministers and officials. We are determined to ensure that a culture of transparency and accountability is fostered within the FCO.' In an unusual riposte Robin Cook published a note to Sir John Kerr affirming that it was 'unfair that officials who cannot speak back should be condemned in the colourful language of political knockabout'. The Foreign Affairs Committee was unrepentant, and in a subsequent special report on its work reasserted its insistence that 'officials understand their constitutional responsibilities to Ministers and Parliament. As we said in our report on Sierra Leone, where these issues were most to the fore, "tenacity has its rewards". By showing that we would not capitulate under pressure we forced the Government to make a number of concessions.'

One further humiliation was imposed upon Robin Cook as a result of the embarrassing disclosure that a copy of the committee's report had been leaked to him in advance of its publication. Ernest Ross, Labour MP for Dundee West, admitted giving Robin Cook a copy and resigned from the Foreign Affairs Committee on 23 February 1999. The following day Robin Cook insisted he had not broken Commons rules in accepting a copy of the report and asserted that he had not made improper use of it. Nonetheless, the Standards and Privileges Committee, in censuring Ernest Ross on 30 June 1999 and suspending him from the Commons for ten days, also delivered a rebuke to Robin Cook for retaining the advance copy of the report. The impact of the entire episode and the incisive manner in which the Foreign Affairs Committee had investigated it were acknowledged by Prime Minister Tony Blair. While he thought it easy to apply 'counsels of perfection' with the advantage of hindsight, he pledged that the government would 'respond carefully' to the recommendations in the report, which among other points suggested a Green Paper on the legal status of mercenaries and arms suppliers.

When the government acted on that suggestion and published a Green Paper on private military companies in February 2002 the Foreign Affairs Select Committee responded in August 2002 with a report based on detailed

enquiries and evidence-holding sessions. Many of its twenty-seven recommendations provoked considerable controversy and added a lively new dimension
to the public debate. It branded as unacceptable the lack of centrally held information on contracts between government departments and private military
armies. Once such information was obtained, the committee recommended
that there could be an international convention to regulate mercenaries so that
they could undertake UN peacekeeping missions, thus relieving over-stretched
British armed forces and make 'a legitimate and valuable contribution to international security'. The Foreign Office response on 31 October 2002 agreed
on the need for centrally held information on mercenaries' contracts with
various government departments and acknowledged the case for regulation.
While there was no difficulty in principle about a UN role for mercenaries, the
Foreign Office believed that for the present the UN would expect a peacekeeping contribution to come from the British armed forces. The committee was
satisfied that its views were taken on board.

Two months after the 'arms for Africa' report one of the most important
scrutinies ever undertaken was launched into the government's performance
on strategic arms controls, which provided a rare example of how Parliament
could have a significant impact on foreign policy. When the government
published its first report on such controls on 25 March 1999, the four select
committees concerned – Foreign Affairs, Trade and Industry, Defence, and
International Development – met on 20 April 1999 to set up a full-scale inquiry into how effective and open the government operations were. Three
members from each committee were assembled and chose as chairman Ted
Rowlands from the Foreign Affairs Committee, former Foreign Office minister
of state and a wily analyst of the Whitehall system, not prepared to be fobbed
off with 'Yes, Minister' tactics. As well as taking evidence from the various
departments the Quadripartite Committee questioned the Foreign Secretary
on policy towards Indonesia and China.

They were exceptionally thorough in seeking opinions from a wide range of
outside experts. The committee received memoranda from many quarters and
questioned in detail representatives from four NGOs: Fiona Weir of Amnesty
International UK, Paul Eavis of Saferworld, Geraldine O'Callaghan of BASIC
(British American Security Information Council), and Ed Cairns of Oxfam.
Their evidence revealed that tear gas could slip through the system under
twelve different categories and, separately, that the International Development
department received fewer than 10 per cent of the licence applications sent to
the Foreign Office and Ministry of Defence by the DTI, giving the impression
that it was not taken as seriously as it should have been. On their advice the

committee visited Stockholm for talks with members of the Parliamentary Council which works with the National Inspectorate of Strategic Products in achieving a model system of control – a visit that pointed to the benefits of establishing a constructive relationship between parliamentary bodies responsible for scrutinizing arms exports.

The first hard-hitting report, published in February 2000, lambasted the government for dragging its feet over the recommendations made in 1996 by the Scott Report on arms exports, saying 'Progress since has been leaden', and called for the theory of parliamentary accountability to be translated more effectively into practice, adding: 'The more transparent the annual reports, the greater reassurance they will give to those concerned.' The committee made the point that the key to the system lay in the detailed assessments on which ministers based decisions to grant or withhold licences in difficult cases, analysing, for example, the integrity of the end user or the risk of items being used for internal oppression. It was emphatic on the need for any committee with a remit to examine licences to see such assessments, since 'without such information individual grants of licences cannot be described as having been scrutinised as fully as they have been within the machinery of Government'.

Consequently, it recommended that the government's reports should go beyond 'bald annual figures on the percentage of cases processed within the department's targets' and give more data on the administrative performance of the Export Control Organization and the other departments involved in the licensing and pre-licensing process.

The third report, published in March 2001, was even more trenchant about the government's behaviour, stating: 'We remain firmly of the view that a serious error of judgement was made in late 1998 and early 1999 in granting several Military List Open Individual Export Licences covering Zimbabwe. We now have also to concede that the Government's response on this point was factually inaccurate.' There was widespread approval both outside and inside Parliament when the report stressed: 'We cannot agree that all "individual casework decisions" by Ministers should be automatically exempt from prior scrutiny.' A letter from Ted Rowlands, as chairman of the Quadripartite Committee, to Robin Cook as Foreign Secretary, which was published as an appendix, registered the committee's deep concern that Parliament should have the right to exert significant influence on ministerial decisions on arms exports. It stated:

We cannot however accept that the danger of damaging bilateral relations with a country can be a sufficient reason not to engage in debate on the merits of exporting goods to that country. In the rare event of the Committee considering that a proposed licence was of such significance as to merit debate in Parliament, we do not think it can be seriously suggested that the sensitivities, real or imagined, of the intended recipient should weigh heavily in the balance against the need for democratic accountability for such important decisions.

Reports by the Foreign Affairs Committee that are published on the order of the House of Commons are presented to the Foreign Office as an important indicator of what Parliament thinks of the conduct of foreign policy. They are carefully assembled – with lists of witnesses, oral evidence and memoranda submitted in advance – by the parliamentary clerks headed by Steve Priestley, who keeps an eagle eye on all the documents, particularly the responses from the Foreign Office, making sure that they come back within two months and that they address the conclusions directly. One of his important roles is in carefully drawing up a table for the chairman listing the specific recommendations of the committee with the response alongside, and an assessment of whatever shortcomings there are. Attempts to avoid a direct answer or to ignore the committee's concerns on an issue such as Gibraltar are met by a request for a full response and if necessary for attendance at a further session of questioning. Statistics are also supplied on the work of the committee for the Sessional Returns on the business of Parliament as a whole, showing that in the session 2000/1 there were twenty-five meetings with attendance by members varying from twenty-three meetings attended by Dr Phyllis Starkey (Lab. Milton Keynes South West) and Sir John Stanley (Cons. Tonbridge and Malling) to one meeting by Diane Abbott (Lab. Hackney North and Stoke Newington).

One of the most interesting reports is the annual one compiled by the Foreign Affairs Committee on the Foreign Office, which makes recommendations as a result of questioning of the Permanent Under-Secretary of State on the administration of the Foreign Office during the year, and which is followed by a report on the responses. While some of the fourteen recommendations in the 2001 report stressed the need for better cost–benefit analyses, there was emphatic recognition of one basic point: 'The Diplomatic Service's greatest asset is its people. At £201,263,000 in 1999–2000 and £195,476,000 in 2000–2001, staff costs account for less than one-sixth of the FCO's total operating costs.' Although the committee recommended finding more outsiders through the pursuit of 'open recruitment and secondment', it added the caveat 'wherever outside experience can add to and not detract from the professionalism of the Service'. This warning reflected an observation to the committee by Viscount Weir, a businessman with vast international experience, to the effect that those brought from the private sector were unlikely to be key people and could well be 'rejects and retreads and those who are for some reason not making it to the top of their company'. Despite Robin Cook's aim of finding people from British industry as suitable ambassadors to countries with strategic markets, the committee admitted that no such talent had been found to take over as heads of mission.

There was surprise in Whitehall that the gap in salaries between the Diplomatic Service and the private sector was not acknowledged to have caused retention problems. What the committee did regard as a matter of concern was the difficulty of finding enough satisfying employment for spouses of diplomats abroad, an issue engendering persistent pressure from the Diplomatic Service Families' Association. Although the Personnel Director, then Denise Holt, had assured the committee that there was 'no evidence that this is causing us serious retention problems', the committee tartly observed that the absence of retention problems was not the same as an improvement in the situation, and added: 'We are, therefore, a little sceptical of the assurances given in oral evidence.' In response to a call for more progress on this issue, the Foreign Office responded that agreements had been reached with ninety-six countries for spouses to work outside the mission, and that under Foreign Office policy, where a spouse overseas bids for employment within the mission with another person and is of equal merit, the spouse should be appointed.

One of the ways in which the Foreign Affairs Committee seeks to set exacting standards for the conduct of foreign policy is in publishing an annual report on the record of the Foreign Office in dealing with human rights issues, which requires a response from the Foreign Secretary. In the 2001 report it took the Foreign Office to task over its unsatisfactory performance 'against the erosion of human rights and democracy in Zimbabwe'. The committee laid it on the line: 'The failure of constructive engagement in Zimbabwe reveals the limits of that policy as an effective diplomatic tool.' The report registered its strong disapproval of the government's failure to promote the tabling of a European Union resolution criticizing China at the UN Commission on Human Rights. It was dismissive of the excuse from the then Foreign Office Minister, Peter Hain, when he gave evidence to the committee, saying: 'There is no point in tabling resolutions which are continually voted down and which do not get anywhere.' The committee retorted: 'We disagree. The tabling of a draft resolution at the Commission of Human Rights is an annual reminder to China of international disapproval of that country's human rights record.'

In his written response in May 2002 the Foreign Secretary blandly re-affirmed that the government remained 'deeply concerned by the situation in Zimbabwe' without offering any positive steps towards dealing with it, beyond stating that there were regular discussions with the countries of the South African Development Community and that constructive dialogue, which the Select Committee report disparaged as a diplomatic lever, would be pursued by a high-level EU troika. The response to the committee's complaint on China was no more positive. While stating that the EU had decided to support a resolution on the human rights situation in China if one were tabled, the Foreign Secretary added dishearteningly: 'The EU's view was that sponsoring a resolution at Geneva would put the dialogue process at risk without improving the human rights situation in China.'

Not prepared to be fobbed off, the committee emphasized its disappointment a year later when it stated in the 2002 Human Rights Report published on 18 March 2003: 'The rate of progress on the Human Rights Dialogue with China remains too slow. We recommend that future Annual Reports [by the Foreign Office] present a more honest picture of what has and has not been achieved by the Dialogue. We also recommend that the FCO give serious consideration to a fundamental re-evaluation of its work with China on the issue of Human Rights, given that the current strategy appears to be yielding few tangible results.'

Despite Donald Anderson's persistence with incisive, painstaking investigations, he was disappointed at the outcome of his committee's scrutiny of the government in his first term as chairman, as he stressed during the debate on the Address to the Queen's Speech on 22 June 2001: 'I was saddened by the extent to which, after very hard work by the Foreign Affairs Committee, many of our reports were almost wholly ignored, even when they were, in my judgement, of great value.' Nonetheless, he was justifiably proud of achieving consensus in the committee on all its reports, with the exception of that on Sierra Leone during the 1997–2001 Parliament. That constructive spirit, it was widely believed, was never more necessary: 'When there is a very large majority and when the democratic spirit demands a well-informed Parliament, ready to ask the Government the right questions, we need to boost the work of select committees.' In his article in *The House Magazine*, Anderson acknowledged a decline in parliamentary influence as almost inevitable: 'With the information revolution, increased technical nature of many problems, speed of events and proliferation of outside bodies, it is hardly surprising that an essentially "amateur" legislature has seen its powers decline.'

Increased powers – as opposed to influence – such as are enjoyed by the American Congress are not favoured at Westminster. There is no disposition in the Foreign Affairs Committee to seek the constitutional powers of Advise and Consent which make the US Senate Foreign Relations Committee a formidable body of politicians. However, there have been signs in recent years that the Foreign Affairs Committee would be prepared to intervene to ensure that the standards for appointments to the Diplomatic Service are maintained at the highest level. It served notice to No. 10 Downing Street about its concern over political appointments to ambassadorial posts when it delivered its annual report on the Foreign Office on 5 November 2002.

It was acknowledged that the policy of other countries in appointing politicians or public figures as ambassadors was rare in the Diplomatic Service, despite the example of Peter Jay mentioned in Chapter 4, and others such as Lord Harlech to Washington and Lords Caradon and Richards to the United Nations in New York. Notwithstanding this, it emphasized its strong opposition to the practice being reintroduced: 'We believe that political appointments are generally detrimental to the Diplomatic Service and can only be justified if the individual concerned is judged to be superior in merit to any FCO candidate.' The committee gave a clear warning that it had the right to summon any designated political appointee to give oral evidence to justify the suitability of the appointment, since its constitution, agreed by Parliament, confirmed that one of its core tasks was to 'consider, and if appropriate report on, major appointments by a Secretary of State or other senior ministers'. Its intentions were bluntly affirmed: 'We intend to consider future political appointments to diplomatic posts.'

For Parliament the right to direct its focus on to any aspect of foreign policy is in itself an indication of the potential influence of the Foreign Affairs Committee, a view highlighted in its annual report on the Foreign Office when it reaffirmed a key conclusion of the report on Sierra Leone: 'We believe that one of the principal justifications for the departmental select committee system is that officials and Ministers are aware that the beam of the select committee searchlight may one day swing in their direction, and that they may have to justify their action – or inaction – when subject to intense scrutiny by a committee such as ours, acting on behalf of Parliament and, beyond that, on behalf of a wider public interest.' This conviction as to what can be achieved by a beam of scrutiny has motivated NGOs to pursue vigorous campaigns in the hope of influencing foreign policy – a matter to be examined in the next chapter.

EIGHT

The Campaigners for Change

Non-Governmental Organisations, both large and small, are essential to this partnership. They can change the language of debate as they have over debt relief; they can drive through significant reform as with the international campaign to ban land mines. Angela Penrose, *The World Today*, September 2001

NGOs have played a vital role both in identifying the problems and in offering solutions, even if their voices are sometimes strident and some of the proposals from the wilder fringes would make matters worse. Peter Hain, *The End of Foreign Policy?*, 2001

THOSE who claim to be the 'conscience of the country' are more prominently in the public eye nowadays than they have ever been. They are not a newly established factor suddenly making their voices heard in seeking to change foreign policy and the way it is conducted. They go back a long way and have an honourable tradition of campaigning for causes abroad and protesting against injustices around the world. In recent years, however, there has been an increasing number of occasions when they are involved together. Moreover, this collaboration is frequently being extended to include close cooperation with the government. Instead of campaigning against Foreign Office policy, NGOs are becoming more and more aware that there are times when their objectives can be attained by working with the government. This has given rise to new labels being applied to these collaborative enterprises, such as 'catalytic diplomacy' by what is termed joint action through an 'epistemic community'. But it is doubtful whether this terminology, created in academic circles where few theorists have actually visited refugee camps in the Sudan, Angola or Ethiopia, conveys anything of the organization behind the determination and devotion of aid workers or campaigners in a hostile environment, which has given the NGOs authority and respect from decades of going it alone.

The importance of partnerships with NGOs was given priority by Jack Straw. One of his first decisions on becoming Foreign Secretary was to make clear to the chief executive officers of the leading NGOs that his door would be open to them. Robin Cook had paved the way for closer relations by holding a working breakfast session with some NGO officers, but there had been only intermittent contact thereafter. Jack Straw called in representatives from eight major NGOs so that he could take soundings from them over a whole range of human rights issues. Regular meetings take place with them so that areas of cooperation can be identified and tabled on an agenda for the future. His standing with many NGOs from his days as Home Secretary enabled them to feel at ease and put forward proposals for sharpening policy on human rights even though their ideas might be regarded as too controversial for public debate. Before the United Nations Commission for Human Rights meets every year at Geneva, the Foreign Office holds a forum for thirty NGO representatives to present proposals for the British delegation to raise.

Senior mandarins such as Sir Michael Arthur, when he was Director General Economic, have stepped up consultations with NGOs. In the run-up to G8 summits executives from organizations such as Oxfam and the Worldwide Fund for Nature (WWF) are called into the Foreign Office so that they can have an input into the policy-making process. During the German presidency of the G8, Sir Emyr Jones Parry, then Political Director, suggested that each government take an expert from an NGO with front-line experience of conflict prevention to the G8 summit. He sat down with twenty NGO representatives and discussed the strategy for the agenda. When it came to the Japanese presidency of the G8 in 2000 he went through specific aspects of the preparatory drafts of the communiqué with the NGOs so that before it ever became public the Foreign Office knew the NGO reaction and thereby found it easier to sell. The same consultation is held with NGOs in advance of a Commonwealth Heads of Government Meeting, so that the government knows what their priorities are on human rights issues.

Such consultation is not seen as inhibiting criticism of government policy in the media but it is acknowledged that while Jack Straw is a good listener others are not always so tolerant of forthright comment. Some NGO executives assert that Prime Minister Blair and Clare Short when she was International Development Secretary were liable to curtail dialogue if they were faced with sharp criticism. This sensitivity was highlighted in the gulf that erupted between NGOs and the government when both Tony Blair and Clare Short were outspoken in denouncing the demonstrations on the debt issue which erupted into violence at the G8 summit in Genoa in July 2001. It was also exemplified at Doha in November 2001 when Clare Short rounded on critics such as War on Want – set up by Harold Wilson and Victor Gollancz in 1951 – who warned that China's admission to the World Trade Organization would mean millions of jobs lost as foreign companies transferred production to

China from Pakistan and Bangladesh, where wages were much higher. 'Don't War on Want understand that Chinese people are human beings and that their journey out of poverty is important? If a lot more people in China get better off, it will create employment for a lot of other people,' she insisted.

Influence with the government varies according to the impact of the campaigns on the public and the NGO taking the lead in them. One of the most successful has been Save the Children, which was launched in London at the Albert Hall in 1919 by two extraordinary women, Eglantyne Jebb and her sister Dorothy Buxton, to send food to starving children facing death on the streets of Germany and Austria after the First World War. It has three advantages which enable it to be effective in its operations in over a hundred countries. It has a substantial income – £110.8 million in the year 2001/2, of which £54.9 million was derived from highly efficient fund-raising. Its patron, Princess Anne, is not a figurehead. She makes hard-hitting speeches about such issues as the cost of drugs needed by poor nations and undertakes some twenty engagements for the fund, including travel abroad each year. It has a dynamic director general in Mike Aaronson, who has good contacts with the Foreign Office through experience as a field coordinator in Nigeria and then a career in the Diplomatic Service for sixteen years before rejoining Save the Children, and a policy director, Angela Penrose, who has made her mark as a deeply committed campaigner at the United Nations as well as with the Foreign Office policy planners. The scale of their activity requires a large, well-trained staff of 1,175 personnel.

Under its programme strategy for the years 2001 to 2005 it targeted special projects such as helping children separated from their parents by conflict in Sierra Leone, Liberia, Guinea and the Ivory Coast to be reunited with their families, safer conditions for mothers and their newborn children in the Gaza Strip, and helping the eight million who lost parents as a result of HIV/Aids, as well as setting up emergency food centres to help children in places such as Angola, Eritrea and Ethiopia. Two projects in particular have prodded the government into a bigger commitment: tackling the problem of children being exploited in hazardous work or being dragooned into domestic labour in cities, and taking rigorous action to have child soldiers in the Congo and Sierra Leone demobilized and reintegrated into their communities with the chance to be educated and trained for jobs.

Their work on behalf of the government, resulting in a programme-partnership agreement for five years, made Save the Children the largest recipient of government funding at around £28 million, a large part of which is negotiated with the Department for International Development (DFID) separately from funds for emergency relief work. They have also received funds from the Foreign Office for human rights projects. The Foreign Office funded a project organized by Save the Children to celebrate the tenth anniversary of the United Nations Convention on the Rights of the Child, which incorporated much of the original declaration drafted by Eglantyne Jebb. A Children's Select Committee modelled on the Foreign Affairs Select Committee was formed in November 1999 with seventeen children asking questions of Foreign Office Minister Peter Hain and issuing a report in parliamentary style.

This cooperation did not prevent Director General Mike Aaronson from calling on the government in December 2001 to push for international monitors to be installed in occupied Palestinian territories to ensure that Israel complies with the Fourth Geneva Convention in its provisions for the protection of civilians and in particular children. His demand for more attention to be paid to the rights of children followed a meeting in Geneva where 114 countries condemned Israel for breaching its obligations under the convention, resulting in the deaths of children. This move was made regardless of the embarrassment it caused the British government, eager to avoid any criticism of the US government, which boycotted the Geneva meeting along with Israel, at a time when solidarity with the Americans was top priority during the operations against al-Qaeda terrorists in Afghanistan.

Equally stretched throughout the world, engaged in helping the poor and feeding the starving, is Oxfam. Established in 1942 as the Oxford Committee for Famine Relief to help victims of the Nazi occupation in Greece, it is one of the largest NGOs, with an income of £187 million in 2000/1, including £10.5 million from the British government. Its 'Cut the Cost' campaign, launched in February 2001, had a significant influence on ending the scandal of drugs being too expensive for poor countries when thirty-nine pharmaceutical companies withdrew from the court case against the South African government. Another of its campaigns to have a major impact was 'Bitter Coffee', which pointed out in May 2001, when the international coffee merchants met at the Park Lane Hilton in London, that with crop prices at a thirty-year low it was the farmers, such as those in Tanzania who could not afford to send their children to school, who suffered. The follow-up campaign in September 2002 with its report 'Mugged – poverty in your coffee cup' launched a coffee rescue plan, urging government and business leaders to take action by destroying surplus stocks and ensuring a fair price for farmers instead of a mere 5 per cent of the retail price.

Under its Director, Barbara Stocking, former chief executive of the Anglia and Oxford Regional Health Authority, there has been a special emphasis on health, which accounts for 10 per cent of Oxfam's programme expenditure, and education, which takes up 5 per cent. Good sanitation facilities and hygiene training have been given priority in health programmes, as has the availability of safe drinking water in Sri Lanka, Rwanda, Bosnia and Kosovo. Oxfam's 'Education Now' campaign was so successful that the government impressed upon its Commonwealth partners the importance of honouring the international commitment to provide free primary education for all children by 2015. The campaign also reinforced pressures on the government to speed up debt relief programmes for Heavily Indebted Poor Countries and to increase bilateral aid focused on educational needs. In over 1,400 projects undertaken in 2000/1, almost half of all expenditure went to countries in sub-Saharan Africa. Always in the forefront of rushing help to the victims of disaster, Oxfam provided seeds and tools for 17,500 farming families made destitute by the Mozambique floods in February 2000, and it was quick to join the Disaster Emergency Committee (DEC) Goma crisis appeal to help victims of the volcano disaster in the Congo.

Some of the other big players in the NGO field, while willing to cooperate in some projects with the government, are at times more confrontational, more prepared for vigorous action in street demonstrations, and more ready to speak out in highly critical terms of government action. Leading the pack in this category is Amnesty International, founded in May 1961 by a British lawyer, Peter Benenson, to take up the cause of political prisoners, with the symbol of a candle in barbed wire evoking the inspiration of the Chinese proverb 'It is better to light a candle than to curse the darkness'. In over forty years it has handled the cases of 47,000 prisoners of conscience and grown from an organization with a staff of nine and a budget of £35,000 to one with 357 staff plus ninety-three voluntary workers, a budget of £15.6 million, and 178,000 members in Britain. No money is accepted from government apart from a small payment for human rights education work.

Amnesty can claim credit for quickening the pace towards the creation of the International Criminal Court. Working closely with the Foreign Office, it made available lawyers to help prepare drafts for the Rome Treaty. Its 'Stamp Out Torture' campaign, launched in October 2000 as a result of recording torture cases in 132 countries in 1999, put pressure on the Foreign Office to make this a priority issue with its European Union partners. This led to Amnesty helping in a joint initiative launched by the British and Danish governments to persuade other governments to sign the United Nations convention against torture. Its campaign was also aided by Redress, a human rights group established by Keith Carmichael in 1992, after his release from detention in Saudi

Arabia, to help survivors of torture to obtain reparations for their suffering. The Foreign Office awarded Redress, which helped 220 survivors of torture to seek justice and reparation in its first eight years and was very active in the moves to establish the International Criminal Court, a grant of £4,000 to help it pursue its campaign at the United Nations.

Amnesty makes available to the Human Rights Department and the UN Department of the Foreign Office the results of its monitoring of political prisoners under arrest, of ill treatment and deaths in custody. Its six-monthly publication *Concerns in Europe* lists cases in eastern Europe where human rights abuses have taken place, such as allegations of torture by police in Georgia. Amnesty also compiles statistics on death sentences and executions, which it supplies to the Foreign Office to strengthen the international campaign to end the death penalty. Its report for the year 2000 showed that at least 1,457 people had been executed in twenty-eight countries and a further 3,058 were under sentence of death in sixty-five countries. With 80 per cent of all known executions having taken place in China, Iran, Saudi Arabia and the United States, the report listed China at the top with at least a thousand executions, while the true figure was expected to be much higher; next was Saudi Arabia with 123 executions, then the USA with eighty-five and Iran with seventy-five. Since Amnesty believes the campaign has helped to increase the number of countries that have abolished the death penalty in law or practice to 108, they have continued to press the British government to support their renewed efforts to convert the other eighty-seven countries retaining the death penalty.

Each September Amnesty publishes a well-researched scrutiny of the government's own record on human rights which provides an interesting comparison with the Human Rights Annual Report published by the Foreign Office in the same month. Amnesty's eighty-four-page audit in 2001 welcomed the Foreign Office's parallel publication but made clear that it expected more with the recommendation: 'Although Mr Straw may wish to avoid the pitfalls encountered by his predecessor's reference to an "ethical dimension", he should stress that promoting respect for human rights is crucial to the national interest and cannot be an optional extra in foreign policy.' While Amnesty praised the government's 'positive contributions' in responding to human rights crises in East Timor, Kosovo and especially Sierra Leone, where it acknowledged that British intervention 'almost certainly prevented a human rights catastrophe', it was highly critical of the UK response to 'gross and systematic human rights violations in Saudi Arabia'. The Foreign Office's 'largely softly-softly approach' reflected what Amnesty termed 'the primacy given to Saudi Arabia's economic, political and strategic importance to the UK'. The government was also criti-cized for not monitoring the use of exported weapons, particularly in Israel, and for not permitting Parliament to scrutinize applications for the export of weapons.

Although Amnesty usually takes great care with its research, it has on occasion aroused suspicion that it rushes to judgement without proper evalu-ation of the facts in a situation. In the heat of the Iraqi invasion of Kuwait in August 1990, Amnesty accepted a propaganda report that Iraqi troops were responsible for newborn babies being killed by destroying incubators in a Kuwaiti hospital. When it became apparent that the report was based on a claim circulated by an American public relations company on behalf of the Kuwaiti government which was totally false, Amnesty had to make a humili-ating climb-down. It faced strong criticism in the 1970s over its concern at the detention of members of the German terrorist organization, Baader-Meinhof, whose operations – bombings, kidnappings and murder – as the Red Army Faction caused the death of over twenty people. The integrity of Amnesty came under suspicion because of misplaced sympathy for terrorists who remained active from their prison cells for an organization that carried out the hijacking of an Air France plane to Entebbe in June 1976 and the hijacking of a Lufthansa plane to Mogadishu in October 1977.

By far the most confrontational of all the NGOs is Greenpeace. Founded in Vancouver in 1971, it has rarely been out of the headlines since its protests against nuclear tests on the Pacific atoll of Mururoa in 1972. The govern-ment has had no more persistent critic on the environment and, therefore, has had to tread very carefully in the way it tries to counter opposition to its environmental policies. After its highly publicized anti-nuclear campaigns, Greenpeace focused attention on the dumping of toxic waste, the killing of whales, and global warming. Although it claims to have almost three million supporters in 158 countries, including about 170,000 in Britain, support in the United States is believed to have dwindled from one million to about 330,000. Greenpeace has attracted worldwide attention from its international headquarters in Amsterdam, where it bases its fleet of campaign ships. In 1982 it established the Greenpeace Environmental Trust to fund scientific research in various countries and finance educational schemes in Britain.

Although Greenpeace received more publicity in the media than most other NGOs, not all the headlines praised it. They lost face in June 1995 in the cam-paign against Brent Spar as 'a toxic time-bomb' when they took a sample from the vent pipe instead of the storage tanks and wrongly asserted that there were over 5,500 tonnes of oil left on the rig, which resulted in Lord Melchett, Greenpeace executive director, apologizing to Shell UK. They clashed with the government in July 1999 when they turned their direct action against experiments on genetically modified crops. After thirty people, including Lord Melchett, were arrested for damaging GM crops at a farm at Lyng near Norwich, Cabinet minister Jack Cunningham undermined their argument by stating: 'How can we possibly have an informed and rational debate when there are people destroying the very evidence we need to conduct this debate.'

The other vigorous NGO opposing the government's nuclear policies, the Campaign for Nuclear Disarmament, which was started in 1958, has not shown the same staying power in keeping in the headlines. Their funding comes entirely from subscriptions as they refuse to accept money from any state possessing nuclear weapons. Unlike some other protest movements, CND insisted on peaceful demonstrations with no provocation of violence and no resistance to arrest, although there has been non-violent direct action by groups cutting their way through security fences. They had their glory days in the 1960s when 100,000 protesters crowded into Trafalgar Square before their Easter 'Ban the Bomb' marches to the nuclear research base at Aldermarston in Berkshire. But chants of support for the arguments propounded by philosopher Bertrand Russell, Labour leader Michael Foot and campaigning journalist James Cameron faded to a whimper long before the Cold War ended.

At its peak in 1983 CND enjoyed success when unilateral nuclear disarmament was confirmed as one of the main pledges of the Labour Party's election manifesto that year. Yet its campaigns did nothing to disrupt the deployment of Cruise and Pershing missiles in Britain and mainland Europe. Despite the persistence of the thirty-six women who marched from South Wales to set up the Women's Peace Camp at Greenham Common in Berkshire in September 1981, the Americans encountered no problems in storing ninety-six missiles at their base. Undaunted, the women maintained their gesture after the missiles went back to the USA in 1991 and did not close their camp until September 2000. Although CND membership subsequently dwindled from 100,000 to 40,000 with a headquarters staff of ten, the protests continued. Their persistence in demonstrating against Britain's nuclear defence resulted in the arrest of Carol Naughton, the CND leader, on the road outside the Trident base at Faslane in Scotland in February 2001 and a subsequent fine of £100.

No less controversial but much less confrontational than either Greenpeace or CND, the highly professional Friends of the Earth, established in 1971, have won a reputation as one of the leading environmental pressure groups. They claim to be the first NGO to launch campaigns against ozone depletion, acid rain and climate change, and promoting the need to save endangered species and tropical rainforests and to protect whales. Their drive to ensure that the natural world and all living things 'be treated with wisdom and respect' is conducted in over sixty countries and is supported by authoritative research which has been made available to governments and business. Executive Director Charles Secrett is proud of a seal of approval from Dr David Slater, Chief Inspector HM Inspectorate of Pollution: 'Technical dialogue is often better from Friends of the Earth than from industry.' At the World Trade Organization meeting in Seattle in December 1999 people were much more impressed by briefs produced by Friends of the Earth than by the slogans of rioting demonstrators whose street fights with police led to 400 arrests. The briefs were the product of research into the arguments behind the proposals for new trade negotiations and the likely impact of the influence of transnational corporations.

Neither controversial not confrontational, the Worldwide Fund for Nature (WWF), which began in 1961 as the World Wildlife Fund, mainly aiming to protect animals and plants facing extinction, is saluted nowadays by government and business as one of the most authoritative and effective conservationist organizations. With its panda logo internationally recognized and a large budget (in 2000 it was $360 million – 20 per cent of it derived from government and aid agencies) it operates in 100 countries with the estimated support of five million people throughout the world. WWF's experts are often consulted at the Foreign Office when briefs are being prepared for a delegation to a summit that has an environmental item on its agenda. However, even when the UK was praised by WWF in November 2001 on becoming the first country in the world to certify that its entire area of national forests complied with the exacting standards of the Forest Stewardship Council set up by WWF in 1993, there was still a sharp reminder of the government's obligations. After ten years of WWF and UK businesses working to promote certified timber and paper products, the government had so far not officially purchased any certified timber. WWF's Conservation Director chivvied Downing Street: 'It is now time for the Government to get its own house in order as one of the largest sectors using timber.'

Religious NGOs have broadened their scope in recent years to play an ever increasing role in partnership with government. Christian Aid, which began as Christian Reconciliation in Europe in 1945, helping refugees, and changed its name in 1964 as a result of the response to Christian Aid Week, works for people of any or no religion in over sixty of the poorest countries. Because of the impact of climate change on the problems of poverty, Christian Aid has made it part of its agenda and was critical of the Kyoto Protocol over its effect on developing nations. Its vigorous Director, Dr Daleep Mukarji, secured

£10.5 million from the government under a three-year partnership-programme agreement to deal with long-term poverty problems. With its income reaching £50 million in the year 2001/2, with 23 per cent coming from grants, including £6 million from the Department for International Development, its staff of 200 has been active in emergency relief for the victims of earthquakes in Gujarat and El Salvador, giving over £1 million in grants to projects in Bangladesh and in programmes to tackle the HIV/Aids pandemic in Africa.

Experience of working at grass-roots level on managing natural resources for poor people in Africa, the Middle East and South America over more than half a century has made the Catholic Institute for International Relations a highly valued partner of the government in its work in the developing world. With a staff of seventy-two and a hundred development workers in the field, its Executive Director, Christine Allen, has assembled a wide range of technical assistance which has made the CIIR a powerful instrument for change. Through its skill-share programme, known as International Cooperation for Development, CIIR has deployed its professional advisers to convey their expertise to others in eleven countries. Almost half of its income of £4,264,000 for the year 2000/1 came from a partnership agreement with the Department for International Development. In recognition of its pioneering work in Nicaragua, El Salvador and Honduras, CIIR was awarded a grant of over £1 million in October 2001 from the National Lotteries Charities Board, the largest grant among £21 million given to seventy-three charities. The funds were assigned to tackling such problems as the lack of safe drinking water, soil erosion and deforestation, which were highlighted by the Hurricane Mitch disaster in 1998. The other main Catholic relief organization CAFOD, set up in 1962 as the English and Welsh arm of Caritas Internationalis, also receives government funding under a programme-partnership agreement amounting to £2 million a year. With an income for the year 2000/1 from voluntary contributions reaching £31 million, it supports 500 development projects in seventy-five countries as well as being active in relief work in Mozambique, El Salvador and India.

Government funding also recognizes the value of another Christian NGO, World Vision, which started in 1950 dealing with the plight of orphans from the Korean War and established itself in Britain in 1979 after helping to handle the problems of the Vietnamese 'boat people'. Its income of £29,297,000 for the year ending September 2001 included government grants of £6,570,000 and funds its activities in over eighty countries, such as emergency relief in the Ethiopian famine in 2000, vocational training for landmine amputees in Cambodia, and health education. As a network of independent agencies rather than a single organization, it operates over a wide field. Its African relief team under Philippe Guiton was one of the first relief groups to reach Goma after the volcano disaster with an immediate grant of £350,000 to enable them to provide blankets, shelter and food plus a supply of clean water in tankers from the Rwandan capital, Kigali.

Large-scale operations, such as that involving many NGOs in the International Campaign to Ban Landmines, have often proved very successful. Although it made a slow start after the initial appeal by Human Rights Watch and Physicians for Human Rights with their publication in September 1991 of *The Cowards' War: Landmines in Cambodia*, it received a tremendous boost from the strong personal commitment of Diana, Princess of Wales, through her visit to Angola in January 1997. The intensified campaign that followed had a huge impact on governments and their peoples, resulting in the Ottawa Treaty being signed by 121 countries and the award of the Nobel Peace Prize for the campaign to Jody Williams in December 1997. That same year 130 NGOs from all over the world met in Oslo and agreed on an action plan to put pressure on governments to secure enough ratifications for the ban to come into force by 2000.

British government funding for landmine clearance was doubled to £10 million. The entire UK stock of anti-personnel landmines was destroyed by February 1998, accompanied by a pledge from George Robertson, then Defence Secretary, that no British soldier would ever lay an anti-personnel landmine again – an example he hoped would eventually be followed by China, the largest producer of landmines, and other countries withholding their signature from the Ottawa Treaty, such as the United States, Israel, India, Pakistan and Iraq. The NGO campaign succeeded in making the ban law before its target date of March 1999, but it failed to win over those six abstainers, who were still among the fifty-one countries not acceding to the treaty by 28 September 2001.

Not all the multi-organizational operations have been an unqualified success. The report of the Disaster Emergency Committee in January 2002 on the Indian earthquake at Gujarat in January 2001, when 20,000 people were killed and one million people made homeless, was critical of the way the UK aid agencies responded. While the £24 million raised to provide 'substantial and timely assistance' was praised, there were lessons to be learned by the twelve agencies involved: Action Aid, the British Red Cross, CAFOD, Care International, Christian Aid, Concern, Help the Aged, Merlin, Oxfam, Save the Children, Tear Fund, and World Vision. The DEC report was emphatic: 'DEC members could have developed more effective local partnerships and thereby achieved greater impact.' The independent evaluation, based on a survey of 2,300 people, stated: 'Even in the relief phase far more people were rescued or assisted by neighbours, government staff and military personnel than by high-profile external search-and-rescue teams and aid agencies. DEC members have ameliorated the suffering and the economic loss but they could have achieved more impact especially in the rehabilitation phase.' DEC Chief Executive Brendan Gormley issued a warning: 'With future DEC appeals when an agency proposes how to spend its share of the money raised it will have to say how it has learned from previous experience.'

Small organizations with narrowly focused objectives can often carry as much weight with government as the large NGOs with their facilities for securing publicity. The Foreign Office and the Department for International Development have given financial and diplomatic support to the work of Article 19, which has earned widespread respect for its efforts to combat censorship and the restriction of freedom of expression. With its international headquarters in London and a regional office in Johannesburg, Article 19 – named after the article in the Universal Declaration of Human Rights asserting: 'Everyone has the right to freedom of opinion and expression' – has a team of advisers and legal experts monitoring, campaigning and litigating in the cause of this basic freedom. In March 2001 it protested in a letter to President Aleksandr Lukashenka of Belarus at the beating up of Dimitri Yegorov, a young journalist who took a picture of riot police in Grodno. Article 19 closely monitored the moves to suppress freedom of expression in Zimbabwe through the Access to Information and the Protection of Privacy Bill in January 2002. Its condemnation of amendments as mere cosmetic changes added to the pressure mounted by the British government for the European Union to issue a threat of sanctions against President Robert Mugabe's regime.

Another small organization rarely in the headlines but assured of support by the Foreign Office when it has a strong case for intervention is PEN, the worldwide association of poets, playwrights, editors, essayists and novelists founded in 1921 with John Galsworthy as its first president. Its objective is to champion the freedom of expression and to campaign for writers harassed, persecuted or imprisoned by governments hostile to such freedom. The original requirement for membership, that an author must have written two books, one of which showed 'considerable literary distinction', was relaxed and membership is now open to 'all published writers regardless of nationality, language, race, colour or religion'. As the number of persecuted writers increased, in 1960 PEN established a Writers in Prison Committee, which by 2002 was monitoring the cases of 900 writers and seeking help from the Foreign Office to take up their plight with the offending governments. It keeps a case list updated daily which is the basis of a service alerting supporters to the plight of individuals whose life and liberty are threatened. In 1973 two Dutch writers founded the PEN Emergency Fund with an annual budget of £35,000 to help persecuted writers and their families. During the Cold War PEN documented the plight of dissident writers in Russia and presented the evidence to the Foreign Office so that their cases could be raised when the Foreign Secretary visited Moscow. The clandestine contacts with samizdat writers working underground that PEN sustained in the face of great risks supplied the Foreign Office with information that was impossible for British diplomats in Moscow, under constant Russian surveillance, to obtain.

By far the most effective of the small NGOs, with a record of achievement that many of the larger organizations would envy, is Global Witness. Under its Director, Charmian Gooch, the small unit formed in 1993 expanded to a staff of sixteen in 2002 to expose the link between environmental destruction and abuses of human rights following its impressive achievements over illegal logging in Cambodia and conflict diamonds in Angola and Sierra Leone. From a few spartan rooms in an office block in North London, Global Witness eschews glossy annual reports and high-profile campaign promotions with celebrities to concentrate on producing authoritatively documented evidence for the government on how natural resources are being exploited by corrupt officials and politicians. Armed with that evidence, they devise a strategy with practical proposals to campaign for international pressure to end the despoliation.

Their first major investigation began in 1995 – when there was a full-time staff of only three people – with incursions into Cambodia with video cameras and hidden tape recorders enabling researchers to talk to villagers, logging company agents, journalists and politicians to gather information about the ecological, social and economic effects of illegal cutting of timber. Every year for the next five years they made field trips to assess the damage as a result of Cambodia's forest cover declining in thirty years from over 70 per cent of the land area to less than 30 per cent. Despite a Cambodian government ban on the export of logs in December 1996, Global Witness showed that over £130 million worth of timber was illegally felled in 1997, almost 50 per cent of Cambodia's annual budget. Their exposé in April 1999, in a document produced in association with Friends of the Earth called 'Made in Vietnam – Cut in Cambodia', won praise from the Foreign Office and the Department for International Development for revealing the vast amount of Vietnamese garden furniture exported to the UK and Norway that came from illegal exports from Cambodia.

Monitoring, which Global Witness undertook on paid contract on behalf of the Department for International Development and the United Nations, eventually created such a volume of international condemnation of illegal logging that the Cambodian government took action against the concessionaires who breached the regulations on illegal timber cutting. It had no choice after the damage from the severe floods of 2000 costing the country £110 million was blamed by the United Nations largely on deforestation. Rosie Sharpe of Global Witness warned: 'Illegal logging has been steadily increasing since late 1999 with the majority of cases committed by legal concessionaires.' Prime Minister Hun Sen called a halt with the announcement on 21 December 2001 that all logging operations had to cease on 1 January 2002. As one campaign ended other timber campaigns were stepped up against Cameroon, Liberia and Congo, but the main focus had already shifted to another bigger scandal under investigation by Global Witness: conflict diamonds.

Global Witness stepped up its campaign over illicit diamond sales funding the war effort of UNITA in Angola when it highlighted the loopholes in United Nations Security Council Resolutions 1173 and 1176 of 1998 which prohibited the export of unofficial Angolan diamonds. In its detailed analysis in a document entitled *Rough Trade* it called for all diamonds being traded to carry a certificate of origin and to be validated by the scrutiny of international experts. Linked to this, it recommended that De Beers, which sells 80 per cent of the world's diamonds, should withdraw sight-holder status (allowing them to deal on sight in legitimate diamonds) from traders dealing in UNITA diamonds. Its statistics impressed the Foreign Office when Charmian Gooch went to meet Richard Clarke, then Head of Policy Planning. Close cooperation developed with regular meetings both inside and outside the Foreign Office on how the strategy should be coordinated in Washington and at the United Nations in New York.

After gathering more information, with details of the amount of buying and the companies involved never before produced in public, Global Witness started lobbying at the United Nations with these disclosures in December 1998 when Gooch and her deputy, Alex Yearsley, gave a briefing to an informal meeting of the UN Security Council. They received encouragement from Sir Jeremy Greenstock, the British Ambassador at the UN, and went on to see other delegations, including the Americans and Canadians. Dianna Melrose, seconded from Oxfam as Richard Clarke's deputy and subsequently his successor, teamed up with the Americans, who were also very concerned at the illicit trade, and worked virtually full time on conflict diamonds for twelve months. The first significant move took her to South Africa with Howard Jeter, US Deputy Assistant Secretary of State, for discussions on the problem with first the South African government, then in Gaborone with leaders from Botswana, Namibia and Angola. This laid the basis for tackling the problem as it spread to Sierra Leone and Congo.

The campaign moved up a gear when Gooch suggested to Dianna Melrose that to get results the major diamond-importing countries, Israel, India and Belgium, had to be confronted and brought face-to-face with the issue. At the Foreign Office Melrose put the proposal to Peter Hain, then Minister of State, who espoused the cause enthusiastically and contacted other governments to get their backing for a meeting in London in June 2000, when even the Russians with a trade estimated at over £1 billion, attended. Recommendations for a global certification and verification system – covering all the technical complexities with an expertise that surprised even the diamond industry – were drawn up by Global Witness in a detailed forty-one-page briefing document partially funded by a £20,000 grant from the Foreign Office. This gave Peter Hain all the material needed to justify demanding resolute action to end the trade, which funded arms purchases for the wars in Africa, when he addressed the International Diamond Manufacturers' Association in Antwerp on 17 July 2000 and insisted that everyone, governments and industry, had 'a moral obligation to act'.

After two years of persistent campaigning Global Witness – supported by the bigger NGOs such as Oxfam and Amnesty – could claim a large share of the credit for an agreement on tough new safeguards endorsed by forty governments, mining executives and members of the diamond industry at Interlaken, Switzerland, on 5 November 2002. Under a programme called the Kimberley Process, taking effect from 1 January 2003, a system was established requiring a certificate of origin for all diamond imports and enforcing a trading ban on anyone exporting or handling diamonds from areas of fighting. Its success, however, was left dependent on the efficacy of the monitoring system put in place to stop evasions such as that reported in the Democratic Republic of Congo, which has no mines yet managed to export an estimated £140 million worth of diamonds to Belgium in 2001.

Such cooperation creates a relationship unimagined in the 1990s when an 'Us' and 'Them' attitude prevailed in most contacts between the Foreign Office and the NGOs. It is welcomed by the smaller NGOs, who have no reservations about working with the government when this increases the prospect of achieving their objectives. NGOs are prepared to put at the disposal of government the sort of information that official diplomatic resources are in no position to obtain without undermining their status in a country. Smaller NGOs see no danger of compromising their integrity and independence by cooperating with the government, especially since they are not concerned to make their case as activists or take part in protest marches. It is not part of their modus operandi to make a public stand against policies espoused by the government. They do their field work, produce the results of their research in pamphlets and brochures, and then present it to the government in the hope of changing policies.

Cooperation by large and small NGOs can sometimes have a greater impact upon government policy than a lone voice of protest, however power-fully armed with evidence. Such was the case in June 2002 when the 'Publish What You Pay Coalition' campaign, fronted by financier George Soros, brought together Global Witness and big NGOs such as Oxfam, Save the Children and Friends of the Earth in a sixty-organization demand for more transparency on the revenues paid to developing countries such as those in West Africa by companies engaged in exploring for oil, gas and minerals. It brought a quick response from Tony Blair. He launched an initiative for full disclosure of payments to national governments and authorities responsible for exploit-ing resources when he addressed the UN Global Compact Round Table on 2 September 2002 at the World Summit for Sustainable Development held in Johannesburg. This alerted the international community to the connection between transparency and poverty in the developing countries and set in train moves to deter corruption by seeking regulations requiring companies extract-ing resources to report payments to governments.

For the big NGO players in the international arena there is, however, a constant dilemma as to how to retain the voice of protest, which inspired their supporters up and down the country to join the movement, when it is in-creasingly important to have access to governments in the policy-formulating stage before decisions are taken at summit meetings. NGOs recognize that their influence can be substantially increased if they are able to be part of a UK delegation at G8 or European Union negotiations, but are anxious not to give the impression to their grass-roots support that the price of participation is a softening of their tone in public. Being present at negotiations can give NGOs an insight into the strategy modifications necessary to win the argu-ment at subsequent meetings. But they are equally aware that contributing to the debate in a delegation risks disclosing some of their own bargaining chips in future rounds.

Cooperation with the British government – and by extension with govern-ments in the developing world – has evoked criticism on occasion among the underprivileged in African countries. By concentrating on humanitarian relief and staying silent about the oppressive regimes in which they operate,

NGOs sometimes face accusations that they help perpetuate oppression and corruption. In an article on NGOs in the journal *International Affairs* in July 2002, two academics, Firoze Manji and Carl O'Coill, asserted: 'Today their work contributes marginally to the relief of poverty, but significantly to undermining the struggle of the African people to emancipate themselves from economic, social and political oppression.' They argued that NGO operations were in some ways part of a system that sacrifices respect for justice and human rights, stating: 'They have taken the "missionary position" – service delivery, running projects that are motivated by charity, pity and doing things for people (implicitly who can't do it for themselves) albeit with the verbiage of participatory approaches.' Their argument implied a choice for NGOs between becoming involved in politics in the developing world or turning a blind eye to the political consequences of their operations: 'NGOs could, and some do, play a role in supporting an emancipatory agenda in Africa, but that would involve them in disengaging from their paternalistic role in development.'

Controverting such criticism, there have been an increasing number of circumstances in recent years when NGOs have been outspoken about the way the government responded to various challenges over human rights abuses or terrorist threats. Eight days after the terrorist attacks in the USA on 11 September 2001, a joint statement urging restraint against the pressures for retaliation was issued by ten major NGOs in London: Christian Aid, Action Aid, Amnesty International, CAFOD, the Catholic Institute of International Relations, Oxfam, the Refugee Council, Saferworld, Save the Children, and the World Development Movement. While expressing shock at the attacks, the NGOs called on the USA and the UK to 'assess carefully the potential impact any proposed military action might have on the poor, the innocent and the voiceless'. When the offensive against the terrorist strongholds in Afghanistan began this plea was followed by an appeal for a bombing pause to enable food to be transported from aid agencies in Pakistan to refugees in Afghanistan. Its rejection – on the grounds that it would allow the terrorists to regroup – provoked some trenchant criticism but the then International Development Secretary Clare Short, usually considered more responsive to humanitarian appeals than her Cabinet colleagues, made equally forceful observations about the priority of ending the inhumane regime imposed by the Taliban and the al-Qaeda terrorists.

Criticism from NGOs continued throughout the anti-terrorist campaign, particularly from Amnesty International, which closely monitored every development in the way the war was waged and prisoners treated. After reports of hundreds of foreign troops fighting with the Taliban being killed after a shoot-out with some prisoners who overpowered their guards and seized weapons at the Qala-i-Jhanghi fort outside Mazar-i-Sharif, Kate Allen, Executive Director of Amnesty, called for an urgent inquiry. Amnesty demanded an investigation 'into what triggered this violent incident, including any shortcomings in the holding and processing of prisoners, and into the proportionality of the response by United Front, US and UK forces'. Despite questions put to US Defense Secretary Donald Rumsfeld and Foreign Secretary Jack Straw about the incident, Amnesty's anxieties about the tough tactics and relentless bombing were not allowed to deter the Americans and their allies from pounding the Taliban forces, nor to moderate the policies drafted in the Pentagon and fully supported in Downing Street.

This drove home the limitations of NGO influence. While there are often occasions when the objectives of government coincide with those of NGOs and make cooperation with them advantageous, there are times when the conscience of the NGOs finds no response in the harsh realities of the world in which the government has to operate. In the last analysis it is the government which is accountable to the people, and the considerations of facing the consequences at the ballot box weigh much more than the headlines achieved by those with fine judgement at the margins of the action, as will be evident from examining the influence of others observing from the sidelines, such as the experts in the think tanks.

NINE

The Influence-seekers

The reach of any think tank or public policy journal is limited by its ability to amplify its message through the mass media. Charles W. Maynes, *Foreign Policy*, Spring 1997

The think tankers' industry is admirable. But in order to be heard above the cacophony of their own, competing voices they are forced to make ever-more overblown, even ludicrous claims. Jonathan Freedland, *Guardian*, 18 April 2001

THINK TANKS used to be called in by the government when 'something had to be done about the Foreign Office'. Bringing it up to date to be more effective in meeting the challenges of a changing world meant summoning the experts, who were supposed to know how to make the Diplomatic Service, which was the envy of other governments, more efficient and even more envied. Three such enterprises were undertaken between 1962 and 1977 – at the instigation first of Prime Minister Harold Macmillan, then of Foreign Secretary Michael Stewart, and lastly of Foreign Secretary James Callaghan – with varying degrees of success depending on the radicalism of the proposals and the strength of the resistance movement organized against them within the Diplomatic Service.

Lord Plowden's inquiry, commissioned by Macmillan, was the first since the Eden reforms of 1943 to assess the sort of Diplomatic Service Britain needed, 'having regard to the changes in the political, social and economic circumstances in this country and overseas'. His report, published in February 1964, with its verdict that Britain should continue to have 'a high degree of world-wide influence' and that 'if our influence is not felt, not only national but international interests and objectives will suffer' was widely acclaimed for creating a unified service and paving the way for the Commonwealth Relations Office to be merged with it. The diplomatic staff were pleased with the provisions for better conditions of service, although there was disappointment that the recommendation for a surplus in staffing levels of 10 per cent above the normal establishment to cover for absences through leave, travel and training was never implemented.

The next think tank investigation, undertaken by Sir Val Duncan on the orders of Michael Stewart, was a radical cost-cutting exercise under the shadow of retrenchment signalled by the withdrawal of British forces from east of Suez. To achieve a projected reduction of 5 to 10 per cent in Foreign Office expenditure, the Duncan Report, issued in July 1969, proposed a substantial retraction of Britain's global diplomatic commitments. It recommended focusing Britain's attention on an Area of Concentration comprising 'about a dozen or so countries in Western Europe plus North America' and leaving the rest of the world, including, amazingly, Japan and South-East Asia, as an Outer Area where 'our need (and ability) to exert political influence will in some (though not all) cases virtually disappear'. For the Diplomatic Service there was the prospect of a division between comprehensive posts, that is missions continuing with a normal complement, and selective posts, those operating like a sub-post-office. Within a year the Labour government was out of office, and when Sir Alec Douglas-Home took over as Foreign Secretary he consigned the report to the archives and turned his attention to what he termed 'the real world': his daily study of the *Racing Post*.

Even more radical changes were proposed when Whitehall's own think tank, the Central Policy Review Staff (CPRS) headed by Sir Kenneth Berrill, Chief Economic Adviser to the Treasury, was unleashed on the Foreign Office by James Callaghan. Its report in 1977 savaged the Diplomatic Service for the extraordinary crime of doing their work to 'an unjustifiably high standard' since they tended to 'err on the side of perfectionism in work whose importance is not always commensurate with the human and material resources'. It recommended a spartan lifestyle for diplomats with the abolition of cocktail parties and large dinner parties; instead drinks at a local bar with officials or a small business lunch at a downtown restaurant were suggested as the best form of hospitality, except in some African capitals 'where lunches at restaurants are not practical'. Its main bombshell was the recommendation that fifty-five posts should be closed, that the Diplomatic Service should be subsumed into the Home Civil Service, and that there should be a small Foreign Service Group staffed from both services. Amid rumblings of revolt after only 14 per cent of 1,400 diplomats polled in a confidential questionnaire stated that they would accept such a merger, the new Foreign Secretary, David Owen, who later observed that 'it was a fatally flawed decision actually to put the CPRS onto the Foreign Office', persuaded Callaghan, by that time Prime Minister, to shelve it.

Thereafter think tanks stayed on the outside looking in at the Foreign Office and, in most cases, keeping at a respectful distance in order to preserve their reputation as independent institutions. The term 'think tank', which originated in the United States during the Second World War when strategic planning took place underground in a tank-like chamber, had come into common currency in 1946 when the Rand Corporation was established with the help of the US government in Santa Monica, California. It came into general usage in Britain when Prime Minister Edward Heath established the CPRS as 'a central capability unit' within the Cabinet Office under Lord Rothschild to coordinate policies across Whitehall and engage in long-term policy projection. The unit survived until Prime Minister Margaret Thatcher abolished it in 1983 and gave her blessing instead to the Centre for Policy Studies. The majority of think tanks that flourished in this era were concerned with national economic policies; in effect they were mainly advocacy organizations promoting ideas from a strong ideological base. With a few exceptions the smaller number of think tanks concerned with foreign, defence and security policy presented themselves as independent institutions.

The origins of think tanks stretch back much farther, to a century before the term was coined. As the oldest institution of its kind, the Royal United Services Institute for Defence Studies (RUSI), founded in 1831 by the Duke of Wellington, has been a pace-setter for all that have followed in the field of international security and defence. Having had the inventor of the machine gun deliver his findings at the RUSI in the nineteenth century, the institute keeps itself at the centre of debate on missile defence in the twenty-first century. Under Director of Studies Dr Jonathan Eyal there are five research teams: Whitehall dialogue, which ranges over defence management, procurement and technology; military sciences; Europe; the Middle East; and Asia. Although independent of government, it has close links with the Ministry of Defence and the Foreign Office which have prompted a glowing commendation from Prime Minister Blair: 'As a facilitator of the exchange of ideas and information and as an educator of policy makers of the present and future the Institute is second to none.'

With a staff of sixteen experts, the RUSI is active in staging conferences with, naturally, a strong emphasis on defence issues for the UK, Nato, the security legacy in eastern Europe of the collapse of communism, and the problems of military procurement. Usually twenty conferences are held in the UK each year, eighteen at its headquarters in Whitehall and two at the Abbey Wood Defence Procurement Centre. Six times a year conferences are held abroad, two of which are convened in the Far East. In October 2002 a major bilateral conference was organized by the RUSI in Singapore, bringing together government ministers, officials, defence analysts and defence industry representatives, and another, smaller one was held in Taiwan. At home there was considerable impact generated by a two-day conference on 'Militant Islam in Asia and its Challenges' organized in November 2002 with the Asia Pacific Foundation and the Centre for the Study of Terrorism and Political Violence at St Andrews University, with a keynote address given by Foreign Office Minister Mike O'Brien.

Next in order of seniority among the think tanks is the Fabian Society, which was founded in 1884 with enthusiastic backing for its socialist ideals from Sidney and Beatrice Webb, George Bernard Shaw and H. G. Wells. Over the years it has had an up-and-down record in making waves in the international arena after its initial cooperation with the trade unions in helping to found the Labour Party and in building support for it with ideas for the party's political and economic strategy. Although after the Second World War the society had powerful figures in the Labour Party, such as Anthony Crosland, who launched the New Fabian Essays in 1952, and despite playing an active part in promoting the decolonization process in Africa, there were periods when it seemed a voice from the past. It became more inward looking, in its own description a 'critical friend' of the Labour Party, more concerned with the direction it was taking on the national political stage and less interested in the international challenges. However, with the advent of the New Labour government in 1997 and some two hundred Fabians as MPs, including a large representation headed by Tony Blair in the Cabinet, it reinvented its international role under the forceful leadership of its General Secretary, Michael Jacobs, at the head of a staff of eight.

One of the most impressive examples of this heightened profile was the convening of a conference entitled 'A New World Order?' at the London School of Economics on 9 February 2002, when four government ministers took part: Peter Hain, Michael Meacher, Paul Boateng and Denis MacShane. The wide-ranging agenda covered 'Afghanistan', with the participation of Tahmeena Faryal from the Revolutionary Association of Women in Afghanistan, 'Russia and the West' with Grigory Yavlinsky, chairman of the Yabloko Party, taking part, 'The State of America' with the US embassy minister Mart Dworken, 'China: the new superpower?' with Xin Shung Kang from the Chinese embassy, as well as other topical issues such as the Middle East, Africa, Islam, globalization and the World Trade Organization. While seeking 'a way forward for progressive thinkers', the Fabian Society insists 'We are neither "on" or "off" message. Some of what we do may be congruent with Government thinking; some not. Good government needs new ideas and public debate.'

For many years the think tank that enjoyed unrivalled prestige in the diplomatic world was the Royal Institute of International Affairs (RIIA), set up with Professor Arnold Toynbee as its Director in 1920 at Chatham House in St James's Square, where Pitt used to live. Its charter defined its objective as 'to advance the sciences of international politics, economics and juris- prudence, and the study, classification and development of the literature of these subjects'. The institute was so zealous in defence of its independence that it insisted from the outset that it was 'precluded by its Charter from ex- pressing opinions of its own'. Nonetheless, suspicions of its closeness to the Foreign Office were strengthened by its mobilization for the war effort in 1939 with a government grant for the establishment of the Foreign Research and Press Service to provide 'raw material in the form of historical background studies and surveys of factors that might come to play a part in the future'. After the war Toynbee's close association with the Foreign Office resulted in the assumption in parts of the Arab world that he had a substantial role in formulating the government's thinking on the Middle East, a perception that was not always advantageous.

Foreign Office links with the Royal Institute of International Affairs are sustained through corporate membership, which enables members of the Diplomatic Service to attend meetings, and through a grant of £50,000 for its research programmes. Three members of the RIIA Council are ex-ambassadors – Sir Leonard Appleyard, formerly in China, Sir John Birch, formerly in Hun- gary, and Richard Tallboys, formerly in Vietnam – and at the top as one of three presidents alongside Lord Robertson and Baroness Williams is the former Foreign Secretary Lord Hurd. It has readily responded to Foreign Office sug- gestions that it host round-table discussions with experts from countries with which the government wishes to improve relations. In some cases manuscripts of certain publications by the institute used to be passed to the Foreign Office for checking by department officials.

By the 1980s financial problems exacerbated by the increased competition over securing funding for programmes were making it difficult for Chatham House to sustain its reputation. Some of the hard choices looming for the in- stitute were kept at bay during the nine-year chairmanship of Lord Tugendhat, owing partly to his persuasive skills in the City and partly to his high stand- ing in European Union circles, dating from his days at the Commission. In September 1992 he stamped the authority of Chatham House on the European policy-making process with a prestigious conference at the Queen Elizabeth II Conference Centre to mark the UK presidency on the theme 'Europe and the World after 1992'. Over four hundred delegates from sixty-five countries took part in the event, which was convened in association with the Foreign

Office and the European Commission and sponsored by leading companies. An even larger conference was organized by Lord Tugendhat in March 1995 in association with the government on the theme 'Britain and the World', which, with speeches by the Prince of Wales, Prime Minister John Major, Dr Henry Kissinger, Foreign Secretary Douglas Hurd, Chief of the Defence Staff Field Marshal Sir Peter Inge, and CBI Director General Howard Davies, once more put Chatham House in the forefront of opinion formers.

Thereafter, beset with trenchant cuts, which among other consequences reduced its renowned library from a staff of thirteen to five and abolished its unique international press cuttings department, run by Deputy Librarian Mary Bone with fine judgement in terms of preserving what could become significant for researchers, Chatham House was left struggling to reassert itself in a leading role as an authoritative institute providing original thinking in international affairs. In recent years its central direction has been diffuse at a time when other mainstream think tanks have focused on the urgent complex challenges – in political, economic and defence terms – facing Britain. While others developed strong leadership for research teams with expertise on the real world in western Europe and security issues in eastern Europe, Chatham House gave the impression in Whitehall of being somewhat semi-detached with the dilettante interest of academe. Forced by financial restraints to let its links with the United States dwindle, Chatham House has sometimes been marginalized at critical periods in international affairs, unable to compete effectively with other organizations with strong connections in Washington.

The pace-maker among the British think tanks with such connections is the International Institute for Strategic Services (IISS), which came into being in 1958 with the help of the Rand Corporation as a genuinely international organization, not one predominantly focused on Britain's role in the world. With membership in over a hundred countries and offices in Washington and Singapore as well as a splendidly refurbished headquarters at Arundel House offering a 210-seat conference salon with high-tech facilities overlooking the Thames on Victoria Embankment, the IISS boasts having relations with the US State Department and the Pentagon that are as close as those it enjoys with the Foreign Office and the Ministry of Defence. Its twenty-four-member Council under chairman François Heisbourg, the distinguished French authority on defence, is truly international, being drawn from fourteen countries, including four members from the UK and three from the USA. The research staff come from eighteen countries. The strength of the American connection is emphasized by the fact that the IISS receives $1 million a year in funding from US foundations.

Quick thinking by the IISS Director, Dr John Chipman, in scrapping the programme for its annual conference in 2001, held the day after the 11 September terrorist attacks, put the institute in prime position, heading think tank analysis of the events that shook the world. Changing the agenda overnight to 'The Strategic Implications of Terror in the Information Age', Dr Chipman and his assistant director, Steven Simon, an authority on the al-Qaeda network from his days as Director of Global Issues in President Clinton's National Security Council, organized the first in-depth debate – in plenaries and working groups – with experts assessing the necessary objectives of a broad-based international counter-terrorism campaign. Policy proposals were fed into the analyses undertaken at both the Foreign Office and the State Department. A month later the IISS staged a conference in conjunction with the Aspen Institute Italia at Arundel House on the global repercussions to the world economy, with Nato Secretary-General Lord Robertson giving the open-ing address to delegates from Europe and the United States.

Its supremacy in the think tank league was strikingly demonstrated on 9 September 2002 when, ahead of everyone else, including the British and American governments as well as other think tanks, it published the first up-to-date, comprehensive assessment of the Iraq crisis in terms of the threat from President Saddam Hussein's nuclear, biological and nuclear arsenal. The glossily produced dossier did not atempt to make a case either way as to whether Saddam Hussein's arsenal was a *casus belli*, nor did it produce a 'killer fact'. But in documenting the potential threat – although subsequently shown to be much less credible by some experts at the Hutton Inquiry – it secured vast media coverage and put director John Chipman on every TV channel. With immaculate timing, exactly a year after the 9/11 terrorist attack in America, the IISS proved how influential a think tank could be.

In an innovative role alongside the tradition of seeking to influence the appraisals made in the course of working out policies, the IISS also developed a para-diplomatic function as a facilitator for meetings that would be difficult for governments to organize. Although defence ministers attend the annual Verkunder Meetings in Europe, there was no similar conference for Asian defence ministers until the IISS stepped in to convene the ground-breaking conference opened in Singapore in May 2002 by its leading statesman, Lee Kuan Yew. It was seen as a form of institution-building disguised as a confer-ence so that ministers from certain countries normally sensitive about being seen together could become accustomed to round-table discussions without problems of protocol as to who should be the host.

Another example of facilitating diplomatic get-togethers is the series of discreet meetings of Indian and Pakistani senior ministry and military officials convened by the IISS in Dubai, one of which took place in January 2002 regardless of the tensions at the time over Kashmir. An IISS conference on the theme 'Prospects for Closer Cooperation in North-East Asia', held in Macao, was an attempt to promote a dialogue about China's relations with the Koreans which received the blessing of – and a financial contribution from – the Foreign Office. It brought together South Korean officials, Western diplomats based in Seoul and Pyongyang, and policy specialists from China, Japan, Britain and the USA. But although humanitarian agencies working in North Korea participated, the North Korean government stayed aloof, deciding not to send any official representatives.

Get-togethers of a different order put the Ditchley Foundation in a class by itself. Instead of operating as a research institute, the foundation, which was established in 1958, organizes high-level exchanges of ideas at weekend conferences for forty decision-makers at Ditchley Park, an eighteenth-century residence in Chipping Norton in Oxfordshire. Although emphatic about its independence from the Foreign Office, insisting that 'no government or agency sets its agenda and funding for its house and operations comes entirely from private sources', the foundation has John Major as chairman of the council, its Director is Sir Nigel Broomfield, former British Ambassador to Germany, and senior mandarins play a leading role at conferences. Originally the themes mainly reflected its founders' aim of promoting close Anglo-American relations, but since the end of the Cold War the agenda has broadened to cover European political and security questions as well as international economic and social issues. After each conference Sir Nigel Broomfield circulates the Director's notes, which are widely studied for their insight into the thinking of the influential delegates.

While most of the fifteen conferences a year are held at Ditchley Park, some are convened in the USA and Canada, since there are American and Canadian Ditchley Foundations. In June 2001 a conference was organized in Normandy at the Château de Canisy in partnership with the Institut Français des Relations Internationales on the theme of Transatlantic Relations, and in May 2002 Lord Tugendhat chaired a Ditchley conference in Budapest in conjunction with the Bertelsmann Foundation on the subject of European Union enlargement. When in October 2000 Ditchley focused on European common foreign security and defence as aspiration and reality, the conference was chaired by former mandarin Sir Michael Alexander with three eminent mandarins from Downing Street – Robert Cooper, William Ehrman and Emyr Jones Parry – and the top UK military representative at NATO, Lieutenant General Sir Michael

Willcocks, taking part. For the conference on the United Nations and its future, Ditchley turned to Britain's former UN Ambassador, Sir Crispin Tickell, as its chairman, and had the current Ambassador, Sir Jeremy Greenstock, as well as the UN Under-Secretary for Political Affairs, Sir Kieren Prendergast, flown over from New York for it. While there is always substantial representation at conferences from the USA, among other delegates from all over Europe, including on occasion Russia, the strong Whitehall and Westminster influence cannot be disguised.

One recent addition to the think tank fraternity seemed designed to have a bigger impact upon the Foreign Office than the others: the Foreign Policy Centre established by Robin Cook as its president and launched in 1998 by Tony Blair as its patron. It set itself the objective of working out 'an inclusive and effective foreign policy' with a new methodology of 'joined-up thinking to create joined-up solutions'. The centre focused its research on six themes: new rules for foreign policy (how to test global policies and 'what should an ethical foreign policy look like?'); a risk and security programme (tackling the new face of terrorism); the new global economy (promoting corporate social responsibility); reforming international cooperation (the role of NGOs); the future of diplomacy (the role of embassies, public diplomacy); and identity (the global nature of Britishness).

As its Director, aiming to provide 'signposts for diplomacy in the information age' through innovative ideas, Mark Leonard claimed that his reports on European reform and public legitimacy influenced EU governments and the European Commission. Inside the Foreign Office, however, his tradition-breaking methodology and his search for 'effective responses to the "new intermestic issues"' (those which cut across the boundaries of nations, regions or departments of state) received a less than rapturous welcome, not surprisingly since they were based on the conviction that foreign policy is too important to be left in the hands of diplomats. Mark Leonard's enthusiasm for rebranding Britain as 'Cool Britannia' struck the Whitehall policy-makers as a cheap gimmick destined for early oblivion. His propositions in 'Going Public' for revitalizing British diplomacy by having the Foreign Office 'unleash the energy of 60 budding ambassadors in Britain's schools, businesses, local authorities, political parties and communities to build deeper links across the world' did not result in working parties being set up to deploy these new envoys. Suggestions that there should be an elected president of the Commonwealth and that its headquarters should be moved to Cape Town or New Delhi were not put on the top of the agenda of the British delegation to the Commonwealth Heads of Government Meeting.

Unabashed, Leonard refused to moderate the scope of his controversial proposals, with the assertion: 'If the Government ends up accepting everything I put forward I will be failing in my job.' The focus of the institution swivels so much that some experiments tax the patience of even its most enthusiastic supporters, such as the idea launched in April 2002 of trying to influence foreign policy discussion by means of fiction with two former advertising executives, Adam Lury and Simon Gibson, writing a novel 'exploring complicated foreign policy issues through storytelling rather than traditional analysis'. While it is genuine in seeking to put ideas across to new audiences, in targeting its message mainly to people through the press, TV and the Internet the centre creates the suspicion that it attaches as much priority to securing big headlines as to provoking a serious discussion among the policy-makers at the Foreign Office. As a consequence it is treated with a great deal of reserve.

This suspicion is generated across the board in varying degrees by all think tanks because of the well-based assumption among directors of institutes that a steady flow of funding depends on frequent reference to a think tank's reports in the media. Large institutes keep a count of every mention and pin articles up on their noticeboards so that visitors get the impression of an organization that carries authority worldwide. One of the boasts at the International Institute of Strategic Studies is that in a good week they could have up to four hundred mentions in newspapers ranging from the *South China Morning Post* to the *Guardian*, the *Los Angeles Times*, and *The Hindu*. Not to be outdone, the Royal Institute of International Affairs boasted that a comment by one of its specialists was picked up by over fifty newspapers and other publications around the world. Since the advent of the Labour government in 1997, with its increased emphasis on securing maximum media coverage for its policies – the day before they are launched, at their launch, and what they mean the day after they are launched – think tanks are also driven to pitch their output so as to command attention in the newspaper summaries circulated in government departments.

Headlines do not matter so much, however, to the small specialized think tanks, where their recognized expertise in a particular field is more likely to carry weight with a department in the Foreign Office. One such institution is the Commonwealth Policy Studies Unit (CPSU), set up in 1999 by Richard Bourne, a widely respected authority on the Commonwealth throughout its fifty-four member states. Housed at the Institute of Commonwealth Studies, a London University research institute, the CPSU has focused on the problems of globalization and information technology, particularly for small countries, issues of democratization and human rights. Its input into policy-making was recognized by a research project funded by the Foreign Office for the

Commonwealth High Level Review, chaired by South Africa's President Thabo Mbeki with cogent recommendations for longer-term election monitoring and a follow-up mechanism.

In preparation for the summit of Commonwealth leaders – scheduled to take place in Brisbane in October 2001 but postponed until March 2002 because of the terrorist attacks in America – the CPSU produced an analysis of the critical issues to be faced by member states in the coming decade. It assembled hard-hitting advice for Britain and its Commonwealth partners on many problems, such as upgrading the quality of governance, greater accountability, helping small states without the human and financial resources to get a fair deal in trade negotiations with the developed world, and effective safeguards for human rights. This distillation into forty-seven pages of the essential requirements for the Commonwealth to stay relevant in the twenty-first century was exactly the sort of manual ministers found useful in focusing the attention of their delegations on the challenges that had to be answered.

One of the most prestigious think tanks, which rarely appears in the headlines but receives assignments from four Whitehall ministries, is the International Policy Institute (IPI) at King's College London. It grew out of the Centre for Defence Studies established by Professor Michael Clarke on 1 August 1990 – the day before Saddam Hussein invaded Kuwait – in order to fulfil contracts with the Ministry of Defence for authoritative analyses of risk assessment and security issues. After directing the centre for ten years, he passed the baton to Paul Cornish and set up the International Policy Institute as an expanded research operation. With a full-time academic staff of forty compared to the centre's fifteen researchers, the IPI has the capacity to supply in-depth assessments at very short notice. It is often called on to provide quick analyses for the Ministry of Defence, the Foreign Office, the Department for International Development, and other government departments. Unlike many academic research organizations, which take months to produce a comprehensive analysis of a situation, the institute can meet a deadline of seven days or less to deliver a detailed report running to twenty or thirty pages.

Following the terrorist attacks of 11 September, the institute became heavily involved in various Whitehall projects on counter-terrorism. Normally, most of its government work comes from the Ministry of Defence, with which it has a standing arrangement to undertake research projects under an enabling agreement. Its next important customer is the Department for International Development under a four-year contract to deal with issues of security, conflict prevention and development. There is a separate programme with the Department of Trade and Industry. Although the Foreign Office is not known as a big spender on research, it keeps in close touch with the institute, and Professor Clarke suggests areas in which it would be appropriate for a research study to be undertaken, resulting in two or three special projects each year. Like other think tanks the institute often acts as a facilitator in arranging speakers for the Foreign Office and setting up conferences such as the Russia–Europe Forum. Most of the work commissioned from the centre taps into its expertise on arms control.

Where the Foreign Office finds it most useful to avail itself of the resources of a think tank is in tracking down evidence of breaches of conventions controlling the export of small arms. When it would be politically embarrassing to disclose material from government intelligence, the Foreign Office calls on the Centre for War Studies to undertake research to produce evidence of arms being illicitly transferred from an eastern European source. Once the evidence of a breach is produced by the centre's researchers and then disclosed in a report that goes into the public domain, the Foreign Office can quote this to substantiate its challenge to the defaulting government.

Publications by think tanks are a significant factor in bringing the resources of independent research to bear upon the government as it responds to developments and reassesses foreign policy. In a class of its own in this category is *The Military Balance*, published every October by the International Institute for Strategic Studies. It is scanned line by line not only in the Foreign Office and the Ministry of Defence but in government departments and defence industry organizations across the world. There is no other assessment of the armed forces of 168 countries and the economics of their defence structure which enjoys such respect as a military reference work. It lists the strengths of the army, navy and air forces of every country as well as armed non-state forces, and details the equipment and weaponry at their disposal. The IISS also publishes a quarterly journal called *Survival,* which carries analyses of strategic issues and is closely read in government departments.

The think tank publication with the longest pedigree is the *RUSI Journal*, first published by the Royal United Services Institute in 1857, which continues to be highly regarded as an authoritative bi-monthly publication on defence and international security matters. The institute also publishes a monthly current affairs journal called *RUSI Newsbrief*, but the pace-maker in this field is Chatham House's *The World Today*, which has been revitalized in recent years by Graham Walker, a journalist with an intuitive sense of news analysis, and given a radical new look by an innovative designer, Martin Colyer. The Royal Institute of International Affairs also publishes a quarterly journal of some 232 pages called *International Affairs*, which has an excellent reputation outside as well as inside the United Kingdom. It is well ahead of others, except when some of its academic contributors give the impression in diplomatic circles that they are more concerned with quoting from the works of their colleagues in academe than in presenting a case from their own observations.

Usage of think tank expertise varies in Whitehall depending on the nature of the challenge facing the government. If there is a military factor in a crisis, the Ministry of Defence is usually much faster and much more subtle than the Foreign Office in its operations. By swiftly calling in experts from think tanks who they know can play a pivotal role in explaining to the public – the electorate – the complexities of a situation, the Ministry of Defence often sets the agenda of any critical debate on government policy. Defence experts from the RUSI, the IISS and the International Policy Institute who are liable to be invited as 'talking heads' on television programmes are given confidential briefings in advance by high-ranking officers or a senior executive such as Oona Muirhead, the Director of Information Strategy, on how the MoD justifies decisions on, for example, bombing targets in Afghanistan or maintaining the no-fly zones in Iraqi airspace.

The MoD is shrewd enough not to try to pressurize its outside experts into taking a 'helpful' line on the government's policy on television; it is content to ensure that have an accurate understanding of the factors that are taken into account by the government in deciding on its policy. There is no attempt to muzzle criticism, but by extending a certain degree of confidence to the experts, beyond what is entrusted to the press, they encourage the 'talking heads' to be more measured and balanced in their assessments than they might otherwise be. This sort of sophisticated operation is not undertaken by the Foreign Office, except on rare occasions when the Foreign Secretary gives a restricted briefing to correspondents – and even then there is a reluctance to disclose any highly confidential material as evidence of the need for a particular course of action being taken by the government. If the Foreign Office had followed the MoD example in taking think tank experts into their confidence about some of the problems that arose in the initial stages of restoring President Kabbah to power in Sierra Leone, the Foreign Secretary would probably have avoided some of the backlash over his arms-to-Africa policy in the House of Commons.

Senior members of think tanks were surprised that the Foreign Office made no attempt at damage limitation over the quandary of the government concerning America's treatment of captured Taliban fighters transported to the US base at Guantanamo in Cuba in November 2001. It was recognized that the government found it awkward to be open about their misgivings over prisoners being initially denied any rights under the Geneva Convention on the grounds that they were being classified as 'illegal combatants'. However, to avoid the political embarrassment of publicly undermining his unqualified military commitment to standing shoulder to shoulder in the coalition with the Americans against the al-Qaeda terrorists in Afghanistan, the Foreign Secretary could have turned to think tank experts to provide a mollifying answer to critics on television and radio. But the Foreign Office allowed itself to be seen shuffling uncertainly from one awkwardly inchoate position to another, instead of explaining in confidence to 'talking heads' that strong reservations about the American policy were being conveyed privately to the US State Department and the Pentagon, and by so doing ensuring that a more balanced picture was being put across to the public in the UK.

One of the factors lessening the potential influence of think tanks is the reluctance of the Foreign Office to involve outsiders at the crucial decision-taking stage. Mandarins shelter behind the myth of the total supremacy of Parliament which inhibits them from discussing any details of a new policy until it is ready to be announced by the government in the House of Commons. Think tanks welcome the opportunity to feed in ideas when ambassadors are called back for regional discussions, as they are much more frequently nowadays, to review policies and assess the prospects for change. But even when brainstorming sessions with outside experts are held it is rare for conclusions to be reached, no matter how compelling the arguments made by think tank experts. If a session is chaired by a senior mandarin at director general level he will usually wind it up with nothing more conclusive than an assurance that the think tank advice will be conveyed to the Foreign Secretary.

Even when a ministerial decision is taken the Foreign Office is hesitant about seeking advice from think tanks on the pitfalls that may have to be guarded against in implementing a particular policy. The knowledge of think tank experts gleaned from their analyses of comparable situations could be harnessed to enable the Foreign Office to avoid the various hazards that a new policy may encounter. It is strange that this does not happen since the Foreign Office does tap into this knowledge at times when a newly designated ambassador is preparing to take up an appointment. Some ambassadors are advised to spend time with think tank experts who can warn him or her of the sort of criticism likely to be faced on launching a new policy on arrival at a post. This influence can be important in widening the perspective beyond the limitations of the Foreign Office briefings.

One significant weakness is long overdue for eradication: a reluctance on the part of the Foreign Office to take advantage of the expertise of think tanks in assessing lessons to be learned from previous crises. This misguided attitude was demonstrated in the way the planning of the Iraq invasion failed to make adequate provision after the fall of the Saddam Hussein regime in April 2003 for tackling the problems of civil disorder quickly and ensuring the safety of charitable organizations required to move into towns deprived of water and medical supplies. Had they been consulted, defence experts in think tanks could have alerted Whitehall planners to the dangers of such scenes of chaos as were shown on television screens day after day from Baghdad and Basra after the coalition forces had crushed organized resistance. One Cabinet minister, International Development Secretary Clare Short, admitted as much when she told foreign journalists in London on 15 April 2003: 'The rapid collapse of the regime was not prepared for. We should have done better.'

Apart from think tanks, the other main agencies seeking to influence foreign policy are associations of like-minded people who engage in lobbying for a specific cause. They fall mainly into two groups: those who operate from inside Parliament as all-party groups focused either on one particular country or on one special subject; and those who operate from outside Parliament with either prominent public figures or MPs among their advocates. In both categories the main objective is to act as an advocacy body or pressure group directed at influencing government attitudes or policies. Their activities vary according to the way in which events focus on a particular subject or the extent to which a country is commanding public attention. In most cases they seek to bring public concern to the attention of the Foreign Office through meetings, delegations to ministers, MPs making representations on behalf of constituents, and backbenchers impressing the front bench with the need to respond to grass-roots anxieties about the damage liable to be caused to party unity by a particular course of action.

All-party groups in Parliament are subject to a number of conditions and must undertake to comply with certain rules. The registration of all-party groups under terms agreed by a resolution of the House of Commons on 17 December 1985 requires them to have at least ten members from the government party and ten from other parties, including six from the main opposition party. They are required to disclose financial benefits from outside sources and 'where a public relations agency provides the assistance, the ultimate client should be named'. Although all-party groups are overwhelmingly composed of backbench MPs, there is no bar on Cabinet members – Tony Blair is chairman and Jack Straw a vice-chairman of the American all-party parliamentary group. Members of the House of Lords are also entitled to join the groups – like anyone else for an annual subscription that 'must not exceed £5' – as is the Speaker and even non-parliamentarians. Parliamentary guidance states that 'Groups flourish and wane according to the interests and enthusiasm of members' – an observation indicative of the extent to which they carry weight in the formulation of foreign policy and the variation in the strength of the representations with which they seek to exert influence.

Since most of the seventy-seven country groups have been constituted under the aegis of the Inter-Parliamentary Union or the Commonwealth Parliamentary Association, there is a strong emphasis on sustaining and developing links between parliamentarians. They do not bluntly proclaim their objective to be that of pressurizing the Foreign Office to support country X against claims by country Y at the United Nations and take its side in any dispute with its neighbours. The official statement of their purposes in the register is usually very bland. The terms set out by the Belarus group are typical: 'To promote friendship and understanding between our countries.' Some, however, acknowledge a political objective, as in the case of the Estonia group, which includes among its aims 'to assist in the process of bringing Estonia into Western institutions'.

The Afghanistan group, formed in 2001, is more explicit than most about its purpose: 'To discuss the future of Afghanistan and provide a forum where all aspects of the rebuilding of Afghanistan can be discussed in a constructive and non-confrontational manner.' The Kashmir group has a sharper edge than many in stating: 'The group monitors human rights abuses in Kashmir and presses Her Majesty's Government to take an active part in the resolution of the conflict.' The most outspoken about its objectives in influencing Foreign Office policy is the Tibet group, which puts its purpose quite unequivocally: 'To put pressure on Her Majesty's Government to encourage negotiations between the Chinese Government and the Dalai Lama and the Tibetan Government in exile, whilst recognising that Tibet is an occupied country which had independent links with Britain.'

One group overflowing with influential people at Westminster is the American group. Besides Jack Straw it has seven former foreign secretaries among its vice-presidents: Lords Callaghan, Carrington, Howe, Hurd, Owen, Pym and John Major. The group lists as one of its activities making arrangements for the exchange of visits between members of the US Congress and MPs. The importance of a warm welcome at Westminster for overseas visitors is stressed by the Malta group, which includes in its aims the commitment 'to ensure visitors to the UK from the Maltese Parliament are properly received'. Wider interchanges are promoted by others, such as the Central Asia group which aims 'to welcome MPs and others from the Parliaments of Tazikistan, Uzbekistan, Kazakhstan, and Turkmenistan'. One of the most active among the promoters of visits is the Israel group, which emphasizes its role in facilitating 'exchanges of views between British and Israeli figures'. The Israeli embassy boasts that at least one out of every three British MPs has visited Israel – at the expense of the Israeli government – and had meetings in the Knesset.

Only twelve of the 150 all-party subject groups are focused on issues concerning foreign policy, and some of these, such as the World Government Group, are marginal to the day-by-day business of the Foreign Office. Traditionally they are expected to keep in close touch with the whips' offices, who are wary of the contacts between subject groups and outside pressure groups, which could result in embarrassing challenges at meetings of the Parliamentary Labour Party or the Conservatives' 1922 Committee. By far the most effective in forcing the Foreign Office to take notice of its pressure on issues is the Human Rights group, chaired by Ann Clwyd, former Labour Party spokesperson on foreign affairs. The feisty Welsh MP, who never lets any embarrassment for the Labour Party inhibit her from making a stand on a matter of principle, clashed with Clare Short over a shortage of relief planes for helping the southern Sudanese and in March 2000 called for Russia to be arraigned before the European Court of Human Rights for its actions in the Chechen war. She was one of the first to demand that fighters from the Taliban forces flown from Afghanistan to America's detention centre in Cuba, Camp X-ray, should be treated as prisoners of war under the Geneva Convention. Ann Clwyd was also ahead of most other NGO representatives in getting in to see the devastation left in the Palestinian refugee camp at Jenin by the Israeli tank incursions into the occupied territories in April 2002, and alerting Westminster to human rights violations.

Outside Parliament there are a large number of associations and organizations seeking support for countries or causes. No lobby in Britain has achieved anything like the influence that the America–Israel Public Affairs Committee (AIPAC) exercises on US foreign policy in the Middle East, as was demonstrated when Congress passed the Jerusalem Embassy Act of 1995 providing for the relocation of the US embassy from Tel Aviv. Nonetheless, the Board of Deputies of British Jews under its Director General, Neville Nagler, a former senior Treasury civil servant, has an impressive record in securing support for Israel. During the premiership of Margaret Thatcher the Board of Deputies had easy access to Downing Street. Its international division makes representations to the Foreign Office regularly, monitors European Union legislation, and ensures that there is a quick response to reports in the press that are regarded as hostile.

Countering the Jewish lobby, the Arabs have no shortage of supporters, many of whom have close contacts with the Middle East experts in the Foreign Office. One of the most active is the Council for the Advancement of Arab–British Understanding (CAABU), which vigorously champions the cause of the Arabs and especially the rights of the Palestinians to self-determination. It was quick off the mark in March 2002 in securing a meeting with Alan Goulty soon after his appointment as UK Special Representative for the Sudan. It also has monthly meetings addressed by senior political figures such as the shadow Foreign Secretary and the Liberal Democrat foreign affairs spokesman. The Middle East Association has established good relations with the Foreign Office and on one occasion provided a useful platform from which Lord Carrington could send back a placatory message to the Saudi Arabian government after the furore over the *Death of a Princess* television documentary in April 1980 had caused a rift in relations.

Some of the long-established associations have sustained positions of trust with successive governments over the years. The European-Atlantic Group has won respect in Whitehall ever since its founding in 1954 as a forum for discussing how to achieve good transatlantic economic, political and defence cooperation. Access to the Foreign Office is eased through the contacts of the eight ex-ambassadors among the vice-presidents serving under its president, the former Foreign Office minister Lord Judd. It holds monthly meetings in committee rooms in the House of Commons and dinners at St Ermin's Hotel in London addressed by authorities on strategy, such as the NATO Secretary-General, the Chief of the Defence Staff and the Supreme Allied Commander Europe. From modest beginnings in 1934 the Greek Cypriot Brotherhood, under the chairmanship of Haris Sophoclides, a well-connected multi-millionaire businessman, has built a widespread reputation in Whitehall and Westminster in promoting the cause of reuniting Cyprus after the division of 1974. It runs seminars on issues such as human rights, and when it holds dinners addressed by the Cypriot Foreign Minister it is seen that the Greek Cypriot Brotherhood can attract a large audience of MPs from all parties.

In assessing the influence of think tanks and advocacy associations it is difficult to quantify with any exactitude their impact upon any particular policy. Whatever the contribution, either through ideas during a brainstorming session at the Foreign Office or by presenting research papers, outside experts often have to put forward recommendations without knowing the precise parameters within which the Foreign Secretary has to operate in a particular situation. Shielding behind the protocol of having to wait for Cabinet approval of policy – which, if there is time for it, is usually a mere formality

– the Foreign Office may choose not to disclose the options being considered to anyone offering advice from outside. At best, advocacy associations can only be influential in helping to create a favourable attitude of mind to their interests in certain situations, and in making the Foreign Office experts have a much clearer understanding than previously of the case they wish the government to espouse.

The expertise of think tanks can sometimes be most effective in an evolving situation which throws up various alternatives in terms of implementing a policy decision. The ability to visualize how a problem may be aggravated by pursuing a particular course of action and the capacity to offer workable alternative strategies are liable to be taken seriously when they come from think tank experts who have a proven record of accurate analysis. For those confronted with providing a Plan B for a Foreign Secretary who finds that the original policy is not working out well, it can be a godsend to have someone from outside presenting a fresh insight. The route through which a new line of thought can be conveyed to the decision-makers is sometimes via an interview on television or an article in a newspaper – an avenue that leads to the next source of potential influence on foreign policy: the power of the media.

TEN

The Power of the Fourth Estate

The information revolution promises to change the routine of our planet as decisively as did the industrial revolution ... challenging estab-lished institutions and values, and redefining the agenda of political discourse.
George Shultz, US Secretary of State, 1989

Foreign policy cannot be conducted in an atmosphere of moral outrage or under constant public scrutiny. It requires realism and confidentiality.
Sir Percy Cradock, *In Pursuit of British Interests*, 1997

AS foreign envoys are escorted into the Ambassadors' Waiting Room on the first floor of the Foreign Office, alongside a large sombre painting of St Cecilia by the Austrian artist Edouard Veith, in readiness to be summoned next door to the Foreign Secretary, their attention is drawn to a table with three news-papers for them to peruse: *The Times*, the *Daily Telegraph* and the *Guardian*. These are not, however, the choice of the Foreign Secretary for his own reading. While he has a daily digest of the press prepared for him, Jack Straw prefers to seek his own enlightenment from three other journals: the *International Herald Tribune*, *Le Monde* and the *Financial Times*. This choice, which includes only one of the eleven British national daily newspapers, may not be intended to indicate a lack of esteem for the others, which account for 96 per cent of the total national daily circulation in the UK. However, it could be taken as a signal to the barons of Fleet Street that the impact of the fourth estate upon the decision-makers in the corridors of power in Downing Street is not quite as influential as they imagine when they boast of the power of the press.

Any suggestion that the press could exercise a significant influence over the policy of the government was dismissed by Walter Bagehot in his biographical study of Robert Peel in 1856 with the rhetorical question: 'Out of the million articles that everybody has read, can any one person trace a single marked idea to a single article?' Much has changed, however, in the last century and a half. Since the terrorist attacks in the USA on 11 September 2001, the interest of the media and the public in international affairs has vastly increased. BBC Radio 4's audience figures have risen sharply. Many more viewers watch television news. The most impressive statistics are those published by the Audit Bureau of Circulations Ltd, which showed that on 12 September 2001 the *Daily Mail* had the highest weekday sale in its history, adding 681,000 copies that day to put its circulation up to over 3,000,000. On the same day the *Sun* added 500,000 extra copies, the *Daily Mirror* 372,000 and *The Times* 275,000.

Despite a steady decline year by year in newspaper circulation, people in the UK read more newspapers per head of population than in any other country in the world, and whatever the views in the Foreign Office about their contents the events of recent years show that what appears in the media cannot be ignored. Sales figures issued by the Audit Bureau of Circulations in November 2003 showed that a total of 12,340,382 national newspapers were sold every day. With each copy being read on average by at least two people, this means that the press is in a position to influence 50 per cent of the population. The same scale of penetration into British households was achieved at the same period on Sundays, with a total circulation of 12,892,359 newspapers. In Whitehall the main focus is on the broadsheets, led by the *Daily Telegraph* with a daily average at that time of 914,169 copies, followed by *The Times* at 631,109, the *Financial Times* at 438,296, the *Guardian* at 392,479, and the *Independent* at 235,491. Their total of 2,611,544 copies a day has a much greater potential impact on the British government than the two main American broadsheets – the *New York Times* with 1,113,000 copies a day and the *Washington Post* with 812,519 copies a day – are likely to have on the US government.

Ministers at Westminster, however, are well aware that the 'heavies' account for only 26 per cent of the national daily sales, and that on many occasions it is the impact of the tabloids reflecting the views of the ordinary voter which creates the climate leading to a call for a change in policy. The three that carry the greatest clout are the *Daily Mail* with a circulation of 2,473,965 in November 2003, the *Sun* with 3,458,269 and the *Daily Mirror* with 1,943,382. If Downing Street's recognition of that factor were ever doubted, Alastair Campbell, the Prime Minister's former Director of Communications and Strategy, put the confirmation on the record when he told the *Guardian* on 17 February 1997: 'The papers that really matter are the tabloids. I think one of the reasons that Tony wanted me to work for him and why I wanted to work for Tony was that we both acknowledge the significance to the political debate of the tabloids.'

Each sector of the media – television, radio and the press – has its own unmatched capacity to make an impact in a specific way. For television it is the ability to bring dramatic live pictures of an event into homes and offices in real time from thousands of miles away. An awareness of the actuality of disasters – natural such as floods and famine or man-made such as the terrorist attack on the twin towers of the Trade Center in New York – is communicated with a forcefulness that no words alone can convey. For radio – and pre-eminently on the *Today* programme on BBC Radio 4 – it is the presenters' persistent inquisition of government ministers in order to unravel the facts from the spin doctors' gloss. For the press it is the investigative skills of specialists in conducting clandestine enquiries with non-quotable sources which make newspapers the prime source of disclosure of circumstances that government ministers, when questioned on the record on television or radio, would not reveal. Occasionally there is an overlap, such as when television and radio follow up exclusive reports in newspapers or when investigative reporters succeed in disclosing secret documents on television before a minister is ready to make them public. But each sector's expertise in establishing its predominant role can build up a formidable pressure on the government in terms of its conduct of policy.

The ability to make the public aware of disasters and thereby influence the response of the Foreign Office and other government departments to them was dramatically demonstrated by the television pictures of a newborn baby, Rositha Pedro, being rescued with her mother from a treetop in flooded Mozambique by a courageous winchman on a South African helicopter in February 2000. Floods from the Limpopo and Save rivers had inundated the country for weeks, but it was the heart-warming television coverage of the rescue which galvanized the world into giving top priority to helping the stricken people. When the urgency of getting relief to the victims was graphically portrayed on television screens the government faced public criticism over why TV crews could get helicopters over the area so much more quickly than it could. Grateful as President Joaquim Chissano was for the international assistance, he admitted: 'It took time.' One disaster management expert observed that if ten skiers had been buried in an avalanche in Switzerland they would not have waited days for helicopters to come to their rescue.

It was the media which exposed the failings of joined-up government in Whitehall over the relief operations and obliged ministers to ensure better co-ordination. They highlighted the delay resulting from a disagreement between the Ministry of Defence and the Department for International Development over the cost of helicopters and the time it would take for the Royal Navy vessel *Fort George* with its Sea King helicopters to get to Mozambique from the Gulf. Initially Clare Short, the International Development Secretary, turned down the offer of four helicopters plus their support facilities because she considered the MoD price of £2.2 million was too high. But after the row spread outside the ministries the price was halved. Even then it took seven days for the *Fort George* to arrive in Mozambique.

On-the-spot reporting on television and in newspapers on the aftermath of the fall of the Saddam Hussein regime in April 2003 aroused widespread public concern at the failure to prepare for the consequences in terms of restoring public order and basic supplies of water. Day after day pictures of the suffering of ordinary Iraqis in Baghdad and Basra put pressure on the British and American governments, who had made no preparations for ensuring the safety of aid workers in supplying humanitarian relief, to take effective action. It was only after the media highlighted the plight of twelve-year-old Ali Ismail Abbas, who lost both arms and was badly burned in an American missile strike, that he was evacuated by air to a hospital in Kuwait City. Even then, Dr Mowafak Gorea, the Baghdad hospital director, made the point: ' You have seen one Ali. But there are a thousand more like him.'

The importance of television's role in making people in the UK aware of events that might easily go unreported was demonstrated in August 1992 by ITN's intrepid correspondent Penny Marshall in exposing the brutality of the Bosnian Serbs against the 7,000 Muslims held in prison camps at Trnopolje, Omarska and Keraterm. The television pictures of emaciated prisoners who had been beaten, tortured and starved that she and her colleague Ian Williams sent back to Britain provoked a sense of outrage that strengthened the resolve of the Foreign Office to bring the camp guards to justice, no matter how long it took. One Muslim survivor, Fikret Alic, paid heartfelt tribute to the bravery of Penny Marshall and her camera crew: 'Until she arrived no one knew around the world what had happened and that we were all prisoners.' Subsequent attempts by the magazine *Living Marxism* to denigrate the ITN achievement by alleging that the film was edited to create the image of barbed wire were denounced in the High Court and led to awards of £150,000 each to Penny Marshall and Ian Williams in libel damages. Their disclosures helped to ensure that the United Nations War Crimes tribunal in The Hague sentenced five Serbs to between five and twenty-five years' imprisonment in November 2001.

It was only after television cameras brought home to people in the West the horror of a mortar attack on a Sarajevo market on 5 February 1994, when sixty-eight people were killed and 167 injured, that Britain and its NATO allies were prodded into international action. The NATO powers declared an exclusion zone for heavy weapons in the Sarajevo area and a more vigorous role was undertaken by the United Nations forces in ensuring high-profile military protection for convoys of food aid. Without the public pressure generated by the media there would not have been the effective enforcement of the no-fly zone over Bosnia which resulted in four Serb aircraft being gunned down by NATO fighter planes on 28 February.

When diplomats are unable to move around freely in areas where an auto-cratic government takes steps to seal them off from prying eyes it is often a courageous reporter who makes the Foreign Office aware of what is happen-ing. Sue Lloyd-Roberts is such a person, taking risks in a hostile environment not just once or twice but several times to find out what the authorities have been hiding. After her fifth visit to Tibet in October 1998 she reported back to the BBC on the Chinese crack-down under the code name 'Strike Hard' which resulted in the arrest of 800 monks and nuns in the Lhasa area. Her reporting in May 2000 from Moldova's orphanages, where she found the children in as much danger from their carers as from their afflictions, was an eye-opener which sent shock waves round Whitehall. A similar tour by her in Romania provided alarming material for Downing Street to consider in assessing its dealings with the government there by revealing that thousands of children had been taken from parents classified as unsuitable because of drug abuse or alcoholism and that there was no difficulty in buying babies in Bucharest.

After the Mugabe government banned the BBC from Zimbabwe one of its correspondents, John Sweeney, entered the country under cover as a bird-watching tourist in February 2002 and compiled a shocking documen-tary of the extent of the violence used against opponents of the regime. His courageous investigations, during which he sometimes hid in the boot of a car to evade police checks on his way to a meeting with opposition leader Morgan Tsvangirai, led to television pictures that revealed brutalities previously sus-pected but never actually confirmed. A clandestine visit to mass graves and eyewitness accounts of how politicians who criticized Mugabe were burned to death in a car provided evidence that supported Prime Minister Blair's call at the Commonwealth summit in Australia in March for Zimbabwe to be suspended from the organization.

BBC correspondents succeed in highlighting complex international issues through taking their camera crews to the heart of the trouble, where Foreign Office diplomats cannot afford to be seen. In exposing intimidation against people campaigning for independence in East Timor, Matt Frei, as the BBC's Asia correspondent, narrowly escaped being hacked by a machete in Septem-ber 1999 when reporting the attacks by the Aitarak militia on protesters in the streets of Dili. His coverage in East Timor, and of the political upheavals in Indonesia after the end of President Suharto's corrupt thirty-year dictatorship, had a powerful impact back at the Foreign Office and on MPs at Westminster. In India the BBC's Mike Wooldridge was often able to convey more graphically than his newspaper colleagues how the tensions over Kashmir affected the stability of the region by contrasting the clashes at the Line of Control with the military build-up by the Pakistani and Indian governments. On-the-spot analysis of such a volatile situation drove home to the government in London the need to take action to prevent repercussions on relations between the two rival communities in Britain.

Nonetheless, the capacity of television to make the government and the public aware of situations in a way that no other branch of the media can do as effectively has its limitations. The selection of what television covers remains highly subjective and often a matter of convenience or accessibility. Viewers wondered why there was so much more time and effort devoted to the Mozambique floods where hundreds died compared to Hurricane Mitch in October 1998, when 17,000 were left dead or missing in Honduras, or the floods in Orissa in October 1999, when thousands died and over one million people were left homeless. For long spells the savage war in Angola and the ugly trade in illicit diamonds to buy weapons rarely featured in television news programmes. The same neglect kept television viewers largely unaware of the plight of the southern Sudanese in their long struggle against the Muslim north, the fight of the Polisario people of the Western Sahara against Morocco for self-determination, or the guerrilla war waged by the Revolutionary Armed Forces of Colombia (FARC).

One explanation for what gives one crisis priority over another is the human interest factor: Mozambique's ordeal gripped people in the West once the rescue of a newborn baby was shown on the television screens. As a basically visual medium, where long, wordy explanations are considered liable to tax the concentration of the average viewer, television makes its impact through dramatic pictures of a swollen river flooding the countryside, even if viewers may not be able to point to the Limpopo on a map. If high-profile aid agency operations funded by donors in the UK are taking place in an area, there is an added incentive for television coverage since it is likely to provide human interest stories, which have the added advantage of boosting the public res-ponse to appeals for contributions. Oxfam's spokeswoman admitted after the floods: 'The world would not have responded as it did had the media not given the prominence it did.' The cost and difficulty of reaching crisis situations are also determining factors. Operating, for example, out of Juba in southern Sudan is far more difficult and expensive than flying over the Limpopo when there are excellent television transmission facilities available only one hour's flight away in Maputo.

Television coverage of conflict is more hazardous in the Congo or Angola than in the occupied territories in Israel – although getting the balance right between the Israeli and Palestinian sides presents additional problems because the Israelis control access to areas where military operations are undertaken, sealing off what they do not want the outside world to see in places such as the Jenin refugee camp in April 2002, and have a much more sophisticated official news management organization than the Arabs. Fluent English-speaking Israeli spokesmen such as Gideon Meir at the Foreign Ministry are always on hand to project Israel as the victim of 'Arab terrorism', shifting the emphasis away from Israel's contravention of UN Security Council Resolution 242, which requires withdrawal from the occupied territories and focusing instead on Israel's need to defend itself against suicide bombers.

The constant demand for changing scenes on television is also a limiting factor on its potential to influence the conduct of foreign policy. After the initial impact of a disaster or a crisis on television screens, interest in the ongoing distress of the victims inevitably diminishes – depressingly quickly for the aid agency staff staying on the ground to offer succour in the camps. All too often it is shrugged off by the cynical explanation of 'compassion fatigue'. While the government and NGOs have to carry on with their commitments to help in all the follow-through operations of resettlement and the provision of welfare and education facilities, news editors believe there is a limit to the viewers' interest in any crisis and require camera crews to change location to focus on the next human interest event.

It is very unusual for television crews to return to the scene of the crisis six or twelve months later to find out what happened to all the outside help and if necessary to prod the government or the aid agencies into more effective effort. This lack of continuity in covering situations is used by governments to justify their reluctance to rush into major changes of policy as a result of public anger aroused by forty-eight hours of television coverage, and enables them to take a stand against the 'something must be done' protesters on the grounds that it is important to consider the long-term implications of any intervention instead of being pressurized by instant judgemental impressions conveyed by television reports.

Media impact by means of the radio, where what matters is the force of per-suasion by words, is not so often affected by continuing shifts of focus, since there is a greater determination to maintain a consistent interest in certain themes, in particular the question of Britain being 'at the heart of Europe'. The ability of the kingpins of the BBC's *Today* programme, John Humphrys and James Naughtie, to sustain their interrogation of ministers on the nuances of European policy in terms of politics, economics and defence has established a reputation – somewhat exaggerated at times – for them in Westminster of setting the agenda for the day. Their command of detail in probing for answers as journalists well grounded in covering conferences gives them a performance rating well above that of opposition MPs questioning ministers in the Commons. There used to be a rule prohibiting discussion on radio or television of any issue scheduled to be discussed in Parliament within fourteen days, but that restriction ended during the turmoil in the Commons during the Suez crisis in 1956.

Ministers are eager to come into the *Today* programme studio – with the exception of the Prime Minister, unless it is in the run-up to elections – as it gives them a platform from which to project their ideas direct to the voting public. In realpolitik terms they, not the editor of the *Today* programme, make the agenda for the day if they are about to deliver a major speech or make a policy announcement later in the day. It enables ministers to put across their main points in advance, then have coverage of the actual statement, and further interviews the next day on the reaction to it. Although John Humphrys and James Naughtie are skilled at picking holes in ministers' arguments and experienced at questioning to find what lies behind the spin, ministers are usually adept at preparing their responses to show themselves in the most favourable light regardless of the sharpness of the questions thrust at them. Where the *Today* programme presenters can score is in switching from the main theme of the day's ministerial speech or official announcement to focus on a new issue disclosed in the morning's newspapers and then trying to extract from the minister an impromptu statement of policy relative to the new development. This strategy can sometimes demonstrate the power of the media to produce a fresh reappraisal of an aspect of government policy – but it is a rare achievement.

Where radio can exert an influence over the climate of opinion being formed on certain issues is through analysis programmes such as *From Our Own Correspondent*, fondly known throughout the BBC as FOOC, which has been on air every week since it was launched on 25 September 1955. Broadcast on Radio 4 and the World Service, the programme has been carefully crafted by editor Mike Popham selecting aspects of situations deserving more in-depth assessment than is possible in the hustle of preparing items for the general newsreel. Correspondents who used to be warned off editorializing are encouraged to analyse the motivating social and political factors in the societies of the countries where they work, and also shed light on the way Britain and its policies are viewed by other nations. These carefully considered observations from experienced correspondents such as Brian Barron, Paul Reynolds, Stephen Sackur and Humphrey Hawksley have often added a new dimension to a minister's considerations as he has pondered the submissions from various posts in the Diplomatic Service. It is odd, however, that sources of serious analytical talent are frequently left untapped elsewhere in the BBC. When air time is given to colourful eyewitness accounts and film coverage of violent action taking place in Africa or the Middle East, the ability of renowned analytical diplomatic correspondents such as Bridget Kendall, Brian Hanrahan and James Robbins to put the situation in perspective has been all too frequently underemployed until a major crisis such as the war in Iraq has erupted.

One source of BBC information of inestimable value to the formulation of policy at the Foreign Office is never mentioned in the programme schedules published in the *Radio Times*: the SWB – Summaries of World Broadcasts provided by the BBC Monitoring Service. The system began at the outbreak of the Second World War at the suggestion of the Ministry of Information, which funded it as part of the intelligence operations to assess the thinking of the Nazi leadership from German broadcasts. By the end of the war the BBC was covering broadcasts in thirty languages every day. Now located at Caversham Park near Reading, the service provides translations of all significant material broadcast in eight different geographic global newsline sectors: Africa, Asia Pacific, Central Asia, Europe, the former Soviet Union, Latin America and the Caribbean, the Middle East, and South Asia.

Its daily output – which until spring 2001 was published in hard copy but is now available to subscribers via the BBC website – is avidly read at the Foreign Office by the Research Analysts Department experts, who assess every nuance in the transcribed speeches and reports on political and economic developments broadcast from radio stations all over the world. It is not focused entirely on items on the regional agenda; the monitoring also covers attitudes to the policies of Britain and other Western countries. The priority interests of the Foreign Office, the Cabinet Office and the Ministry of Defence are regularly notified to Caversham Park as tasking programmes, but the expertise of the linguistic experts is of such a high order that they are largely left to make their own judgement of what is significant enough to transcribe. Closely linked to their work is a special supervisory department assessing the ever increasing number of broadcasting stations, particularly in eastern Europe. The Foreign Media Unit is responsible for checking the reliability rating of the media being quoted on the newly emerging radio stations to make sure that the service is not disseminating reports from inaccurate sources.

The monitors' operations are not conducted as if they are merely engaged in academic research to provide background material. They have a highly acute sense of news values in detecting shifts in policy. Monitors are experts in their specialized field, keeping themselves up to date with the jockeying for political influence, social changes and economic developments in the country under their surveillance. While they do not sacrifice accuracy for speed, they can compete with the news agencies, as they proved when the Russian department at Caversham Park was the first to report the communist hardliners' bid to oust President Mikhail Gorbachev in the coup of 19 August 1991. At that time there was confusion about the outcome, which was compounded for several hours by television pictures that seemed to indicate that the conspirators had been successful – enough to convince some Western statesmen to pay tribute to Gorbachev in the past tense. But Gorbachev's reliance on the BBC World Service and its reports of the resistance by the reformists under Boris Yeltsin stiffened his resistance to his captors' demands. It was Visnews transmitting a defiant broadcast by Boris Yeltsin which helped to turn the tide against the plotters.

The reputation of the BBC Monitoring Service – and its importance to the Foreign Office – stems from its total reliability. The Foreign Office depends upon it, trusting its accuracy in the face of any contradiction from other usually reliable sources. Never was its accuracy more crucial than on 15 February 1991 when newspapers and television bulletins blazoned the announcement from Saddam Hussein's Revolutionary Command Council, broadcast on Baghdad Radio, purporting to accept United Nations Security Council Resolution 600 of 2 August requiring complete withdrawal of Iraq's troops from Kuwait. Exultation, however, was short lived. A few hours later an authoritative BBC Monitoring Service translation from Arabic enabled the Foreign Office to reject the Saddam Hussein ploy as it contained a number of conditions for any Iraqi withdrawal which were unacceptable. The episode made the Foreign Office much more cautious about reports in the media, and even more careful to scrutinize the facts behind any story under big headlines in a newspaper before offering any official reaction to it.

Foreign Office funding for the monitoring operations was substantially increased in October 2002 as a result of the crises over Afghanistan, Iraq and the war on terrorism. An extra £1.7 million a year was allocated in a three-year funding agreement, with £1.2 million targeted on improved monitoring of Islamic broadcasts as well as other sources in the Afghanistan region. Armed with a grant of £5 million a year assigned for the development of new services up to 2005/6, the BBC was able to develop its online portal as the single entry point for all the products of its monitoring operations from 3,000 sources in 100 languages and 150 countries round the clock. Andrew Hills, the operations director, hailed it as 'a real vote of confidence in the value of our work'.

Where the opportunity to have an impact on policy is often neglected is in probing for facts behind international scandals. While BBC News reported the domestic political flurries over events leading to the departures from office of Peter Mandelson and Keith Vaz, it trailed cautiously behind the newspapers eagerly investigating the involvement of the Prime Minister and the Foreign Office in the purchase of a Romanian steel plant by Lakshmi Mittal, an Indian billionaire who made a donation of £125,000 to Labour's election fund. It was the enterprising correspondent of *The Times*, Richard Owen, who secured a statement in Bucharest on 18 February 2002 from the Privatization Ministry about a letter drafted by the Foreign Office and signed by Tony Blair following meetings between Ambassador Richard Ralph and Mr Mittal over his £300 million bid. This prompted Boris Johnson, forthright editor of *The Spectator* and Conservative MP for Henley, to berate the BBC: 'when a fantastic story lands in their lap, like the Mittal affair, they seem incapable of bringing a new fact into the human domain. When you watch or listen to BBC accounts of the scandal, everything is related as if it were some distant row conducted in the newspapers.'

These strictures were validated by the fact that the biggest scoop following the invasion of Iraq came not from television or radio but from a newspaper. Although the BBC had the largest team of British correspondents in Baghdad once the city had been taken by the coalition forces, it was David Blair of the *Daily Telegraph* whose enterprise enabled him to find what eluded other journalists: a box of seemingly incriminating documents at the Iraqi Foreign Ministry. His rummaging in the archives, revealing papers that pointed to vast payments from Saddam Hussein's intelligence services to Labour MP George Galloway through a Jordanian intermediary, resulted in a series of exclusives for the newspaper beginning on 22 April 2003 which left all others in the media trying to catch up.

This determination to be constantly on the lookout for what is going on behind closed doors makes newspapers effective as watchdogs and gives them the unique capability of bringing influence to bear on the conduct of foreign policy. It was the persistent digging of the press into the ramifications of John Major's government involvement in soft loans for the construction of the Pergau dam hydroelectric project in Malaysia in return for a large contract for British arms which led to pressure for a complete review of Britain's aid policy. A report based on secret memos from Wimpey in the *Sunday Times* alleging widespread bribery resulted in British firms being banned from bidding for Malaysian government contracts for over six months. A High Court decision in November 1994 branded British aid funding for the dam as 'an abuse of the aid programme'. A row with Saudi Arabia, disclosed in the *Daily Mail*, which caused the withdrawal of British Ambassador Sir James Craig and put exports worth £1 billion a year in jeopardy because of the TV documentary *Death of a Princess* in April 1980, resulted in much more awareness in the Foreign Office of the harm a television programme can have on diplomatic relations and the need for moves on damage limitation in advance.

After the Scott Inquiry in 1996 into arms exports to Iraq, which was assiduously attended by Robin Cook as shadow Foreign Secretary, it was assumed that the Labour government would be wary of being found by the press to be less than ethical about its arms policy. But it was caught out as a result of pressure mounted in various newspapers, led by the *Guardian*, which disclosed that Hawk jets had been used by the Indonesians for internal repression in East Timor. Despite a bland statement by Baroness Symons as Defence Procurement Minister that the Indonesians should be allowed to attend an arms trade fair in the UK in September 1999 to look at 'self-defence' equipment, the press campaign reached such a level of condemnation that the Foreign Office 'advised' the Ministry of Defence to ensure that the Indonesians did not turn up. To avoid further embarrassment for Robin Cook, it was quietly arranged that the Indonesian defence chiefs should let it be known that they had decided not to attend.

Newspapers are prepared to devote much more time and resources than television or radio to investigating controversial or illegal activities and bringing pressure for action against them to be taken internationally. The exposure of the trade in illicit diamonds funding wars in Africa from Angola to the Congo and Sierra Leone was an example of how the press can build up strong pressure for government intervention against corruption. Following up the painstaking investigation by the enterprising NGO Global Witness, newspapers led by *The Times*, *Financial Times* and the *Guardian* revealed the sinister ramifications of the conflict diamond business. The spotlight of the press showed that Oryx, a company with diamond operations in the Congo registered in the Cayman Islands, had a profit-sharing arrangement with Osleg, a Zimbabwean government company that had as a director General Vitalis Zvinavashe, the chief of staff for the 10,000 Zimbabwean troops in the Congo.

These disclosures in June 2000 enabled the Foreign Office to make it clear to the London Stock Exchange how damaging it would be to have the City appear to be giving approval to any dealings in 'conflict diamonds'. This made impossible any listing of Oryx on the Alternative Investment Market through its reverse takeover of Petra Diamonds. Further disclosures in *The Times* that a Ghanaian diplomat, Dr Moses K. Z. Anafu, who just happened to be in Zimbabwe organizing the Commonwealth observer team for the elections, was one of the nominated directors of Oryx led to his recall and resignation as Assistant Director of International Affairs at the Commonwealth Secretariat.

The intensity of media pressure has been vastly increased by the acceleration of communications and the ability of journalists to send words and pictures from virtually anywhere in the world without all the facilities of an international press centre. In a remarkably short time, the days of journalists with a portable typewriter and a notebook taking their copy to a cable office for transmission at the Empire rate of one penny a word gave way to their sending reports by telex and waiting for call-backs so that they could clarify garbled sections, then the use of special telephone lines to dictate articles to copy-takers who required foreign names to be spelled out slowly, and finally to today's do-it-yourself operations by correspondents on their own with the high-tech facilities of laptop computers, Marisat and satellite telephones and portable satellite ground stations.

For the government this communications revolution through what is termed 'smart' news technology means less 'thinking time' for responding to the developments in a rapidly changing international crisis. With journalists able to send instant reports free from controls imposed by ministries or military commands, their information reaches viewers, listeners and readers and begins to mould public opinion often before the Foreign Office has received its own account from embassies or operations headquarters. The hustle to catch up at the Foreign Office in London can heighten the pressure on decision-makers to reach conclusions without protracted committee meetings. Although the Foreign Office insists that it always takes a measured view of the immediate and longer-term consequences involved in any situation, and will not be thrown off course by calls for instant responses, the constant flow of outside information from the media can make it difficult to stand firm against the tide of opinion calling for action to be taken immediately. As Foreign Secretary Douglas Hurd admitted: 'Ministers of the major Powers now work in a constant snowstorm of information. They are required to take within hours, often more or less in public, decisions which their predecessors were able to mull over for weeks in private.'

One of the most poignant illustrations of the media accelerating government response to a crisis occurred on 7 April 1991 when Prime Minister John Major read graphic reports in the Sunday newspapers at Chequers of the plight of 30,000 Kurds fleeing from what Massoud Barzani, leader of the Democratic Party of Kurdistan, called the genocide campaign of President Saddam Hussein's troops. The television pictures of women and children huddling on the muddy slopes of the hills of northern Iraq without food or shelter so moved the Prime Minister that he telephoned his private secretary, Stephen Wall, at home in Wimbledon to insist that a way must be found to bring urgent help to them. An emergency meeting was convened with Sir John Weston, the Political Director, and Stephen Wall in the Prime Minister's flat on the top floor of Downing Street on 8 April, the morning they were due to fly to Luxembourg for a European Community Council meeting.

As they wrestled with the problem it was agreed that some sort of secure area had to be created for the Kurds. Sir John Weston suggested 'safe en-claves', protected places where the Kurdish refugees could be shielded from marauding Iraqi troops and have food and medicines made regularly avail-able. The phrase was amended to 'safe havens' on the advice of Sir David Hannay, Ambassador to the UN, because of the risk of it being interpreted as creating a separate mandated territory, and by the time they went into the European Council meeting they had a proposition sufficiently well planned to win the support of their European partners. John Major deliberately did not reveal his hand in advance to the Americans so that he could take the safe havens proposals to them with the momentum of the full support of the Europeans.

With media pressure mounting hour by hour, it was impossible for the US administration to ignore the distress of the Kurds, which was portrayed on television screens and reported graphically in newspapers. Royal Navy Marine commandos were patrolling in northern Iraq within days, and des-pite his initial reluctance President Bush bowed to the public demand for humanitarian aid and agreed to the deployment of ground troops. Once the differences over the wording of a resolution at the United Nations Security Council had been overcome the screen round the Kurds was complete, with about seventy British, American and French jet fighters patrolling the skies to keep Iraqi intruders away from the safe havens.

Relations between media and government face their most severe test in time of war. For perfectly valid reasons the basic priority for any government is to ensure that media activity does not create added danger for the forces engaged in battle or seriously undermine the confidence of the public in the ability of the forces to achieve their objective. At the same time the media's role is to convey the reality of what is happening and not lose their objectivity or credibility by being uncritical recipients of government officials' hand-outs with sanitized accounts of operations. The government expects the media to put loyalty to their country first while the media rate their first priority as get-ting at the truth regardless of who is right – always provided that in doing so the disclosures do not risk the lives of the forces. This clash of interests often results in resentment in the Foreign Office at journalists pursuing a course of action that complicates the official conduct of public relations.

There was no disguising the anguish in Downing Street at the BBC's World Affairs Editor John Simpson courageously staying in Belgrade during the allied bombing of Yugoslavia. Reporting the damage in the areas where some of the civilian victims were killed, he insisted that he was accurately interpreting what the situation was like from his vantage point and not making political commentaries. To avoid accusations of any distortion, the BBC was careful to preface the presentation of his dispatches with the warning that he was operating under the rules laid down by the Yugoslavs. Similarly, there was no mistaking the anger in Washington at the way Peter Arnett continued bravely reporting the situation in Baghdad as he saw it for Cable News Network (CNN) during the Gulf War. Nonetheless, the perceptive reporting by John Simpson and Peter Arnett of what was happening on the spot, and the local reaction to it, provided Downing Street with an extra dimension in their assessments of the way their conduct of policy was being judged elsewhere.

In this symbiotic relationship where each side recognizes the need for coexistence and, within certain limits, cooperation, the impact of the media is circumscribed by the fact that the allied governments control the extent of access to military information and the timing of its release. Although almost 1,500 journalists were sent to Saudi Arabia to cover the Gulf War, official access to front-line areas was limited to 198 journalists who had media pool accreditations. Those not accredited to combat units had to make do with rewriting the pool reports and fleshing out the official accounts of actions given at the daily briefings with their background knowledge. Some enterprising journalists circumvented the ground rules laid down by the military briefers. Two experienced British correspondents, Alistair Stewart and Sandy Gall of Independent Television News (ITN), and Bob McKeown of Columbia Broadcasting System (CBS) did not wait to be escorted into liberated Kuwait. Regardless of the risks, they made their own way into Kuwait and reported in vivid terms from the liberated city, not only before the official announcement of its liberation but before the American and British troops arrived.

In paying tribute to the bravery of the Independent Television News war correspondent Terry Lloyd, who was killed under fire near Basra on day three of the Iraq war in March 2003, Stewart Purvis, ITN chief executive, explained that the decision to operate with correspondents not tied to Ministry of Defence commands was the result of the restrictions experienced in the Gulf War in 1991. 'People who were embedded were not able to file any meaningful reports,' he insisted. 'The fact is that in Gulf War 1 the majority of detailed and accurate reports was done from people on their own.' While the protection of military escorts usually guarantees safety, the view of many veterans from Fleet Street is that there is a price to pay in that at times you can be limited to reporting only what is officially approved.

With the advance in media technology eyewitness accounts on television and radio and in newspapers conveyed the impression that the public had a ringside seat in the Iraq war. As there were 500 journalists accredited and 'embedded' with the American and British forces there was round-the-clock coverage, reports often being filed under extremely perilous conditions. Closeness to the action at times made it difficult for correspondents to distance themselves sufficiently to be objective, especially alongside servicemen who were protecting them and on occasion helping them put on anti-chemical warfare gear. Editorializing becomes hazardous in the confusion of battle when there is a tendency on the military side to count on patriotism in situations where there is no absolute certainty. In response to criticism of the BBC at the end of the first week of the Iraq war, Richard Sambrook, Head of News, acknowledged that it was difficult at times for reporters to distinguish true reports from false ones.

Courageous and graphic on-the-spot reporting from Baghdad by experienced correspondents such as Lindsey Hilsum of Channel 4 News, David Chater of Sky News, John Irvine of ITN, and Rageh Omaar of the BBC had a widespread impact, not just on public opinion but on the way the government's media experts had to advise ministers. This was never more clearly demonstrated than when the marketplace in the Shaab district of Baghdad was devastated in a missile strike which killed seventeen civilians and injured a further thirty on 26 March. Apart from arousing anger at a time when public support for the cause was politically important, it created fresh doubts over the Anglo-American commitment to conducting their operations with maximum effort to avoid 'collateral damage'. Moreover, the vivid and extensive media coverage undermined Anglo-American attempts to assuage strong feelings in the Arab world over the enormous might of the allied bombing with the argument that it was being directed not against the Iraqi people but at their rulers.

On the other side, television pictures of captured American and British service personnel being humiliated had an equally dramatic impact on public opinion in the West. On the very night that the Qatar-based Arab TV company al-Jazeera was hailed for its 'fearless and independent reporting' in being awarded the Best Circumvention of Censorship prize by the Index of Censorship in London, there was a furore over its screening live pictures of the bodies of two British soldiers being scorned by jubilant Iraqi crowds. At

Central Command in Qatar, Air Marshal Brian Burridge was scathing in his condemnation of the TV station for what he termed blatant violation of the Geneva Convention.

It compounded the outrage provoked forty-eight hours earlier when al-Jazeera showed five captured American personnel bewildered at being questioned in front of Iraqi television cameras. These incidents presented a challenge for media executives in assessing their responsibilities in times of conflict. Some stations refused to show live pictures degrading combatants in the vulnerable position of prisoners. Others had second thoughts after an initial screening and reverted to still pictures. Al-Jazeera defended its action on the grounds that it was showing the reality of war and was not beholden either to the Iraqis or to the Americans and British – an argument given more credence subsequently when the Iraqi regime banned two of its correspondents and later an American tank fired on the al-Jazeera office in Baghdad, killing a correspondent. Its stand was supported by some who pointed out that the Americans had shown scant concern for the rights of prisoners when captives from Afghanistan were shown being marched blindfolded and chained on a path to Guantanamo's Camp X-ray in Cuba in 2002. Rights and wrongs apart, these events generated more controversy about the role of the media and its effect upon the conduct of government.

Editors were often faced with contrasting accounts which were not easy to verify, especially when the coalition forces' spokesmen were eager to avoid negative headlines about advances being bogged down or civilians being bombed. While reporters with front-line units described what they saw as fierce fighting, the military spin doctors outside the country at Central Command in Qatar played it down as skirmishes. Clarity was scarce at times on the American side, as when a US official spokesman stated that American troops were 'involved in multiple incidents with multiple casualties that we are trying to sort out'. Irked by 'unhelpful' television reporting, Defence Secretary Geoff Hoon retorted in an article in *The Times* on 28 March that 'instant pictures can mislead'. He insisted that disconnected snapshots failed to convey 'the big picture', and instead of providing an accurate account sometimes had the opposite effect. His conclusion had ominous implications for press freedom: 'Free media access does not always equate to a balanced picture reaching the viewer or reader.'

Government irritation with the media reached a peak when ministers were dismayed to find that exhilaration at the fall of Baghdad was quickly overtaken by widespread public concern over reports of looting and civil disorder which appeared beyond the control of the coalition forces. Graphic reporting from Baghdad by journalists such as Robert Fisk, the authoritative Middle East correspondent of the *Independent*, and well-documented accounts of the chaos in Mosul by Catherine Philip in *The Times* on 12 April under the headline 'This is not liberation, this is destruction' had an impact that worried Downing Street. After what was described in Fleet Street as 'private sniping' against the reporting from Iraq, Tony Blair's aides went on the record to criticize the experienced BBC Defence Correspondent Andrew Gilligan for the way he described the lawlessness on the streets of Baghdad despite the presence of coalition forces in the city. After complaints were rebutted by the BBC stating that Andrew Gilligan had witnessed events at first hand and that similar reports had been sent from Iraq by other news organizations, proof of the media having an impact was demonstrated by the decision to allocate more military personnel to the problem of ending civil disorder and restoring the authority of police.

During the bombing campaign in the Gulf War in 1991 US Defense Department officials chose material for release to the media which they considered best illustrated the effectiveness of the raids. The clips made impressive viewing on television screens around the world as explosions were recorded apparently in the centre of the target frame. Not until months after the war was it disclosed that only 7 per cent were spot on and that 75 per cent of the 'free-fall' bombs failed to hit their target. The allied bombing of the al-Ameriya bunker in Baghdad on 13 February 1991 was described at official government briefings as a successful operation against a strategic command centre. This was dutifully reported by the media, which had no independent means of checking the statement, and was justified by Prime Minister John Major as an attack on 'a legitimate military target playing a part in the Iraqi war effort'. Subsequently it was shown that the victims were 300 civilians killed in a bomb shelter.

A week later, on 20 February, it was disclosed that an American A-10 tank-buster warplane had fired on two British armoured carriers, killing British soldiers. Amid the chagrin it was officially stated that such a tragedy from 'friendly fire' was an extremely rare event. Again this was reported by the media as a statement of fact, since there was no way of verifying it. Yet six months later, on 13 August, the Pentagon revealed that thirty-five of the 148 Americans who died and seventy-two of the 467 wounded in the Gulf War were the victims of 'friendly fire'. This belatedly disclosed statistic was three times more than previously admitted and ten times higher than had been recorded in any previous war. It was not the media who got the facts wrong, but their credibility suffered from the disclosure that they were 'taken in' – however innocently – by the official version given out at the time.

No one nowadays denies that television pictures of a tragic event have the power to focus the attention of decision-makers on a particular situation. As Foreign Secretary Douglas Hurd acknowledged in January 1993: 'Like it or not, television images are what forces foreign policy makers to give one of the current 25 crises in the world greater priority.' It was impossible to ignore the impact of television's live tracking of the first flight of Scud missiles directed at Israel on 17 January 1991 and the alarm at some speculative comment that they might be carrying chemical weapons. Yet there is a tendency to overrate the influence of television on how foreign policy decisions are taken. As James 'Scotty' Reston of the *New York Times* observed: 'Our power is smaller than our reputation.' While he was Foreign Secretary, Douglas Hurd repeatedly faced demands from the media that 'something must be done', but he was always wary of allowing policy to be determined by what he called 'the white-hot flame of indignation'.

One of the myths that keeps being quoted as evidence of the importance of the so-called CNN factor is the assertion that the horrendous television pictures of the massive carnage of Iraqi troops dive-bombed in their convoys on the Jahra–Basra road at Mitla Ridge forced the allies to end the Gulf War instead of going on to Baghdad. The television film was taken on 26 February 1991. President Bush announced the cessation of hostilities against Iraq on 27 February with a statement on television: 'Kuwait is liberated. Iraq's army is defeated. Our military objectives are met.' However, the television footage of the devastation on the Mitla Ridge was not screened in the USA or Britain until 1 March.

President Bush took the decision to end the war after discussions with General Colin Powell, Chairman of the Joint Chiefs of Staff, but without any consultations with the British – although Foreign Secretary Douglas Hurd was in Washington, he played no part in the decision-making process, being informed just before the announcement that the decision had been taken. Even if President Bush was aware of the television film – and if not he would certainly have received reports about the devastation – the public had not seen it at that stage and were still expecting the troops to head right into Baghdad. In consequence, the CNN factor had no influence. President Bush was not under public pressure to suspend military action.

There were two cogent arguments that influenced the US administration in their decision not to continue the offensive against the Iraqis right to their capital. The authorization for launching military action on 16 January 1991 against the forces of Saddam Hussein was UN Security Council Resolution 678 of 29 November 1990, which mandated the use of 'all necessary means' to

ensure Iraq's complete withdrawal from Kuwait. There was no UN mandate to
proceed to Baghdad and take action to overthrow the regime of Saddam Hussein. Apart from doubts over the international legality of any operation against
Baghdad there were a number of practical concerns. Foremost among these
was the fear of heavy casualties and being drawn into a political quagmire
by having to hold Baghdad until agreement was reached on a government to
take over from the current regime, and the danger of losing a large measure
of support in the Arab world over such intervention.

Every military campaign produces a different pattern of pressures on the
government. Thus the war in Afghanistan begun with the launch of Operation
Enduring Freedom on 7 October 2001 against the Taliban and the al-Qaeda
network of terrorists generated much less visual pressure through television
than the Gulf War. After the Tomahawk missiles had been fired from US ships
there was not much for the cameras to convey except the flashes of bombs
exploding under the murky black skies and guns firing into the scrubland surrounding Kabul. It was the reporting of various incidents that aroused public
anxiety over human rights violations which brought influence to bear on the
American and British governments. Reports of refugees being left starving
because relief trucks could not reach them led to appeals from NGOs for a
halt in the bombing to enable food and medicines to be delivered to them,
but Downing Street stood firm against any concessions.

More pressure was mounted on the government following media reports in
November of large-scale casualties following a shoot-out after a revolt by 300
foreign Taliban prisoners who grabbed weapons at Qala-i-Jhangi, a nineteenth-
century fort turned into a prison camp 10 miles from Mazar-i-Sharif. Evidence
that some of the Taliban prisoners had died with their hands tied behind their
backs provoked demands, led by Amnesty International, for an independent
inquiry. As before, the government did not yield. Where they met much more
sustained concern, however, was over the treatment of prisoners transported
to Guantanamo's X-ray camp in Cuba. Television pictures of men, their beards
shaved off, being led shackled and blindfolded from planes into metal cages
in the open air resulted in severe criticism of the government in British newspapers and aroused anger among human rights campaigners. Newspapers
highlighted the embarrassment of Tony Blair at being forced to accept that
the Americans were making all the rules concerning the prisoners.

Editorials highly critical of the American decision to describe the captives
as 'illegal combatants' instead of prisoners of war, and the refusal to allow
five Britons in the camp access to a lawyer, forced Prime Minister Blair off
the fence. Initially, No. 10 Downing Street stated: 'The Prime Minister accepts

that the prisoners are highly dangerous; they are inevitably being treated in a rigorous way to ensure there is no repeat of Mazar-i-Sharif.' But after taking the line that the prisoners should be treated according to 'international norms', he bowed to the pressure and acknowledged that they were entitled to humane treatment in accordance with the Geneva Convention, regardless of how they were described.

As there was no let-up in the criticism the White House was obliged to concede that the captives were covered by the Geneva Convention. It was significant that British media pressure secured a shift in policy which was revealed on 24 February 2002 when Charles Moore, editor of the *Daily Telegraph*, conducted the first British newspaper interview with Donald Rumsfeld, US Defense Secretary, after al-Qaeda's terrorist attacks. The US government agreed that British prisoners could be repatriated on condition that they stand trial in the UK and be made available for further American interrogation. On 17 January *The Times* had demanded that the Criminal Justice (Terrorism and Conspiracy) Act of 1998 should be used to prosecute people for crimes committed outside Britain.

Where the government takes exception to the influence of the press is when it makes it more difficult to pursue political objectives by virtue of creating what politicians claim are misconceptions. Much of this criticism is focused on the way the European Union is portrayed in the press, a number of newspapers being vigorously opposed to further European integration. With its reputation for being strongly pro-European, the Foreign Office finds it hard that press statements should be accepted at face value, particularly when many newspapers are suspicious of reporting what the Establishment considers 'good news' about Europe. Lord Hurd highlighted the problem at a conference organized by the *Guardian* and the Club of Three in London in February 2002 when he said: 'The Europe of perception is part of the Europe of substance. Those who have responsibility for perception have a major role.'

Philip Gould, Tony Blair's pollster, maintained that the media had become increasingly aggressive over a whole range of issues and that politicians had in consequence become more defensive. Professor Jo Grobel, Director of the European Institute for the Media in Dusseldorf, asserted: 'While politicians are bringing Europe together, the media are widening the gap.' Assessing the government's difficulties over its European policy, Lord Hurd went so far as to suggest that the Prime Minister might have to warn the public that 'certain newspapers are working against your interest and you should repudiate them'. Whether he meant that the readers should stop buying newspapers that were against the Prime Minister's policies or that they should bombard their newspaper with letters urging it to support him was not made clear. However, Deputy Prime Minister John Prescott's solution in an interview with the *Financial Times* on 12 March 2002 was to behave as if one could ignore the press. 'The Government has to get on with it, keep its eye on the ball, and be answerable to the electorate in four years' time. We can't allow ourselves to be mesmerised by papers who declare themselves simply to be the opposition.'

One of the developments held in some quarters to be responsible for much of the critical attitude taken to European issues in the British press is the fact that most of the reports on European matters are written nowadays by political correspondents working in the Westminster lobby. They are seen in pro-European circles as belonging to an insular culture that resents any moves that dilute the supremacy of Westminster and yield more power to Brussels. It used to be the practice that the coverage of all European issues as well as international matters was automatically assigned to the diplomatic staff, who concentrated on foreign affairs and left domestic politics to the lobby corres-pondents at Westminster. It was rare for political correspondents to leave Westminster and travel abroad on assignment, except occasionally for bilateral visits of the Prime Minister. Diplomatic correspondents were accustomed to travelling with the Foreign Secretary to Brussels and accompanying him on his plane when he embarked on more extensive visits overseas. This gave them the opportunity to probe the thinking of the Foreign Secretary and question the senior mandarins off the record about policies during the long flights. These correspondents also talked to other foreign ministers and their ambassadors to keep abreast of shifts in policy, which the political correspondents confined to the Westminster lobby did not have time to do.

In recent years, however, the pattern of newspaper coverage of international affairs has changed so radically that the diplomatic correspondent is at risk of being classified as an endangered species. Whereas the *Daily Telegraph* used to have five experienced journalists on their diplomatic staff there is now only one. The *Daily Mail*, which once had a diplomatic staff of three journalists, no longer has a diplomatic correspondent at all. The *Daily Express* and the *Daily Mirror*, which had travelling diplomatic correspondents, now do without one. *The Times*, the *Guardian*, the *Independent* and the *Financial Times* have reduced their diplomatic staff to just one correspondent. Part of the responsibility for this decline lies with the Foreign Office. Diplomatic correspondents have been excluded from the main Foreign Office buildings and confined to a separate press conference room which is only infrequently used because there are no longer any regular briefings.

There has always been a certain amount of suspicion of the press in the

Foreign Office. It was typified by Selwyn Lloyd as Foreign Secretary when he wrote to Prime Minister Harold Macmillan stating: 'We must get out of the habit of feeling obliged to provide information or answer questions simply because newspaper correspondents press us to do so.' Gradually, trust was extended to the diplomatic correspondent of *The Times*, who was given a private briefing every day and handed telegrams from ambassadors. He was allowed to take notes from the telegrams, and on one occasion his report contained a meaningless sentence unaltered from an ambassador's telegram which had been garbled in transmission and left uncorrected.

When the News Department was strengthened, with a high-flyer from the Diplomatic Service at its head as the Foreign Secretary's spokesman, the daily programme provided for a briefing of news agencies at 12.30 p.m., which was conducted on the record, and an off-the-record afternoon briefing for the Three o'Clock group – all the national newspapers plus the BBC. In his six years as Foreign Secretary, Lord Howe established a relaxed, confident relationship of trust and cooperation between the Foreign Office and the press, both on his travels with correspondents and at home. That 'special relationship' – which recognized the need for understanding of the competing interests on both sides while not inhibiting criticism from the correspondents – was allowed to become steadily eroded after Lord Howe left office and deteriorated sharply during Robin Cook's time at the Foreign Office.

Only the 12.30 p.m. news agencies briefing survives today. There is no daily session with the Foreign Secretary's spokesman sitting round the table facing questions on current problems from experienced diplomatic correspondents, as happens with the lobby correspondents and the Prime Minister's spokesman. While the Foreign Office downgraded briefings, No. 10 Downing Street announced a modernization of the lobby system in May 2002, stating: 'We have got to be less buttoned-up, far more open.' Greater access was promised by making the 11 a.m. briefing open to all comers, including the foreign press, and by providing more expertise at the 4 p.m. briefing in a Gothic turret at the House of Commons to accredited political correspondents. The enlargement of the morning briefing to all specialists, not just political journalists, emphasized the drift of the media away from the Foreign Office.

The air of detachment was maintained by the Foreign Office in its policy of assigning anything it considers newsworthy, as well as speeches and appointments, to its website. Face-to-face questioning occurs at best only once a week on a 'Don't phone us, we'll phone you' basis. The official explanation was that the News Department – renamed the Press Department in 2002, which some cynical journalists took as an indication that its priority was no longer dealing with news but getting the right spin in the press – is so busy because of a constant demand for broadcast interviews with ministers, and these are what the Foreign Office now regards as 'the main means of making statements on policy to the media'. The assumption that newspaper correspondents should be content with writing articles based on answers to questions from broadcasting interviewers once they have appeared on the Foreign Office website is not one that goes down well with journalists trained in Fleet Street to assess the priorities of the day, ask their own questions and develop their own stories.

This devaluation of respected diplomatic correspondents explains why the conduct of policy by the Foreign Office receives such a small percentage of the column inches in newspapers as compared to the days when diplomats who became outstanding ambassadors, such as Sir Donald Maitland, Sir John Leahy, Sir Christopher Meyer and Sir Ivor Roberts, were in the department, meeting trusted correspondents every day and discovering the major interests liable to make news for the Foreign Office. Many ambassadors on leave, who used to stop in the corridors to talk to correspondents who had visited their embassies and bring them up to date with the situation in their region, bemoan the contact lost by keeping the press at arm's length outside the building. They enjoyed the challenge of the cut and thrust of question and answer from correspondents whose business it was to know their area and the political forces at work there.

The problem was emphasized by the Young Turks in the Foresight Report when they stated: 'Effective media handling will be a key policy tool and an essential part of achieving foreign policy objectives.' The solution is simple: an identity card allowing the small number of established diplomatic correspondents in the media access to all members of the Press Department on the ground floor of the building would overcome any security concerns (the official reason for the change) and enable members of the department to meet the press instead of merely providing a telephone answering service. Since lobby correspondents do not create any security problems by having access to Downing Street's press office it is difficult to justify the exclusion of diplomatic correspondents from the Press Department of the Foreign Office. Despite the high degree of security precautions at the US State Department, accredited correspondents are not denied access. In an era where the benefits of New Labour's joined-up government are continually being advocated, it is strange that the Foreign Office has persisted in its disjointed attitude to the press.

In a percipient article in the *Independent* on 7 January 2003 under the headline 'Our Diplomats need a posting to the real world', Mary Djevsky highlighted the strange attitude to the press as evinced by the handling of the media at the special conference of ambassadors held in London. Who were chosen by the Foreign Office to brief the envoys about relations between foreign embassies and the media? she asked. 'A senior BBC correspondent, the head of the BBC World Service and the UK edition editor of the *Financial Times* – a trio whose background and priorities closely resemble those of the diplomats themselves. Why not the *Mirror*, the *Sun* or ITV?' she went on to observe.

Diplomats do not try to reach agreement on any serious issue by negotiating on the telephone; they meet around a table and establish a rapport face to face. For the Foreign Office to achieve a better understanding of the way it conducts its policies it needs to return to daily face-to-face encounters with diplomatic correspondents, whose journalism can have considerable impact on the influential people at home and abroad who read their newspapers. Senior mandarins would do well to adopt the benchmark applied by the Young Turks in the Foresight Report to determine best practice for the Foreign Office in its relations with the media: 'Apply the What would the *Sun* say? test.' One of the challenges facing the new generation of Young Turks on their way to becoming the new mandarins will be whether they can give that mantra pride of place when they reassess their priorities ... after the revolution.

ELEVEN

After the Revolution

The opportunities have never been better for British leadership in Europe and beyond ... The next ten years could see British influence in the world at its highest for a long time. Britain in 2010, Foresight Report, 2000

The FO generates an esprit de corps without which it could not maintain its high standards in so many trying and difficult posts ... Yet that very spirit, so essential for life in the Diplomatic Service, can envelop like a cocoon. It is that which breeds what appears, at times, to be superciliousness. Lord Owen, *Time to Declare*, 1991

NO matter what sort of revolution occurs – political, industrial or technical – its evolution is always difficult to predict. None more so than the quiet revolution that almost surreptitiously overtook the Foreign Office after it had been bound by tradition for centuries. When the Young Turks discovered how far their revolution had spread throughout the Diplomatic Service they became worried about how the momentum could be maintained, especially in the light of the philosopher Hannah Arendt's warning that 'the most radical revolutionary will become a conservative on the day after the revolution'. Their concerns were eased by the way the new Permanent Under-Secretary, Sir Michael Jay, in his first twelve months in 2002, carried out his commitment, made on the day he took over in January, that the revolution would not stop or run out of steam. His creation of a new Strategy and Innovation Directorate sent a message throughout the Foreign Office and its members abroad that there was a new vision to carry forward what the Young Turks had set out to achieve in their Foresight manifesto.

However innovative the modernization programme, and however radical the reforms introduced as a result of the revolution, the Young Turks and their successors, continuing in the spirit of Foresight, had to ensure that the changes enhanced the ability of the Foreign Office to achieve its objectives in two different directions. In all its activities – reactive and proactive – the Foreign Office has two distinct roles, one abroad, the other in Whitehall. Abroad, there is no problem of definition. Put at its simplest, the Diplomatic Service flies the flag around the world and is Her Majesty's government's representative in every capital. Its function is to conduct the policies of the government in other countries, assess how the policies of other countries could affect the UK, assist British citizens, and promote the economy by serving the interests of British business. In Whitehall the role of the Foreign Office is more complicated, partly because the boundaries between foreign policy and domestic interests are often difficult to determine. In some matters it is obvious that the Foreign Office takes the lead role; in others – constantly changing and increasing because of the complexities of issues concerning the environment, international crime, drugs, HIV/Aids, conflict prevention, trade, etc. – there has to be a degree of sharing in the conduct of policy. As the Young Turks recognized, the Foreign Office's relationship with the rest of Whitehall is one demanding constant attention. 'The more we have our own agenda in cross-Whitehall issues, the harder it becomes for us to be an honest broker,' they admitted.

One consequence of the terrorist attacks in New York and Washington was that international affairs climbed higher up the government agenda than had appeared likely when the Foresight Report came out twenty-one months earlier. In theory, this should automatically have put the Foreign Office in an even more pivotal position than before. But anyone studying the ever-changing scene in Downing Street should be wary of thinking that the consequences of any development there, however predictable, are necessarily automatic. Over recent years No. 10 Downing Street has acquired a steadily increasing role in the setting and conduct of foreign policy. While all prime ministers in their first term are prepared to delegate most of the problems on the international agenda to the Foreign Secretary, as Margaret Thatcher did in 1979 with her trusted Lord Carrington so that she could concentrate on the economic problems at home, this situation does not usually last long. Subsequently, when Thatcher became fully aware of the interconnection between foreign and domestic issues, she took command on the international stage in her second term – as did Tony Blair. This prime ministerial predominance in the international arena became even more pronounced when the political kaleidoscope was totally changed after 11 September 2001, especially since Jack Straw was very much a newcomer with a domestic affairs background suddenly plunged into the complexities of foreign affairs. Until then Tony Blair had limited his interventions mainly to questions of Britain's place in the European Union. Thereafter the tide of events – and his own determination to influence them personally – resulted in his role being extended to cover the entire international spectrum. At the Foreign Office both politicians and senior mandarins officially welcomed *con spirito* having a prime minister deeply interested in the conduct of foreign policy and prepared to travel widely to win support for it. In private, there was no disguising the concern of some mandarins that the traditional lead role of the Foreign Office was in danger of being eroded.

This risk has been highlighted by the way in which the Prime Minister's Office has been augmented since the start of Blair's second term. In the Foresight Report there was speculation that events could lead to the creation of a separate Prime Minister's Department. Such a development was suggested as the means of strengthening the Prime Minister's policy team by Clive Whitmore in a paper in 1982, and again by Sir Kenneth Berrill in 1985, seven years after his report on the Foreign Office criticized diplomats for working to 'an unjustifiably high standard'. In fact, the development has apparently already happened, since Blair has established 'a Prime Minister's Department in all but name' according to Dr Anthony Wright, Labour chairman of the Commons Public Administration Committee. The new set-up at No. 10 Downing Street incurred the wrath of the Commons Transport Committee, headed by the redoubtable Mrs Gwyneth Dunwoody, especially when the Prime Minister refused to let her question Lord Birt, his transport adviser, in February 2002. The committee's view of the expanded organization at No. 10, which is known in Whitehall as 'the Centre', was scathing: 'Never in peacetime has a prime minister gathered about himself such an assembly of apparatchiks unaccountable to Parliament.'

Officially unperturbed by the concept of an enlarged Prime Minister's Office, the Foresight visionaries took comfort from their assumption that 'it will never be able to contain the expertise of policy departments' in the Foreign Office. However, in acknowledging that size may not be everything in terms of the amount of expertise at the Foreign Office's command, they sought to calm any anxieties by emphasizing the quality of Foreign Office advice from two outstanding diplomats working closely with the Prime Minister – Sir Stephen Wall, his European affairs guru, and the former European Union ambassador Sir Nigel Sheinwald moved from Brussels to succeed Sir David Manning as foreign policy adviser when the latter was promoted to Ambassador in Washington. With a senior mandarin from the Treasury, Jeremy Heywood, heading the policy directorate as principal private secretary to the Prime Minister, the Whitehall professionals were confident about preserving their pre-eminent position.

Some of that confidence was undermined when what is termed the 'No. 10 Organogram' was released as a sort of plain man's guide to where the power really lies in the corridors of power in Downing Street. The troika has as its head Jonathan Powell, the Prime Minister's trusted chief of staff, formerly in

Washington as a member of the Diplomatic Service. This position gave him supreme authority over all Civil Service officials in No. 10. Next in the rankings – until his resignation in September 2003 – was Alastair Campbell, an influential journalist who became Blair's press secretary before being promoted to Director of Strategy and Communications. Within his fiefdom was the No. 10 press office, the Strategic Communications Unit responsible for statements and speeches, and the Research and Information Unit. Although the reorganization after Alastair Campbell's departure was presented as moving away from the era of spin, the main difference was that it was more low key and less professional. The third part of the troika is the Government and Political Relations division with Baroness Morgan as its director, charged with ensuring smooth coordination with the party, the whips, the National Executive Committee and the trade unions. All three political appointees – not accountable to Parliament – have been accorded the necessary ranking by the Prime Minister to override any advice proffered by civil servants.

Criticism at Westminster that Prime Minister Blair had become presidential in surrounding himself with a large staff whose allegiance is exclusive to him personally did not cause much sleep to be lost at No. 10 Downing Street. With the decline of decision-making in Cabinet there is more pressure nowadays for a strong central authority to take charge of a problem – whether it is over Northern Ireland, sending troops to Afghanistan, or going to war in Iraq – and this usually requires a decision by the Prime Minister on his own. To take such decisions does not necessarily mean becoming presidential, the Prime Minister's entourage maintain. Having a Prime Minister's Department at No. 10, whether or not it is so called, is not, it is argued, a presidential move. There are constitutional precedents for such a department not giving rise to suspicions of presidential aspirations in countries such as Canada, Italy and Germany.

Where the balance of influence between the two sides of Downing Street is determined is in the Prime Minister's political entourage having the clout born of being Blair's close advisers before he came to office. They need not bow to the Establishment. Although the phrase was Margaret Thatcher's, 'One of Us' remains the password to power in Tony Blair's Establishment. In consequence, the advisers' influence is a major constraint on the Foreign Office's room for manoeuvre and can be at times a formidable obstacle to be overcome when the Foreign Office seeks to have the stamp of approval from No. 10 for its policies at a time of crisis. It used to be accepted that the Foreign Office was the first in line to be consulted on any international problem on the ground that it 'knows how to deal with foreigners'. Not so any longer. There is stiff competition in Whitehall with other ministries claiming to have the requisite technical expertise to ensure that Britain's best interests are secured in an international forum.

Working relations with other departments in Whitehall are acknowledged in the Foreign Office to be much more challenging nowadays. No longer do other ministries turn automatically to the Foreign Office in the first instance when an international issue commanding their attention arises. Partly this is due to the lingering elitism inside the Foreign Office in handling discussions with 'outsiders', which, as Lord Owen perceived in the course of his time as Foreign Secretary, sometimes amounts to superciliousness. One senior mandarin admitted: 'We still have colleagues in Whitehall who regard us as arrogant prats. We cannot afford that.' Foresight recognized it was necessary to end 'the cult of separateness' and acknowledged: 'We are still too quick to define ourselves as different and the only ones who understand "abroad".' The change in attitude in the rest of Whitehall is also due to the fact that other departments have established their own networks abroad, especially in the European Union, and have burnished their own skills at the negotiating table in wheeling and dealing to secure their own objectives, which they claim they know best how to achieve.

The Foresight planners recognized the need in the Foreign Office for what they termed 'a step change in expertise'. Since the report was completed there has been a determined effort to extend and deepen the expertise of the Diplomatic Service beyond skills in difficult languages and knowledge of political, cultural and regional aspects of countries where other departments have to become involved. Teams of specialists in disarmament able to deploy their expertise in negotiations on mutual and balanced force reductions are no longer in much demand now that the conventional military confrontation between the West and the communist world is over. Instead the Foreign Office realizes it needs to have specialists on environmental problems such as water, pollution and climate change, on population problems such as ethnicity and migration, on international crime such as drugs and money laundering, on trade, terrorism and counter-terrorism. It has also resulted in embassies being required to be more focused on the UK government's international agenda across the board, not confining themselves to traditional foreign policy questions but adapting their resources to cover the interests of other departments in Whitehall. To do so effectively ambassadors have been urged to take on responsibilities directly with each Whitehall ministry whose interests are involved.

Even though the Foreign Office is renowned for its expertise on the European Union and in particular the techniques of being a skilful player in complex negotiations with the Brussels bureaucracy, it realized that its resources were inadequate to deal with the increasing workload accruing from the EU involvement with so many ministries. This resulted in a much larger pool of people in the Diplomatic Service acquiring EU expertise at a much earlier stage in their careers. By increasing the number of first-posting appointments to the UK delegation in Brussels, more people are being given a career anchor in the EU which will ensure that there is always an experienced corps of first secretaries in London with the necessary training to deal with the complexities of coordinating policies among several Whitehall departments.

Nevertheless, there are more occasions nowadays when the Foreign Office is being outflanked by other ministries on issues that were formerly regarded as exclusively the preserve of its ministers and experts. When the Commonwealth Relations Office was merged into the Foreign Office in 1968, for example, all political questions concerning African countries, whether they were inside or outside the Commonwealth, were considered to be solely within the purview of the Foreign Office. During Conservative governments the Overseas Development Administration was under the Foreign Office with a senior minister, not a member of the Cabinet, in charge. That changed in 1997 when the Labour government established the Department for International Development (DfID), with its secretary a member of the Cabinet. While Peter Hain, during his first period as Foreign Office Minister, immersed himself eagerly in African affairs, Cook took little interest in Africa at the outset and usually just skimmed through telegrams from African posts. It was only when Robin Cook was caught up in the arms-to-Sierra Leone scandal that he took the trouble to keep abreast of developments in that part of Africa. By then the International Development Department had established itself as a major player throughout not just Africa but also most parts of the Commonwealth.

While Cook and Jack Straw have participated in joint Anglo-French forays into Africa with their French opposite numbers, this collaboration has been treated in African capitals as mainly cosmetic. Apart from an inevitable involvement in the crisis over Zimbabwe, Straw showed little concern for what was happening in Africa during his first year at the Foreign Office. When Tony Blair fulfilled his pledge to make a partnership with Africa a major priority item in his second-term agenda, the minister to whom he turned was his International Development Secretary, not his Foreign Secretary. It was a natural choice, as Clare Short was highly respected by African leaders and knew the sub-Saharan regions of the continent and their peoples well from the days when she was married to Alex Lyon, one-time MP for York with a extensive reputation as an

African expert, who died in 1993. She was the first Cabinet minister to visit the Democratic Republic of the Congo in August 2001.

When Tony Blair went ahead with a brainstorming session on Africa at Chequers only a week after the terrorist attacks in America on 11 September 2001, the Foreign Office was represented by a junior minister, Baroness Amos. The principal adviser at his side was Clare Short as he assessed the problems with six presidents – Olusegun Obasanjo of Nigeria, Abdoulaye Wade of Senegal, Joaquim Chissano of Mozambique, John Kufuor of Ghana, Benjamin Mkapa of Tanzania, and Festus Mogae of Botswana. The change in status between the Foreign Office and the International Development Department was confirmed when Blair embarked on a tour of Nigeria, Ghana, Senegal and Sierra Leone in February 2002, when again he had Clare Short at his side. Her enthusiastic commitment to tackling the problems of the African continent was much more evident than that of the junior ministers handling the region in the Foreign Office.

One significant example of Clare Short taking over from the Foreign Secretary was when she flew to the Great Lakes region in February 2002 and pulled off a diplomatic coup in Kisangani by negotiating an agreement with Goma rebel forces to allow United Nations observers to have access to Kinshasa and Kindu in the eastern sector of the Democratic Republic of the Congo (DRC). It was a bold move designed to push forward the peace process under the Lusaka and Arusha agreements, which until then had been locked in stalemate. With the support of the European counterparts accompanying her, Hilde Johnson from Norway and Eveline Herfkens from the Netherlands, Clare Short secured pledges from President Joseph Kabila of the DRC, President Paul Kagame of Rwanda, President Yoweri Museveni of Uganda, and President Pierre Buyoya of Burundi to keep the momentum going in a bid to rid the region of conflict. This was the kind of diplomatic initiative that used to be undertaken by the Foreign Office, but Short and the experts in her ministry clearly demonstrated they were able to go farther than the Foreign Office in linking moves to secure political stability with development projects, such as funding the restoration of the railway line between Kinshasa and Kindu.

Cooperation between Chancellor of the Exchequer Gordon Brown and Clare Short, which stemmed from a natural political partnership in the party, often left the Foreign Office marginalized in the implementation of other major government initiatives in the developing world. Clare Short's robust views on globalization gave her a stronger voice than Jack Straw in Cabinet alongside Gordon Brown. She was supported by experts at DfID who, on occasion, carried much more authority than a Foreign Office director dealing with globalization issues. Working together with Gordon Brown when the British government took the lead on debt relief for Heavily Indebted Poor Countries (HIPCs) and set standards for other developed countries on this issue, Short acquired considerable status in promoting political stability in a number of disadvantaged African countries which would normally have turned first to the Foreign Office for help in solving their problems.

This influential role did not survive long once the Prime Minister became convinced that war was the only logical outcome of the Iraq crisis. Short's political credibility was undermined on 9 March 2003 – eight days before the Anglo-American deadline to the Saddam Hussein regime – by her threat to resign after condemning Blair's policy as 'extremely reckless'. After she performed a U-turn on resignation following her assertion on BBC radio that 'I will not uphold a breach of international law or this undermining of the UN and I will resign from the government', her authority in Cabinet was diminished. When she bowed to the inevitable by resigning on 12 May 2003, her departure and replacement by the low-profile Foreign Office Minister, Baroness Amos, devalued the influence of DFID as a ministry and boosted Jack Straw's position in the Cabinet. With the further downgrading of DFID six months later on the appointment of Hilary Benn, a grey figure without the flair of his former firebrand Cabinet minister father Tony, to succeed Baroness Amos on her promotion on 7 October 2003 as Leader of the House of Lords, Jack Straw faced no serious challenge inside the Cabinet as long as he dutifully emulated every attitude struck by the Prime Minister. However, even with a more prominent role in the international arena, being an emissary of a dominant prime minister so highly rated in Washington often left Straw in a merely supportive role.

Difficulties in defining who takes the lead in cross-cutting issues have sometimes shown that the Foreign Office writ does not extend as far as it assumed was the case. This was publicly demonstrated to the embarrassment of the Foreign Office when leaked documents disclosed a serious clash with the Ministry of Defence in January 2002. Ever since the Maastricht Treaty in 1991 set out the European Union's aspirations for a common foreign and security policy there has been a political tug of war in Whitehall over who decides when a situation demands a foreign policy decision or a military commitment. When Defence Secretary Geoff Hoon agreed in November 2000 to commit 12,500 troops to the rapid reaction force – 20 per cent of the total strength – plus if required eighteen warships and seventy-two combat planes in readiness for use in 2003, it was assumed at the Ministry of Defence that it would have a major say in their deployment. The clash over when to commit troops came to a head over the crisis in Macedonia, when the Foreign Office wanted British troops to join a peacekeeping mission. A letter from Geoff Hoon's office on 22 January 2002 to Sir David Manning, then the Prime Minister's foreign affairs adviser, which was leaked to the *Sunday Telegraph*, vigorously opposed the position taken by the Foreign Office, which argued that as 'the bandwagon is rolling' with France and Italy eager to take the lead it would be damaging to be left out. The Ministry of Defence emphasized its resentment of Foreign Office intervention by stressing that 'Military advice is that the fledging ESDP [European Security and Defence Policy] mechanism is not ready to undertake an operation of this magnitude and risk.' Clearly rankled by the Foreign Office being ready to plunge ahead regardless of military intelligence indicating that the situation in Macedonia was deteriorating, the ministry's letter drew its own line in the sand: 'There would be a real risk that the EU's first mission would end in failure or rescue by a re-engaged NATO, which would be disastrous in presentational terms.' Even although Blair eventually overruled Geoff Hoon for the sake of a political trade-off with the French at the EU summit in Barcelona in March 2002, it was a sharp reminder for the Foreign Office that other ministries do not automatically defer to it or accept its assessment as the final verdict. The episode also drove home the point that the Foreign Office has to be constantly aware that other Whitehall departments are much less ready than they used to be to accept that it should have a leading role in handling European issues.

Another challenge being faced as a result of the new circumstances in which the Foreign Office has to operate is how to make a significant input in the conduct of policy abroad where another government department is taking the lead. Nowhere has this been more relevant than at the international conferences convened to work out the terms of implementing the Kyoto agreement on climate change. Although as Environment Minister Michael Meacher had experts from his department well versed in the intricacies of issues such as 'carbon sinks' and emission levels of greenhouse gases, the Foreign Office recognized that it had to develop its own expertise or find itself marginalized at such conferences. In its dealings with the Department for Environment, Food and Rural Affairs (DEFRA) across the board, the Foreign Office acknowledged that it had to have experts capable of holding their own with others round the conference table.

For the Foreign Office to maintain its prime position in Whitehall it knows it has to demonstrate its value by showing it has the necessary skills not only in the techniques of international negotiations but also in terms of technical knowledge of the issues under negotiation. While the environment specialists from DEFRA know how to play their hand, the Foreign Office's credibility in the rest of Whitehall depends on its ability to maximize its political contacts in other capitals to pave the way for Britain to get a good hearing at conferences. It is often a matter of the Foreign Office having people with the capability to size up where the technical hurdles to Britain's objectives lie and then focusing on where the trade-offs can be found in other areas. This can involve a round of diplomatic bargaining in which the Foreign Office has to exercise all its skills in avoiding a scenario in which some players feel too much has been sacrificed in their own specialized area for an overall settlement to be viable.

Yet when there is a case where Britain's interests are being damaged by European Union regulations or lack of EU law enforcement, Whitehall ministries sometimes prefer to pursue the matter directly in Brussels and only use Foreign Office lobbying as a follow-up. DEFRA Secretary Margaret Beckett took action herself in March 2002 when British beef exporters were still prevented from selling meat products in Europe two months after the EU ban imposed during the foot-and-mouth outbreak was lifted. With France refusing to take British beef, in defiance of a ruling of the European Court of Justice, and the EU dragging its heels over enforcing penalties against the French, the DEFRA bypassed the Foreign Office and sought a relaxation of abattoir regulations from the EU Food Safety Commission to allow British meat exports to other EU countries. By putting the case for part-time abattoir operations instead of the full-time regulatory requirement in order to make a limited resumption of exports to countries such as Italy, the DEFRA experts believed they could break the stalemate faster than through diplomatic intervention by the Foreign Office.

Transatlantic trade disputes which erupt with the sudden imposition of protectionist tariffs by the US government used to ring alarm bells first at the Foreign Office, because of the anxiety to maintain as much as possible from the legacy of the so-called special relationship. They would entail the immediate deployment of the diplomatic skills of commercial ministers in Washington, such as the emollient Sir Derek Thomas. Then the Foreign Secretary would weigh in, as Sir Geoffrey Howe did in January 1987 when he flew to Bermuda for talks with Secretary of State George Shultz which resulted in averting extra levies, including 200 per cent on gin, which would have meant UK companies losing £50 million in exports. On major international issues such as the American counter-measures against suppliers of equipment to Russia's Urengoi pipeline in June 1982, Foreign Office protests were ratcheted up to prime ministerial level with Margaret Thatcher taking the case to the White House.

Nowadays it is the Trade and Industry Department which moves in first and leaves the Foreign Office to lobby its Washington contacts in the second wave. This was demonstrated when President George W. Bush announced in March 2002 new tariffs of up to 30 per cent on steel imports, affecting almost 10 per cent of the world market for steel. Trade Secretary Patricia Hewitt did not wait to see what the Foreign Office were going to do. She telephoned EU Trade Commissioner Pascal Lamy in Brussels at once to coordinate a quick European response, not waiting for a lengthy legal challenge at the World Trade Organization. Her speedy intervention set the agenda for 'urgent and appropriate action' threatening retaliation against the USA 'to safeguard British and European steel producers and workers against a flood of steel imports'.

The way in which the Foreign Office will have to earn its spurs in Whitehall in the years ahead was succinctly put by one senior mandarin thus: 'We have to work with the rest of the departments in Whitehall and sell our relevance day in and day out, explaining why European policy handled through us is better handled.' The days when the Foreign Office believed its job was simply to get it right and then leave it to the political masters to sell it to the rest of the government are long gone. Whenever policy advice is set out for a minister it now has attached to it guidance on how to sell it, indications of what sort of opposition may have to be faced, and how best to overcome resistance to it in other parts of Whitehall. For an adviser to suggest that the Foreign Secretary should write a newspaper article paving the way for a change of policy and countering possible resistance to it in advance would have been inconceivable in the days before the Foresight Revolution. Now it is mainly a question of which newspaper should be used this time, or an application of the 'What would the *Sun* say?' test.

Keeping the momentum of change going inside the Foreign Office after the revolution depends not just on recruiting the best potential new mandarins from a wide spectrum of society, it requires a constant flow of new blood – and new ideas – into the system at all levels. So far no one has been bold enough to implement the Ham Whyte 'Up or Out' Plan – proposals for maintaining flexibility in the Diplomatic Service which were set out in the valedictory dispatch of a former favourite of Fleet Street as Head of the News Department on his retirement in 1987 as high commissioner to Singapore. Sir Hamilton Whyte advocated the abandonment of the system under which the vast majority entering the Foreign Office from university at the age of twenty-two were expected to stay in the Diplomatic Service for their entire working life.

His argument was blunt:

We need to change the terms on which we recruit. To take people in the twenties with tenure to 60 (short of defection, sexual aberration *or senility*) is in this day and age plain crazy. How do we know what they, or the world, or our requirements will be in 30 years' time? We need a regime more like that of the Royal Navy over the years: Up or Out, depending on individual performance, number of ships and number of hands and variety of skills required. In the F.O. we are skilful (mostly) at moving people to the top. But below that we create frustration and inefficiency by being unable to retire decently those we could do without. This impairs promotion prospects for the middle ranks where the pressure of work is greatest and increases the temptation among those we can least spare to peel off for higher salaries. Let those who prefer the security of the Home Civil Service or the fast track into the City go their separate ways. For those with a taste and flair for government service overseas and a career very different from that of the Whitehall commuter or the business whiz-kid, greater upward mobility and more scope to get round pegs in round holes should offset the prospect of having to find a new niche in middle age.

The classic case against the Ham Whyte 'Up or Out' Plan has always been that the Treasury cannot afford the cost of large numbers taking early retirement. However, more and more people in the Foreign Office are acknowledging that if investment banks can accept a higher rate of attrition and take in people on a short-term basis of five or ten years then it should be possible in Whitehall. The lack of flexibility is apt to produce a certain style of mindset which has many advantages for ensuring a coordinated – and predictable – approach to the conduct of foreign policy at different levels and in various places. The disadvantage is that the mindset results in hesitancy over innovation, a tendency to become entrenched in diplomatic procedures, and a propensity to 'play safe' and avoid taking risks.

To get rid once and for all of the perception of diplomats as pinstriped obsequious mandarins conniving to get their way with ministers it is imperative for the new generation of mandarins to adopt the mantra of one former Young Turk: 'Being a diplomat does not always mean being diplomatic.' While it is recognized that the Foreign Office inculcates certain specific skills that cannot be acquired anywhere else, it has become increasingly apparent since the Foresight revolution that there is a large range of other skills elsewhere which until then had not been properly valued by the Foreign Office. One of the consequences the mandarins observed in the highly competitive climate of large organizations in the private sector was the continuous recycling of skills. As a result the Foreign Office has been encouraging a significant expansion of people moving out of Whitehall's insulated atmosphere into the private sector and welcoming a large number of temporary attachments from it into the Foreign Office.

Despite the advances under the modernization programme, however, there are areas where the Foreign Office still shows a reluctance to dispense with some of the practices of the past century. In one particular respect it preserves a studied detachment from modern methods of communication. American visitors waiting to be escorted into the Foreign Secretary's room express amazement at seeing attendants trundling antiquated trolleys along the corridors distributing boxes of telegrams. They move at a measured pace, as if they were delivering second-class letters, amid the hum of the IT inside the diplomats' rooms. The end of the paper regime is not in sight yet, for although there is no shortage of computers throughout the buildings Jack Straw admitted that he did not use one very often and that when he was studying a situation he preferred to read about it on paper, not on screen. Another sign that modernization still has some way to go is that telegrams and submissions are all too often still couched in a stilted form of language typical of the cautious cast of mind and the ponderous way of thinking that have been passed from one generation to the next in the Civil Service. There remains in some quarters a disinclination to be direct in setting out arguments for a course of action, despite a persistent campaign by Sir John Kerr to strike out the phrase 'I feel that ... ' and insist that what the Foreign Office wants is not feelings but well-thought-out considerations.

Although some old habits – and some working practices – are taking a long time to be abandoned, Matthew Kirk's new technology projects have had an enormous impact in accelerating the revolution, not just in terms of performance but in attitudes as well. Recent statistics show that the British send more e-mails than any other people in Europe, with everyone in an office dealing on average with 180 each day – and more are sent in the Foreign Office than in any other part of Whitehall. It has broken down barriers inside the Foreign Office and abroad between one post and another, as well as between the perimeter and the centre. As one IT expert put it: 'The old hierarchical system dividing one rank from another all the way up to the directors general is being steadily eaten away by the technology termites.'

Nowadays the lowliest aspiring mandarin is able to send an e-mail direct to a director general, bypassing his head of department, and the answer is transmitted to the sender directly, without going back down through the traditional chain of command. This means that ideas can flow more freely and more quickly without requiring submissions to be given initialled approval all the way up the line. The knowledge management system through PRISM enables people to seek information about a complex situation from someone who developed expertise in it in a previous posting by e-mailing a query directly to another post, without the triangular process of going through London and being delayed by the time factors. This allows posts at the periphery to complete in twenty minutes a transaction that would sometimes have taken two days under the old system.

With the new state-of-the-art technology that puts the Foreign Office, which used to be ten years behind others in Whitehall, well ahead of the rest of the government departments there is a requirement for greater vigilance than ever before to preserve quality control in the advice given on the conduct of foreign policy and accountability for the ultimate responsibility in tendering that advice. The ability of anyone to send a submission by e-mail without clearing the draft with a superior has been ground-breaking and has made life in isolated posts much more interesting. But in the end someone must be held responsible. A department in London which sees an e-mail impinging on its area of operation can intervene and register a different point of view. But not even the Permanent Under-Secretary can obliterate what the junior member of the service has submitted in an e-mail as recommended policy. All he can do is to set out his reasons for opposing a particular course of action and add his own recommendations.

In the end the Foreign Secretary has the choice of accepting the innovative ideas in the e-mail sent by the embassy or following the recommendations either of the department or of the PUS. This flexible system enables everyone with a legitimate case for having an input into the resolution of a problem to contribute to the shaping of the policy advice sent to ministers. At the same time it preserves the essential record of the various stages through which a decision is taken in the Foreign Office, thereby retaining the virtue of visibility from the old system of annotated written submissions in the days of telegrams, dispatches and records of meetings. While 60 per cent of all communications at the Foreign Office are shredded as inessential for the records in the National Archives at Kew, the new technology ensures that, once a policy submission goes to the Foreign Secretary with the various additions from the department and the PUS, it goes simultaneously to the archives. Thus historians in future will be able to judge the record of the Foreign Office from the archives as they are made available under the thirty-year rule.

They will also have the material to assess how successfully the Diplomatic Service evolved after the revolution inspired by the Young Turks when they set out their vision of a truly modernized Foreign Office in the Foresight Report in January 2000. After the first flush of success by the Young Turks there was scepticism among the old Whitehall warriors, who believed the revolution would quickly run out of steam. But Foresight's renewal as the key element in the Innovative Diplomacy Unit within the Directorate of Strategy and Innovation was designed to give it its second wind. With a team of six under Simon Elvy, Foresight signed up 300 activists to keep up the pressures for change with ideas on policy, how to deliver them with a flexible use of people and resources, and the continued struggle to break down hierarchical barriers. Questionnaires are sent out, as the original Young Turks used to do, in order to sound out staff abroad on how to make the most of Foreign Office talent. Lunchtime discussions are held in the Locarno Room on a variety of topics from how the Consular Service can meet public expectations to the problems of consistency in human rights policies.

With the intake of increasingly diverse new mandarins from a wide variety of backgrounds adding approximately 250 young diplomats to the staff of the Foreign Office – equivalent to almost 10 per cent of the UK-based staff– in the first decade since the Young Turks began their campaign for change, there are good grounds for the confidence of their successors that the impetus of the revolution will be sustained and carried forward indefinitely. 'Foresight is here to stay,' the activists insist. In view of the high standards set for the new mandarins to be the *crème de la crème* in Whitehall there is also every reason to expect that future foreign secretaries following in the footsteps of Lord Carrington will echo his encomium: 'I admired the men and women in the Foreign Office and felt it a privilege to work with them. They were outstanding and in my experience their quality exceeds that of any other Department – and any other Foreign Office.'

APPENDIX 1 **The Foreign Office Hierarchy**

Permanent Under-Secretary of State and Head of
the Diplomatic Service

|

Group Chief Executive, British Trade International

|

Directors General

1. Corporate Affairs
2. Economic
3. Europe

4. Defence/Intelligence
5. Legal Adviser
6. Political

|

Directors

1. Africa
2. Americas/Overseas Territories
3. International Security
4. Wider Europe
5. Mediterranean, Europe
   Bilateral, Resources
6. FO Services

7. Global Issues
8. Middle East/North Africa
9. Asia Pacific
10. South Asia
11. Personnel
12. Information
13. Finance

|

UK Special Representatives

1. for Afghanistan
2. for Cyprus
3. for Georgia

4. for Nepal
5. for Sudan
6. for Iraq

The Foreign and Commonwealth Office Organogram

Sir Michael Jay* Permanent Under-Secretary (PUS) and Head of the Diplomatic Service			**Simon Fraser*** Director, Strategy and Innovation	– Strategy and Innovation – Research Analysts
			Richard Stagg* Director, Information	– Islamic Media Unit – Library Information Services – Online Communications – Parliamentary Relations and Devolution – Partnerships and Network Development Unit – Press Office – Public Diplomacy Policy – Records and Historical
	John Sawers* Director General, Political	**Nick Baird** Assistant Director, Europe Internal		– Common Foreign and Security Policy – Economic
		Linda Duffield Director, Wider Europe		– Eastern – Eastern Adriatic – OSCE
		Edward Chaplin Director, Middle East and North Africa		– Middle East – Near East and North Africa
		John Buck Director, Iraq		– Iraq Policy Unit – Iraq Security Sector Unit – Iraq Operations Unit
		James Bevan Director, Africa		– Africa (Equatorial) – Africa (Southern)
	Peter Collecott* Director General, Corporate Affairs			– Estates Strategy – IT Strategy – Protocol – Security Strategy
				– Local Staff Management – Medical and Welfare – PROSPER – Personnel Management Development
		Simon Gass* Director, Resources		– Financial Compliance – Internal Audit – Prism Programme – Procurement Policy – Resource Accounting – Resource Budgeting – Quality and Efficiency
		Stephen Sage Chief Executive, FCO Services		– Client Services – Estates and Security – Finance – Human Resources – ICT – People and Best Practice – Promotions and Events – Strategic Planning – Supply Chain
		Paul Sizeland Director, Consular Services		– Assistance – Crises – Passports and Documentary – Resources Group – Services Quality

Sir Michael Jay* Permanent Under-Secretary (PUS) and Head of the Diplomatic Service	Graham Fry* Director General, Economic	Robert Culshaw Director, Americas	– Latin America and Caribbean – North America – Overseas Territories
		Tom Phillips Director, South Asia	– Afghanistan – South Asia
		Nigel Cox Director, Asia Pacific	– China and Hong Kong – North-East Asia and Pacific – South-East Asia
		Philippa Drew Director, Global Issues	– Aviation, Maritime and Energy – Environmental Policy – Commonwealth Coordination – Science and Technology – Human Rights Policy – United Nations
		Creon Butler Chief Economist	– Economic Relations
			– UK Visas
	William Ehrman* Director General, Defence and Intelligence		– Whitehall Liaison
		Edward Oakden Director, International Security	– Counter-terrorism Policy – Drugs and International Crime – Counter-proliferation – Security Policy – Service Advisers and Attachés
	Kim Darroch Director General, European Union Policy	Dominick Chilcott Director, Mediterranean Europe, Bilateral, Resources	– EU (external) – EU (internal) – EU (Mediterranean)
		Michael Wood Legal Adviser	– Legal Advisers

Sir Stephen Brown* Chief Executive	– British Trade International

* Members of the FCO Board of Management, along with two non-executive members: Allan Gormley, Chairman, BPB Industries, and Lucy Neville-Rolfe, Director of Corporate Affairs, Tesco.

Afghanistan Unit: set up to help Afghanistan achieve stability, security and prosperity.

African Department (Equatorial): political and economic relations with thirty-two countries plus Economic Community of West African States (ECOWAS), East African Community (EAC), Africa Union, and Inter-Governmental Authority for Development (IGAD).

African Department (Southern): political and economic relations with fifteen countries plus Southern African Development Community (SADC).

Aviation, Maritime & Energy Department: air services agreements, Law of the Sea, fisheries, Channel Tunnel, global energy and nuclear technologies.

British Trade International: trade support services operated jointly by the Foreign Office and the Department of Trade and Industry incorporating four groups – Invest UK, Trade Partners UK, International Group, and Business Group.

Central and North-West European Department: political and bilateral economic relations with fourteen countries.

China Hong Kong Department: relations with China and the Special Administrative Region of Hong Kong.

Commonwealth Coordination Department: policy procedures and practices relating to the Commonwealth and liaison with the Commonwealth Secretariat.

Consular Directorate: supervision of consular services, protection and assistance for British nationals abroad, passport policy, compensation claims against other governments by individuals or companies, and electoral registration overseas.

Counter-terrorism Policy Department: crisis management and policy coordination with other governments.

Diplomatic Service Families' Association: voluntary group working with FO administration on welfare and social matters to achieve 'best-practice family-friendly policy'.

Directorate for Strategy and Innovation: created in 2003 to set clear goals for the Foreign Office and pursue them in innovative and effective ways.

Drugs & International Crime Department: coordination of government policies to combat the drugs trade and cooperate with international organizations.

Eastern Adriatic Department: relations with Albania and states that emerged from the former Yugoslavia.

Eastern Department: policy on Russia, Ukraine, the South Caucasus, Central Asia, Moldova, Belarus and Caspian energy issues.

Economic Policy Department: analyses global trends, commodities markets, globalization, debt relief, money laundering, asset confiscation and relations with international economic organizations such as the IMF and G8.

e-Media Unit: heads the FO's Internet strategy and is responsible for the FO's web platform.

Environment Policy Department: environmental issues connected with sustainable development, globalization, climate change and biodiversity.

Estate Strategy Unit: handles all FO property in the UK and abroad.

European Union Department (Bilateral): political and economic relations with European nations including the Holy See, Monaco and San Marino.

European Union Department (External): relations between EU member states and third countries.

European Union Department (Internal): analysis of the EU's institutional and economic proposals.

Executive Agency: organization of Wilton Park conferences on international issues.

FCO Association: handles welfare and staff social matters.

FCO Services: support services in London and abroad including the following:

> *Conference and Visits Group*. Management of events and visits plus all hospitality services.
>
> *Consultancy Group*. All consultancy services for maximum efficiency at home and overseas including security arrangements at posts plus a vetting unit for security clearance of staff.
>
> *Estate Group*. Property management for buildings overseas.
>
> *Finance Group*. Central financial management for all FO services.
>
> *Human Resources Group*. Personnel management and training.
>
> *Information Management Group*. Supervises information systems.
>
> *Language Group*. Formerly Language Training Centre responsible for language training, translation and interpreting.
>
> *Strategic Planning Branch*. Corporate marketing and communications.
>
> *Support Group*. Supplying furniture, vehicles and equipment and making travel arrangements.
>
> *Technical Group (Implementation)*. Installing communications and security systems.
>
> *Technical Group (Support)*. Technology systems maintenance.

Financial Compliance Unit: accounting for expenditure on Whitehall guidelines.

Human Rights Policy Department: implementation of human rights obligations throughout Whitehall as well as abroad and liaison with NGOs.

Internal Audit Department: watchdog on expenditure.

IT Strategy Unit: technology investment and budgets.

Latin America and Caribbean Department: political and economic bilateral relations.

Legal Advisers: supervision of UK interests, treaties and international litigation in terms of international law.

Middle East Department: relations with nine countries in the region.

Near East and North Africa Department: political and economic relations with eleven Arab countries and Israel.

Non-proliferation Department: nuclear treaties, chemical and biological weapon conventions, and policy on conventional arms sales.

North American Department: relations with the United States and Canada.

North-East Asia and Pacific Department: relations with Japan, North and South Korea, Australia, New Zealand and twelve other countries.

OSCE and Council of Europe Department: policy on Europe and European security.

Overseas Territories Department: responsibility for what used to be called dependent territories.

Parliamentary Relations and Devolution Department: handling relations with select committees and preparing answers to parliamentary questions.

Personnel Directorate: supervising recruitment, training, career planning, promotion, discipline, welfare, pay and pensions, and local staff management.

Press Office: formerly the News Department, responsible for briefing media and issuing ministerial statements.

Prism Programme: organizing the global online management information system.

Protocol Division: deals with diplomatic missions, their privileges and immunities, ceremonial events, and royal visits.

Public Diplomacy Policy Department: policy presentation guidance to posts, administration of grants to the BBC World Service.

Purchasing Policy Department: buying goods and services.

Quality and Efficiency Unit: value-for-money reviews and efficiency targets.

Records and Historical Department: records custody and historical advice.

Research Analysts: specialist expertise on policy.

Resource Accounting Department: funding of posts and payment of salaries.

Resource Budgeting Department: monitoring of expenditure and measuring performance.

Science and Technology Unit: advising posts on science and technology.

Security Policy Department: nuclear and conventional arms control, defence policy, defence attachés.

Security Strategy Unit: counter-measures and security education training.

South Asian Department: bilateral relations with seven countries.

South-East Asian Department: political and economic relations with eleven countries.

Trade Union Unit: staff interests with the Diplomatic Service Whitley Council.

UK Visas: joint operations with the Home Office supervising appointments at overseas posts.

United Nations Department: policies at the UN and Security Council, peace-keeping, sanctions, war crimes, and the Government Diamonds Office.

Whitehall Liaison Department: coordination with the Cabinet Office and other ministries.

APPENDIX 4 **European Policy Division**

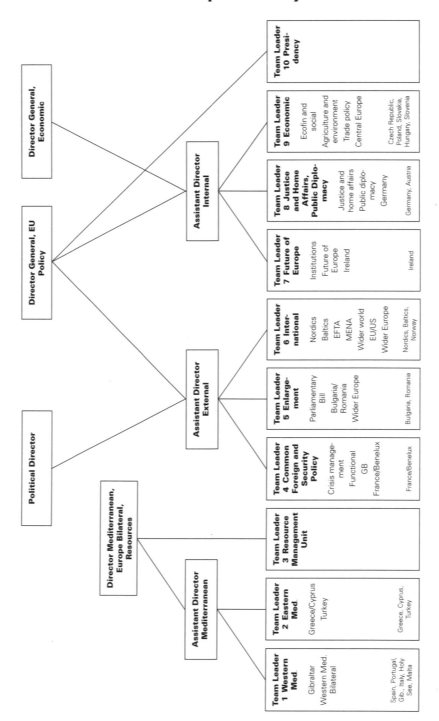

Bibliography

There are so many books covering various aspects of foreign policy that rather than over-burden the reader I have confined the following list of recommended reading to those volumes particularly relevant to this study.

Adamson, David (1989) *The Last Empire*, London: I. B. Tauris.

Andrew, Christopher, and Oleg Gordievsky (1990) *KGB: The Inside Story*, London: Hodder & Stoughton.

Bulloch, John, and Harvey Morris (1989) *The Gulf War*, London: Methuen.

Burrows, Bernard (2001) *Diplomat in a Changing World*, London: The Memoir Club.

Callaghan, Lord (1981) *Time and Chance*, London: Collins.

Carrington, Lord (1988) *Reflect on Things Past*, London: Collins.

Carstairs, Charles, and Richard Ware (1991) *Parliament and International Relations*, London: Open University Press.

Clark, Eric (1973) *Corps Diplomatique*, London: Allen Lane.

Clarke, Michael (1992) *British External Policy-making in the 1990s*, London: Macmillan.

Coles, John (2000) *Making Foreign Policy*, London: John Murray.

Cradock, Percy (1997) *In Pursuit of British Interests*, London: John Murray.

— (2002) *Know Your Enemy: How the Joint Intelligence Committee Saw the World*, London: John Murray.

Dickie, John (1964) *The Uncommon Commoner: A Study of Sir Alec Douglas-Home*, London: Pall Mall.

— (1992) *Inside the Foreign Office*, London: Chapmans.

— (1994) *Special No More*, London: Weidenfeld & Nicolson.

— (1997) *The Boys on the Bongo Bus*, Luton: University of Luton Press.

Eban, Abba (1998) *Diplomacy for the Next Century*, New Haven, CT: Yale University Press.

Feltham, R. G. (1977) *Diplomatic Handbook*, Harlow: Longman.

Freedman, Lawrence, and Michael Clarke (eds) (1991) *Britain in the World*, Cambridge: Cambridge University Press.

George-Brown, Lord (1971) *In My Way*, London: Gollancz.

Gladwyn, Lord (1972) *Memoirs*, London: Weidenfeld & Nicolson.

Hannay, David (1996) *The Growth of Multilateral Diplomacy*, London: Historians Occasional Papers No. 13, FCO.

Harris, Kenneth (1987) *David Owen: Personally Speaking*, London: Weidenfeld & Nicolson.

Harris, Robert (1990) *Good and Faithful Servant: The Unauthorised Biography of Bernard Ingham*, London: Faber.

Heath, Edward (1998) *The Course of My Life*, London: Hodder & Stoughton.

Henderson, Nicholas (1984) *The Private Office*, London: Weidenfeld & Nicolson.

Henderson, Nicholas (1994) *Mandarin*, London: Weidenfeld & Nicolson.

Hennessy, Peter (2000) *The Prime Minister: The Office and Its Holders since 1945*, London: Penguin.

— (2002) *The Secret State: Whitehall and the Cold War*, London: Penguin.

Hiro, Dilip (1992) *Desert Shield to Desert Storm*, London: HarperCollins.

HM Stationery Office: *Plowden Report* (London: Cmnd. 2276, 1964), *Duncan Report* (London: Cmnd. 4107, 1969), *Berrill Report* (London: Cmnd. 7308, 1977), *FCO Departmental Report 2002* (London: Cm. 5413, 2002), *FCO Departmental Report 2003* (London: Cm. 5913, 2003), 'UK International Priorities: A Strategy for the FCO' (London: Cm. 6052, 2003).

Howe, Geoffrey (1994) *Conflict of Loyalty*, London: Macmillan.

Hurd, Douglas (1997) *The Search for Peace*, London: Little, Brown,

Kavanagh, Dennis, and Anthony Seldon (1999) *The Powers behind the Prime Minister*, London: HarperCollins.

Kissinger, Henry (1994) *Diplomacy*, London: Simon & Schuster.

Major, John (1999) *An Autobiography*, London: HarperCollins.

Marshall, Peter (1997) *Positive Diplomacy*, London: Macmillan.

Melissen, Jan (ed.) (1999) *Innovation in Diplomatic Practice*, London: Macmillan.

Moorhouse, Geoffrey (1977) *The Diplomats*, London: Jonathan Cape.

Nicolson, Sir Harold (1963) *Diplomacy*, Oxford: Oxford University Press.

Pimlott, Ben (1992) *Harold Wilson*, London: HarperCollins.

Rawnsley, Andrew (2000) *Servants of the People: The Inside Story of New Labour*, London: Penguin.

Satow, Sir Ernest (1979) *Guide to Diplomatic Practice*, 5th edn, ed. Lord Gore-Booth, London: Longman.

Sharp, Paul (1997) *Thatcher's Diplomacy*, London: Macmillan.

Smith, Geoffrey (1989) *Reagan and Thatcher*, London: Bodley Head.

Smith, Hedrick (1989) *The Power Game; How Washington Works*, London: Collins.

Stone, Diane (1996) *Capturing the Political Imagination: Think Tanks and the Policy Process*, London: Frank Cass.

Stone, Diane, Andrew Denham and Mark Garnett (eds) (1998) *Think Tanks across Nations*, Manchester: Manchester University Press.

Thatcher, Margaret (1993) *The Downing Street Years*, London: HarperCollins.

Thayer, Charles (1960) *Diplomat*, London: Michael Joseph.

Thorpe, D. R. (2003) *The Life and Times of Anthony Eden*, London: Chatto & Windus.

Trevelyan, Humphrey (1971) *Worlds Apart*, London: Macmillan.

— (1973) *Diplomatic Channels*, London: Macmillan.

Tugendhat, Christopher, and William Wallace (1988) *Options for British Foreign Policy in the 1990s*, London: RIIA.

Wheeler, Nicholas J. (2002) *Saving Strangers: Humanitarian Intervention in International Society*, Oxford: Oxford University Press.

Young, Hugo (1989) *One of Us*, London: Macmillan.

Index